THE

LIFE

YOU'VE
ALWAYS
WANTED

Resources by John Ortberg

An Ordinary Day with Jesus
(curriculum series, with Ruth Haley Barton)

Everybody's Normal Till You Get to Know Them
(book, audio, curriculum)

Faith and Doubt
(book and audio)

God Is Closer Than You Think
(book, audio, curriculum)

If You Want to Walk On Water,
You've Got to Get Out of the Boat
(book, audio, curriculum)

The Life You've Always Wanted
(book, audio, curriculum)

Living the God Life

Love Beyond Reason

Old Testament Challenge
(curriculum series, with Kevin and Sherry Harney)

When the Game Is Over, It All Goes Back in the Box
(book, audio, curriculum)

[EXPANDED EDITION]

THE LIFE YOU'VE ALWAYS WANTED

spiritual disciplines
for ordinary people

JOHN ORTBERG

ZONDERVAN®

WILLOW
Willow Creek Resources

ZONDERVAN.com/
AUTHORTRACKER
follow your favorite authors

ZONDERVAN®

The Life You've Always Wanted
Copyright © 1997, 2002 by John Ortberg

Requests for information should be addressed to:

Zondervan, *Grand Rapids, Michigan 49530*

ISBN 978-0-310-61212-4

All Scripture quotations, unless otherwise noted, are taken from the *New Revised Standard Version Bible*, copyright © 1989 by the Division of Christian Education of the National Council of the Churches of Christ in the United States of America. All rights reserved. Used by permission.

Scripture quotations identified as NIV are taken from the *Holy Bible: New International Version*®. NIV®. Copyright © 1973, 1978, 1984 by International Bible Society. Used by permission of Zondervan. All rights reserved.

All rights reserved. No part of this publication may be reproduced, stored in a retrieval system, or transmitted in any form or by any means—electronic, mechanical, photocopy, recording, or any other—except for brief quotations in printed reviews, without the prior permission of the publisher.

Interior design by Melissa Elenbaas and Todd Sprague

Printed in the United States of America

08 09 10 11 12 13 14 • 21 20 19 18 17 16 15 14 13 12 11 10 9 8 7 6 5 4 3 2 1

To Windsor House, in fulfillment of a long-time promise:
Chuck, Kevin, Jerry, Don, Tommy, Guy, and Rich.
And to Nancy.

CONTENTS

PREFACE

How do I grow? What does a spiritually mature person even look like? Why does it seem so hard, and go so slowly? Will I ever really be any different?

To paraphrase Lew Smedes: If you have ever been frustrated with what you know of spiritual life, ever wondered if real change is possible, ever felt confused or stuck—you're my kind of person. I wrote this book for you.

The Christian gospel insists that the transformation of the human personality really is possible. Never easy. Rarely quick. But possible. I see it happening in people sometimes—occasionally even in myself.

It begins to happen anytime people become intensely serious about learning from Jesus how to arrange their lives. Wise people across the centuries have devoted themselves to this. But the Way of Jesus needs to be restudied and reapplied to every age and social setting.

This book is an attempt to make some of that wisdom accessible to people who live in a world of freeways and corporate ladders and Nintendo rather than monasteries and deserts. I hope you will take it as an invitation to live Christ's Way, because it is the only invitation that really matters.

I want to thank several people who read all or parts of this manuscript, and offered encouragement or suggestions to make it a better book. They include Max DePree, Scott and Laurie Pederson, Lee Strobel, Dieter Zander, Sam Reeves, Jodi Walle, Richard Foster, Bill Hybels, Mickey Maudlin, and John Sr. and Kathy Ortberg.

Thanks to John and Linda Anderson for their gracious offer of a wonderful place in which to write. My wife, Nancy, has offered a patient and unceasing ministry as a sounding board for a constant flow of random ideas.

Jack Kuhatschek of Zondervan has been a joy to work with and a fountain of feedback and stimulation, without which this project would have been impoverished. Jim Ruark as well has brought clarity and precision.

In particular, I want to express a debt of gratitude to Dallas Willard, whose thinking and writing about spiritual formation have had an enormous impact on my life and ministry, as it has on so many others. (In fact, one of my private working titles for this book was *Dallas for Dummies*.) While I wouldn't want to saddle him with any of its deficiencies, much of whatever merit this book has is due to him.

CHAPTER 1

"WE SHALL MORPH INDEED"
The Hope of Transformation

Now, with God's help, I shall become myself.
SØREN KIERKEGAARD

I could not quiet that pearly ache in my heart that I
diagnosed as the cry of home.
PAT CONROY

I am disappointed with myself. I am disappointed not so much with particular things I have done as with aspects of who I have become. I have a nagging sense that all is not as it should be.

Some of this disappointment is trivial. I wouldn't have minded getting a more muscular physique. I can't do basic home repairs. So far I haven't shown much financial wizardry.

Some of this disappointment is neurotic. Sometimes I am too concerned about what others think of me, even people I don't know.

Some of this disappointment, I know, is worse than trivial; it is simply the sour fruit of self-absorption. I attend a high school reunion and can't choke back the desire to stand out by looking more attractive or having achieved more impressive accomplishments than my classmates. I speak to someone with whom I want to be charming, and my words come out awkward and pedestrian. I

I am disappointed with myself. . . . I have a nagging sense that all is not as it should be.

am disappointed in my ordinariness. I want to be, in the words of Garrison Keillor, named "Sun-God, King of America, Idol of Millions, Bringer of Fire, The Great Haji, Thun-Dar the Boy Giant."

But some of this disappointment in myself runs deeper. When I look in on my children as they sleep at night, I think of the kind of father I want to be. I want to create moments of magic, I want them to remember laughing until the tears flow, I want to read to them and make the books come alive so they love to read, I want to have slow, sweet talks with them as they're getting ready to close their eyes, I want to sing them awake in the morning. I want to chase fireflies with them, teach them to play tennis, have food fights, and hold them and pray for them in a way that makes them feel cherished.

I look in on them as they sleep at night, and I remember how the day really went: I remember how they were trapped in a fight over checkers and I walked out of the room because I didn't want to spend the energy needed to teach them how to resolve conflict. I remember how my daughter spilled cherry punch at dinner and I yelled at her about being careful as if she'd revealed some deep character flaw; I yelled at her even though I spill things all the time and no one yells at me; I yelled at her—to tell the truth—simply because I'm big and she's little and I can get away with it. And then I saw that look of hurt and confusion in her eyes, and I knew there was a tiny wound on her heart that I had put there, and I wished I could have taken those sixty seconds back. I remember how at night I didn't have slow, sweet talks, but merely rushed the children to bed so I could have more time to myself. I'm disappointed.

And it's not just my life as a father. I am disappointed also for my life as a husband, friend, neighbor, and human being in general. I think of the day I was born, when I carried the gift of promise, the gift given to all babies. I think of that little baby and what might have been: the ways I might have developed mind and body and spirit, the thoughts I might have had, the joy I might have created.

I am disappointed that I still love God so little and sin so much. I always had the idea as a child that adults were pretty much the people they wanted to be. Yet the truth is, I am embarrassingly sinful. I am capable of dismaying amounts of jealousy if someone succeeds more visibly than I do. I am disappointed at my capacity to be small and petty. I cannot pray for very long without my mind drifting into a fantasy of angry revenge over some past slight I thought I had long since forgiven or some grandiose fantasy of achievement. I can convince people I'm busy and productive and yet waste large amounts of time watching television.

These are just some of the disappointments. I have other ones, darker ones, that I'm not ready to commit to paper. The truth is, even to write these words is a little misleading, because it makes me sound more sensitive to my fallenness than I really am. Sometimes, although I am aware of how far I fall short, it doesn't even bother me very much. And I am disappointed at my lack of disappointment.

Where does this disappointment come from? A common answer in our day is that it is a lack of self-esteem, a failure to accept oneself. That may be part of the answer, but it is not the whole of it, not by a long shot. The older and wiser answer is that the feeling of disappointment is not the problem, but a reflection of a deeper problem—my failure to *be* the person God had in mind when he created me. It is the "pearly ache" in my heart to be at home with the Father.

Universal Disappointment

One of the most profound statements I have heard about the human condition was one I first encountered when I was only five years old. It was spoken by my hero, Popeye the Sailor Man. When he was frustrated or wasn't sure what to do or felt inadequate, Popeye would simply say, "I yam what I yam."

Popeye was not a sophisticated guy. He had never been in therapy and was woefully out of touch with his shadow self and his inner child. He did not have much education as far as we know. He knew who he was: a simple, sea-faring, pipe-smoking, Olive Oyl-loving

I am in a state of dis-appointment. I am missing the life that I was appointed by God to live.

sailor man, and he wouldn't pretend to be anything else. He "owned his story," as Lewis Smedes puts it. "I yam what I yam."

But I always thought there was a note of sadness in Popeye's expression. It was generally offered as an explanation of his short-comings. It does not anticipate much growth or change. It doesn't leave him much of a shot at getting to be what he yam not. "Don't get your hopes up," he seemed to say. "Don't expect too much. I yam what I yam—and [he would add in his bleakest moments] that's all that I yam."

That is the sad cry of the human race. You have said those words, in your own way, and so have I. This is the struggle between disappointment and hope.

Dis-appointing God

The word itself is apt: I am in a state of dis-appointment. I am missing the life that I was appointed by God to live—missing my calling. And I have dis-appointed God. I have removed him from the central role he longs to play in my life; I have refused to "let God be God" and have appointed myself in his place. I yam what I yam.

But that's not all that I am. I am called to become the person God had in mind when he originally designed me. This is what is behind Kierkegaard's wonderful prayer, "And now Lord, with your help I shall become myself." This book is about spiritual growth. It is about that holy and mysterious process described by the apostle Paul when he said he was "in the pain of childbirth until Christ is formed in you." The goal of such growth is to live as if Jesus held unhindered sway over our bodies. Of course, it is still *we* doing the living. We are called by God to live as our uniquely created selves— our temperament, our gene pool, our history. But to grow spiritually means to live increasingly as Jesus would in our unique place—to perceive what Jesus would perceive if he looked through our eyes, to think what he would think, to feel what he would feel, and there-fore to do what he would do.

The goal of this book is to help us to grow spiritually. But it is hard to write about spiritual formation in a way that captures the urgency of the subject. Too often people think about their "spiritual lives" as just one more aspect of their existence, alongside and largely separate from their "financial lives" or their "vocational lives." Periodically they may try to "get their spiritual lives together" by praying more regularly or trying to master another spiritual discipline. It is the religious equivalent of going on a diet or trying to stick to a budget.

The truth is that the term *spiritual life* is simply a way of referring to one's life—every moment and facet of it—from God's perspective. Another way of saying it is this: God is not interested in your "spiritual life." God is just interested in your life. He intends to redeem it.

God's Work of Art

One of the great works of art in the Western world is Michelangelo's *Pietà*, a marble statue of an anguished Mary holding the crucified Christ. Some years ago a fanatic nationalist rushed upon the masterpiece and began smashing it with a sledgehammer. Although the damage was significant, Vatican artists were able to restore the statue to near-perfect condition.

You were created to be a masterpiece of God. Paul writes, "For we are God's *poiēma*"—a word that can mean God's "workmanship," or even God's "work of art." God made you to know oneness with him and with other human beings. God made you to be co-regent with him—to "fill the earth and subdue it," to "have dominion" over creation under his reign and with his help. It is the goodness of God's work in creating us that makes our fallenness so tragic. This is why my disappointment in myself runs so deep.

But God is determined to overcome the defacing of his image in us. His plan is not simply to repair *most* of our brokenness. He wants to make us new creatures. So the story of the human race is not just one of universal disappointment, but one of inextinguishable hope.

Inextinguishable Hope and the Gospel

Frederick Buechner once wrote that every age has produced fairy tales. Something inside us believes, or wants to believe, that the world as we know it is not the whole story. We long for the reenchantment of reality. We hope that death is not the end, that the universe is something more than an enclosed terrarium. So we keep spinning and repeating stories that hold the promise of another world.

But these stories don't simply demand that another world exists. A common feature of fairy tales is that the enchanted world is not far away. You step into a wardrobe and you're in Narnia. You walk through a forest and stumble on a cottage with seven dwarfs. This other world turns out to be far closer than you thought.

In fact, the stories that endure are the ones that most deeply touch this longing inside us. Buechner quotes J. R. R. Tolkien:

> It is the mark of the good fairy-story, of the higher or more complete kind, that however wild its events, however fantastic or terrible the adventures, it can give to the child or man that hears it, when the "turn" comes, a catch of the breath, a beat and lifting of the heart, near to (or indeed accompanied by) tears, as keen as that given by any form of literary art.

Furthermore, fairy tales are not just stories about the transformation of the world around us. They are usually about the transformation of the central characters: frogs becoming princes, ugly ducklings becoming swans, wooden marionettes becoming real boys. George MacDonald gives to his hero, Curdie, the magical gift of being able to tell by the touch of someone's hand what he or she is turning into.

These are all features, Buechner says, that the gospel has in common with fairy tales, with this one great difference: The gospel is true.

Jesus' announcement of the gospel is simply the announcement of the existence and availability of another dimension of existence, another world. "The kingdom of God has come near," he said. "Repent, and believe in the good news." The Good News—the word we translate "gospel"—is that this fallen world as we know it is not the whole story. There is another realm. It is as real as the chair I sit in and the book you read.

These words of Jesus announce the great "turn" in the history of the world. The lid is off the terrarium. Anytime someone heard Jesus say them—really heard them—these words would bring a catch of the breath, a beating and uplifting of the heart, and sometimes tears. They still do.

> **The story of the human race is not just one of universal disappointment, but one of inextinguishable hope.**

The good news is especially that this world—the kingdom of God—is closer than you think. It is available to ordinary men and women. It is available to people who have never thought of themselves as religious or spiritual. It is available to you. You can live in it—now.

This means in part that your story is the story of transformation. You will not always be as you are now; the day is coming when you will be something incomparably better or worse.

C. S. Lewis expressed that hope this way.

> It is a serious thing to live in a society of possible gods and goddesses, to remember that the dullest and most uninteresting person you can talk to may one day be a creature which, if you saw it now, you would be strongly tempted to worship, or else a horror and a corruption such as you now meet, if at all, only in a nightmare. All day long we are, in some degree, helping each other to one or other of these destinations. . . . There are no *ordinary* people. You have never talked to a mere mortal. Nations, cultures, arts, civilizations—these are mortal, and their life is to ours as the life of a gnat. But it is immortals whom we joke with, work with, marry, snub, and exploit—immortal horrors or everlasting splendors.

This is why Jesus came. This is what spiritual life is about. This is your calling—to become what Lewis calls an "everlasting splendor."

The Need to "Turn Aside"

God holds out the possibility of transformation. One day when the human race had not heard a word of hope for a long time, a man named Moses walked past a shrub. He had seen it before, perhaps a hundred times. Only this time it was different. This time the "turn" comes; this time the wardrobe opens into Narnia; this time the bush is on fire with the presence of God.

And Moses said, "I must turn aside and look at this great sight, and see why the bush is not burned up." Everything turned on Moses' being willing to "turn aside"—to interrupt his daily routine to pay attention to the presence of God. He didn't have to. He could have looked the other way, as many of us would. He would have just missed the Exodus, the people of Israel, his calling, the reason for his existence. He would have missed knowing God.

> Moses had seen the shrub before, perhaps a hundred times. Only this time it was different.

But he didn't miss it. He stopped. He "turned aside."

God said he wanted to begin a new community of human existence, and he wanted Moses to lead it. He wanted Moses to go to Pharaoh, the commander-in-chief of a superpower, and tell him that his vast Israelite labor force is no longer available.

But God's sense of timing seemed strange to Moses. Forty years ago maybe—forty years ago he was young and strong and the product of the greatest education the advanced civilization of Egypt could produce. Forty years ago he had powerful connections and high hopes. But now he was a nobody, an anonymous shepherd in a forgotten desert, rejected by his own people and a fugitive from the Egyptians.

"Who am I that I should go to Pharaoh?" Moses asked. "Nobody knows me. I am slow of speech and slow of tongue. I am disappointed in myself. I yam what I yam."

God said to Moses what he has said to you and me and millions of other Moseses: "I know all about that. It doesn't really matter much. For *I* will be with you. Your guilt and your inadequacies are no longer the ultimate truth about you. *You are what you are—but that's not all that you are. You are what you are, but you are not yet what you will be.* I will be with you."

To which Moses responded, logically enough: "Who are you? What if I go to the people and tell them the God of our fathers has sent me, and they ask me his name—what should I tell them?"

And God answered: "I am what I am." God wanted to be known intimately, by name. This same God had already been active in human history, ready to transform anyone then or now who is willing to turn aside before a burning bush: "I am the God of Abraham and Sarah, of Isaac and Rebekah; I am the God who cares for my people. I have seen the misery of my children when they thought I was not looking. I have heard their groans when they thought I was not listening. I am the God who saw you in the reeds when you were hidden, in the desert when you fled as a fugitive." For this is the God who hides in burning bushes and speaks in a still small voice.

"Get your hopes up!" God says. "You know me. I yam what I yam."

Transformation the Goal

A few years ago, the dominant interest of six-year-olds in the United States was a group of teenage superheroes called the Mighty Morphin Power Rangers. The shows were an unlikely hit—originally produced on a very low budget in Japan, then badly dubbed into English.

The key to the show's appeal was the characters' ability to "morph." Ordinarily they were normal adolescents, but as needed they could access a power beyond themselves to become martial arts heroes for justice. Their rallying cry in moments of crisis was "It's morphing time!" and they would be transformed with the ability to do extraordinary things.

The show became such a huge hit that the term *morph* has begun creeping into magazine articles and everyday conversations and may become part of our permanent vocabulary. It became a standard phrase around our house if someone was in need of serious attitude adjustment: "It's morphing time."

Of course, it is not just six-year-olds who want to morph. The desire for transformation lies deep in every human heart. This is why people enter therapy, join health clubs, get into recovery groups, read self-help books, attend motivational seminars, and make New Year's resolutions. The possibility of transformation is the essence of hope. Psychologist Aaron Beck says that the single belief most toxic to a relationship is the belief that the other person cannot change.

The possibility of transformation is the essence of hope.

This little word *morph* has a long history. It actually comes from one of the richest Greek words in the New Testament, and in a sense this little word is the foundation of this whole book. *Morphoo* means "the inward and real formation of the essential nature of a person." It was the term used to describe the formation and growth of an embryo in a mother's body.

Paul used this word in his letter to the Galatians: ". . . until Christ is *formed* in you." He agonized until Christ should be born in those people, until they should express his character and goodness in their whole being. Paul said they—like us—are in a kind of spiritual gestation process. We are pregnant with possibilities of spiritual growth and moral beauty so great that they cannot be adequately described as anything less than the formation of Christ in our very lives.

Paul used another form of this word when he told the Christians in Rome that God had predestined them to be "conformed to the image of his Son." This word, *summorphizo*, means to have the same form as another, to shape a thing into a durable likeness. Spiritual growth is a molding process: We are to be to Christ as an image is to the original.

Still another form of the word appears in Romans when Paul says we are not to be conformed to the world around us but "*transformed* by the renewing of your minds." This word is *metamorphoo*, from which comes the English word *metamorphosis*. A creeping caterpillar is transformed into a soaring butterfly—yet as the children of God we are to undergo a change that makes that one barely noticeable.

When morphing happens, I don't just *do* the things Jesus would have done; I find myself *wanting* to do them. They appeal to me. They make sense. I don't just go around trying to do right things; I *become* the right sort of person.

These are audacious statements. Ordinary people can receive power for extraordinary change. It's morphing time, Paul says.

To help people remember this, I developed a little liturgy at a church I served. I would say to the congregation, "It's morphing time." They would reply, "We shall morph indeed."

The primary goal of spiritual life is human transformation. It is not making sure people know where they're going after they die, or helping them have a richer interior life, or seeing that they have lots of information about the Bible, although these can be good things. Let's put first things first. The first goal of spiritual life is the reclamation of the human race. It's morphing time.

Not only that, but this goal can be pursued full-time. For a long time in my own life a very bad thing happened: I had reduced my "tools for spiritual growth" to a few activities such as prayer and Bible study or a few periods of the day called a quiet time. I took an embarrassingly long time to learn that every moment of my life is an opportunity to learn from God how to live like Jesus, how to live in the kingdom of God. I had to discover that there are practical, concrete ways to help me "turn aside." Elizabeth Barrett Browning wrote:

> Earth's crammed with Heaven,
> And every common bush afire with God,
> But only he who sees takes off his shoes—
> The rest sit round it and pluck blackberries.

The purpose of this book is to help you learn how to use every moment, every activity of life, for morphing purposes.

A Case Study: The Morphing of Mabel

It can be helpful to see how God brings about transformation in the lives of ordinary people, so I would like to introduce you to a friend of a friend of mine. Her name is Mabel. This is what my friend, Tom Schmidt, wrote:

"The state-run convalescent hospital is not a pleasant place. It is large, understaffed, and overfilled with senile and helpless and lonely people who are waiting to die. On the brightest of days it seems dark inside, and it smells of sickness and stale urine. I went there once or twice a week for four years, but I never wanted to go there, and I always left with a sense of relief. It is not the kind of place one gets used to.

"On this particular day I was walking in a hallway that I had not visited before, looking in vain for a few who were alive enough to receive a flower and a few words of encouragement. This hallway seemed to contain some of the worst cases, strapped onto carts or into wheelchairs and looking completely helpless.

"As I neared the end of this hallway, I saw an old woman strapped up in a wheelchair. Her face was an absolute horror. The empty stare and white pupils of her eyes told me that she was blind. The large hearing aid over one ear told me that she was almost deaf. One side of her face was being eaten by cancer. There was a discolored and running sore covering part of one cheek, and it had pushed her nose to one side, dropped one eye, and distorted her jaw so that what should have been the corner of her mouth was the bottom of her mouth. As a consequence, she drooled constantly. I was told later that when new nurses arrived, the supervisors would send them to feed this woman, thinking that if they could stand this sight they could stand anything in the building. I also learned later that this woman was eighty-nine years old and *that she had been here, bedridden, blind, nearly deaf, and alone, for twenty-five years*. This was Mabel.

"I don't know why I spoke to her—she looked less likely to respond than most of the people I saw in that hallway. But I put a flower in her hand and said, 'Here is a flower for you. Happy Mother's Day.' She held the flower up to her face and tried to smell it, and then she spoke. And much to my surprise, her words, although somewhat garbled because of her deformity, were obviously produced by a clear mind. She said, 'Thank you. It's lovely. But can I give it to someone else? I can't see it, you know, I'm blind.'

"I said, 'Of course,' and I pushed her in her chair back down the hallway to a place where I thought I could find some alert patients. I found one, and I stopped the chair. Mabel held out the flower and said, 'Here, this is from Jesus.'

"That was when it began to dawn on me that this was not an ordinary human being. Later I wheeled her back to her room and learned more about her history. She had grown up on a small farm that she managed with only her mother until her mother died. Then she ran the farm alone until 1950 when her blindness and sickness sent her to the convalescent hospital. For twenty-five years she got weaker and sicker, with constant headaches, backaches, and stomachaches, and then the cancer came too. Her three roommates were all human vegetables who screamed occasionally but never talked. They often soiled their bedclothes, and because the hospital was understaffed, especially on Sundays when I usually visited, the stench was often overpowering.

"Mabel and I became friends over the next few weeks, and I went to see her once or twice a week for the next three years. Her first words to me were usually an offer of hard candy from a tissue box near her bed. Some days I would read to her from the Bible, and often when I would pause she would continue reciting the passage from memory, word-for-word. On other days I would take a book of hymns and sing with her, and she would know all the words of the old songs. For Mabel, these were not merely exercises in memory. She would often stop in mid-hymn and make a brief comment about lyrics she considered particularly relevant to her own situation. I never heard her speak of loneliness or pain except in the stress she placed on certain lines in certain hymns.

"It was not many weeks before I turned from a sense that I was being helpful to a sense of wonder, and I would go to her with a pen and paper to write down the things she would say. . . .

"During one hectic week of final exams I was frustrated because my mind seemed to be pulled in ten directions at once with all of the things that I had to think about. The question occurred to me, 'What does Mabel have to think about—hour after hour, day after day, week after week, not even able to know if it's day or night?' So I went to her and asked, 'Mabel, what do you think about when you lie here?'

"And she said, 'I think about my Jesus.'

"I sat there, and thought for a moment about the difficulty, for me, of thinking about Jesus for even five minutes, and I asked, 'What do you think about Jesus?' She replied slowly and deliberately as I wrote . . . :

> I think about how good he's been to me. He's been awfully good to me in my life, you know. . . . I'm one of those kind who's mostly satisfied. . . . Lots of folks wouldn't care much for what I think. Lots of folks would think I'm kind of old-fashioned. But I don't care. I'd rather have Jesus. He's all the world to me.

"And then Mabel began to sing an old hymn:

> Jesus is all the world to me,
> My life, my joy, my all.
> He is my strength from day to day,
> Without him I would fall.
> When I am sad, to him I go,
> No other one can cheer me so.
> When I am sad He makes me glad.
> He's my friend.

"*This is not fiction.* Incredible as it may seem, a human being really lived like this. I know. I knew her. *How could she do it?* Seconds ticked and minutes crawled, and so did days and weeks and months and years of pain without human company and without an explanation of why it was all happening—and she lay there and sang hymns. *How could she do it?*

"The answer, I think, is that Mabel had something that you and I don't have much of. She had power. Lying there in that bed, unable to move, unable to see, unable to hear, unable to talk to anyone, she had incredible power."

Here was an ordinary human being who received supernatural power to do extraordinary things. Her entire life consisted of following Jesus as best she could in her situation: patient endurance of suffering, solitude, prayer, meditation on Scripture, worship, fellowship when it was possible, giving when she had a flower or a piece of candy to offer.

Imagine being in her condition and saying, "I think about how good he's been to me. He's been awfully good to me in my life, you know.... I'm one of those kind who's mostly satisfied." This is the Twenty-third Psalm come to life: "The LORD is my shepherd, I shall not want."

For anyone who really saw Mabel—who was willing to "turn aside"—a hospital bed became a burning bush; a place where this ordinary and pain-filled world was visited by the presence of God. When others saw the life in that hospital bed, they wanted to take off their shoes. The lid was off the terrarium. Then the turn came, with a catch of the breath, and a beating of the heart, and tears. They were standing on holy ground.

> **Here was an ordinary human being who received supernatural power to do extraordinary things.**

Do you believe such a life is possible for an ordinary human being? Do you believe it is possible for you? This is promised in the gospel—the Good News proclaimed by Jesus: "The kingdom of God has come near; repent, and believe in the good news." The good news as Jesus preached it is that now it is possible for ordinary men and women to live in the presence and under the power of God. The good news as Jesus preached it is not about the minimal entrance requirements for getting into heaven when you die. It is about the glorious redemption of human life—your life.

It's morphing time.

CHAPTER 2

SURPRISED BY CHANGE
The Goal of Spiritual Life

If you are weary of some sleepy form of devotion,
probably God is as weary of it as you are.
FRANK LAUBACH

"Spirituality" wrongly understood or pursued is a major
source of human misery and rebellion against God.
DALLAS WILLARD

The Man Who Never Changed

Hank, as we'll call him, was a cranky guy. He did not smile easily, and when he did, the smile often had a cruel edge to it, coming at someone's expense. He had a knack for discovering islands of bad news in oceans of happiness. He would always find a cloud where others saw a silver lining.

Hank rarely affirmed anyone. He operated on the assumption that if you compliment someone, it might lead to a swelled head, so he worked to make sure everyone stayed humble. His was a ministry of cranial downsizing.

His native tongue was complaint. He carried judgment and disapproval the way a prisoner carries a ball and chain. Although he went to church his whole life, he was never unshackled.

A deacon in the church asked him one day, "Hank, are you happy?"

Hank paused to reflect, then replied without smiling, "Yeah."

"Well, tell your face," the deacon said. But so far as anybody knows, Hank's face never did find out about it.

Occasionally, Hank's joylessness produced unintended joy for others.

There was a period of time when his primary complaints centered around the music in the church. "It's too loud!" Hank protested—to the staff, the deacons, the ushers, and eventually the innocent visitors to the church.

We finally had to take Hank aside and explain that complaining to complete strangers was not appropriate and he would have to restrict his laments to a circle of intimate friends. And that was the end of it. So we thought.

A few weeks later, a secretary buzzed me on the intercom to say that an agent from OSHA—the Occupational Safety and Health Administration—was here to see me. "I'm here to check out a complaint," he said. As I tried to figure out who on the staff would have called OSHA over a church problem, he began to talk about decibel levels at airports and rock concerts.

"Excuse me," I said, "are you sure this was someone on the church staff that called?"

"No," he explained. "If anyone calls—whether or not they work here—we're obligated to investigate."

Suddenly the light dawned: Hank had called OSHA and said, "The music at my church is too loud." And they sent a federal agent to check it out.

By this time the rest of the staff had gathered in my office to see the man from OSHA.

"We don't mean to make light of this," I told him, "but nothing like this has ever happened around here before."

"Don't apologize," he said. "Do you have any idea how much ridicule I've faced around my office since everyone discovered I was going out to bust a church?"

Sometimes Hank's joylessness ended in comedy, but more often it produced sadness. His children did not know him. His son had a wonderful story about how he met his wife at a dance, but he never told his father because Hank did not approve of dancing.

Hank could not effectively love his wife or his children or people outside his family. He was easily irritated. He had little use for the poor, and a casual contempt for those whose accents or skin pigment differed from his own. Whatever capacity he once might have had for joy or wonder or gratitude atrophied. He critiqued and judged and complained, and his soul got a little smaller each year.

Do We Expect Transformation?

Hank was not changing. He was once a cranky young guy, and he grew up to be a cranky old man. But even more troubling than his lack of change was the fact that nobody was surprised by it. It was as if everyone simply expected that his soul would remain withered and sour year after year, decade after decade. No one seemed bothered by the condition. It was not an anomaly that caused head-scratching bewilderment. No church consultants were called in. No emergency meetings were held to probe the strange case of this person who followed the church's general guidelines for spiritual life and yet was nontransformed.

The church staff did have some expectations. We expected that Hank would affirm certain religious beliefs. We expected that he would attend services, read the Bible, support the church financially, pray regularly, and avoid certain sins. But here's what we didn't expect: *We didn't expect that he would progressively become the way Jesus would be if he were in Hank's place.* We didn't assume that each year would find him a more compassionate, joyful, gracious, winsome personality. We didn't anticipate that he was on the way to becoming a source of delight and courtesy who overflowed with "rivers of living water." So we were not shocked when it didn't happen. We would have been surprised if it did!

Most of us want to be changed, to become more like Christ. But is it happening? According to a Gallup poll, nine of ten Americans say they pray daily, and 84 million Americans—almost a third of the population—say they have made a personal commitment to

We were not shocked when change didn't happen. We would have been surprised if it did!

Christ as Savior. But as William Iverson writes, "A pound of meat would surely be affected by a quarter pound of salt. If this is real Christianity, the 'salt of the earth,' where is the effect of which Jesus spoke?"

Because by and large we do not expect people to experience ongoing transformation, we are not led to question whether perhaps the standard prescriptions for spiritual growth being given in the church are truly adequate to lead people into a transformed way of life.

I believe we need to say that this state of affairs is simply not acceptable. It is not God's plan for his community. As C. S. Lewis said in another context, we are "like an ignorant child who wants to go on making mud pies in a slum because he cannot imagine what is meant by the offer of a holiday at the sea. We are far too easily pleased."

In fact, Hank's problem is not just that he is failing to change. His problem—and the problem of all of us who become "far too easily pleased"—is that we may end up changing in ways that leave us worse off than before.

The Danger of "Pseudo-Transformation"

The great danger that arises when we don't experience authentic transformation is that we will settle for what might be called *pseudo-transformation*. We know that as Christians we are called to "come out and be separate," that our faith and spiritual commitment should make us different somehow. But if we are not marked by greater and greater amounts of love and joy, we will inevitably look for substitute ways of distinguishing ourselves from those who are not Christians. This deep pattern is almost inescapable for religious people: If we do not become changed from the inside-out—if we don't morph—we will be tempted to find external methods to satisfy our need to feel that we're different from those outside the faith. If we cannot be transformed, we will settle for being informed or conformed.

Boundary-Marker Spirituality

James Dunn notes that in the first century A.D. a vast amount of rabbinic writing focused on circumcision, dietary laws, and Sabbath keeping. This seems odd, because no devout rabbi would have said these matters were at the heart of the Law. They knew its core: "Hear, O Israel: The LORD is our God, the LORD alone. You shall love the LORD your God with all your heart, and with all your soul, and with all your might." So why the focus on these three practices?

The answer involves what might be called "identity" or "boundary markers." Groups have a tendency to be exclusive. Insiders want to separate themselves from outsiders. So they adopt boundary markers. These are highly visible, relatively superficial practices— matters of vocabulary or dress or style—whose purpose is to *distinguish* between those inside a group and those who are outside.

For example, imagine that you were driving through the Haight-Asbury district of San Francisco in the 1960s. If you came to a stoplight and a Volkswagen van pulled up next to you, plastered with peace signs and "Make Love Not War" bumper stickers and driven by a long-haired, tie-dyed, granny-glasses wearer, you would have known you were driving next to a hippie. If it were the 1980s and you were to see a BMW with a driver wearing Gucci shoes, a Rolex watch, and moussed hair and nibbling on brie, you would know you were driving next to a yuppie. Bikers, too, are recognizable by their preference in fashion color (black), fabric (leather), skin ornamentation (tattoo), and beverage of choice ("great taste, less filling"). Farmers and doctors and politicians and rock stars all have their own ways of distinguishing who is in their fraternity or sorority.

With this in mind, the importance of circumcision, dietary laws, and Sabbath keeping in the first century becomes clear. These were the boundary markers; the highly visible, relatively superficial practices that allowed people to distinguish who was inside and who was outside the family of God. What is worse, the insiders become proud and judgmental toward outsiders. They practiced what might be called a "boundary-oriented approach" to spiritual life: Just look at people and you will know who are the sheep and who are the goats. This is pseudo-transformation.

Spiritual Life Defined by Its Center

With Jesus it was not so. Jesus brought a message that spoke to the deepest longings of the human heart to become not simply conformed to a religious subculture but transformed into "new creatures." Instead of focusing on the boundaries, Jesus focused on the center, the heart of spiritual life. When asked to identify what the law is about, Jesus' response was simply "Love God, love people." He named a fundamentally different way of identifying who are the children of God: "Do they love God, and do they love the people who mean so much to him?"

Jesus' early followers understood this clearly. The apostle Paul wrote to the church at Corinth about the significance of having many spiritual "markers" but lacking the center: "If I speak in the tongues of mortals and of angels, but do not have love, I am a noisy gong or a clanging cymbal. And if I have prophetic powers, and understand all mysteries and all knowledge, and if I have all faith, so as to remove mountains, but do not have love, I am nothing." John put it even more bluntly: "Everyone who loves is born of God and knows God. Whoever does not love *does not know God*, for God is love."

This is why the religious leaders of Jesus' day so often fought with him about circumcision, dietary laws, and the Sabbath. Jesus was not just disagreeing with them on how to interpret the Law. He was *threatening their very understanding of themselves as the people of God*.

Boundary Markers in Our Day

The search for identity markers did not die out in the first century. The church I grew up in was a fine church, and I am deeply in its debt, but we also had our own set of markers there. The senior pastor could have been consumed with pride or resentment, but as long as his preaching was orthodox and the church was growing, his job would probably not be in jeopardy. But if some Sunday morning he had been smoking a cigarette while greeting people after the service, he would not have been around for the evening service. Why? No one at the church would have said that smoking a single Camel was a worse sin than a life consumed with pride and resentment. But for us, cigarette-smoking became an identity marker. It was one of the ways we were able to tell the sheep from the goats.

> Instead of focusing on the boundaries, Jesus focused on the center, the heart of spiritual life.

That is why the marker held an emotional charge far beyond its theological significance. For the pastor to smoke a cigarette would have caused a scandal, not because we were so naive that we thought it an evil thing to do, but because it would have violated an unspoken boundary marker. It would have threatened our sense of identity.

Of course, many beliefs and values will inevitably divide those who choose to follow Christ from those who don't. Jesus himself said he came not "to bring peace, but a sword." But what makes something a boundary marker is its being seized upon by the group as an opportunity to reinforce a false sense of superiority, fed by the intent to exclude others.

Religious boundary markers change from generation to generation. The Christian college I attended in the late seventies still had in effect a rule against the performance of jazz music on campus, a regulation instituted in the early twentieth century. Fifty years later, no one was willing to rescind it for fear of appearing to compromise essential beliefs. The irony is that students were perfectly free to listen to punk rock or heavy metal—but Louis Armstrong was off-limits. On Sundays the tennis courts were locked up, but for some reason the volleyball court was left accessible. As a tennis player, I always maintained that volleyball was the more worldly of the two sports, as it was more closely associated with California and was often played on the beach.

If you give it much thought, whether your religious background is liberal or conservative, Protestant or Catholic, you can probably come up with your own set of identity markers.

A boundary-oriented approach to spirituality focuses on people's position: Are you inside or outside the group? A great deal of energy is spent clarifying what counts as a boundary marker.

But Jesus consistently focused on people's *center*: Are they oriented and moving *toward* the center of spiritual life (love of God and people), or are they moving *away from* it? This is why he shocked people by saying that many religious leaders—who observed all the recognized boundary markers—were in fact outside the kingdom of God. They were—like Hank—increasingly dead to love. And this is why Jesus could say that "the tax collectors and the prostitutes" who were a million miles away from the religious subculture, but who had turned, converted, and oriented themselves toward God and love, were already in the kingdom.

This was the great irony of his day: The "righteous" were more damaged by their righteousness than the sinners were by their sin.

The Distortion of Spirituality

The misunderstanding of true spirituality has caused immense damage to the human race. Tragically, it is possible to think we are becoming more spiritual when in fact we are only becoming more

> The misunderstanding of true spirituality has caused immense damage to the human race.

smug and judgmental. Pseudo-transformation means becoming what Mark Twain once called "a good man in the worst sense of the word." Winston Churchill, told that a political opponent of his by the name of Cripps—who was widely disliked for his smug self-righteousness—had just stopped smoking cigars, commented, "Too bad. Those cigars were his last contact with humanity."

(Another time, the story goes, Churchill saw Cripps passing by and remarked, "There, but for the grace of God, goes God.")

Getting clear on what spiritual life looks like is no casual affair. This is life or death to the soul. Sheldon Vanauken wrote that the strongest argument for Christianity is Christians, when they are drawing life from God. The strongest argument against Christianity? Also Christians, when they become exclusive, self-righteous, and complacent.

Dallas Willard writes,

> How many people are radically and permanently repelled from The Way by Christians who are unfeeling, stiff, unapproachable, boringly lifeless, obsessive, and dissatisfied? Yet such Christians are everywhere, and what they are missing is the wholesome liveliness springing from a balanced vitality with the freedom of God's loving rule. . . . Spirituality wrongly understood or pursued is a major source of human misery and rebellion against God.

So how do I know if I am settling for pseudo-transformation instead of the real thing? In the gospel according to Matthew, Jesus offers a list of warning signs in capital letters. Here are a few that I find helpful.

1. Am I spiritually "inauthentic"?

"Woe to you. . . . For you clean the outside of the cup and of the plate, but inside they are full of greed and self-indulgence."

Inauthenticity involves a preoccupation with *appearing* to be spiritual.

Someone once asked me whether I thought that the church where I worked might be worldly.

"What do you mean by 'worldly'?" I asked him.

"Well, you use drama, and people are used to that in the world. And you play contemporary music just like they're used to hearing. So how will they know you're any different? Everybody knows that as Christians we're supposed to be different from people in the world by being more loving and more gentle, and everybody knows that we're not. So don't we have to do something to show we're different?"

In other words, if we can't be *holy*, shouldn't we at least be *weird*?

I act like that. I recently reread a letter I had written to a friend many years ago. Most of the letter was a review of current activities, and it sounded casual and natural. Then I wrote a few lines at the end about God and my spiritual life. But they didn't feel natural. They felt calculated and artificial, as if I were saying things I thought a spiritual person is *supposed* to say.

I realized I have a hard time even *talking* about God without trying to convince people I'm "spiritual." I try to hide my sin. I work harder at making people think I'm a loving person than I do at actually loving them.

A little boy went to Sunday school, where he knew the sort of answers you're supposed to give to questions. The teacher asked, "What is brown, furry, has a long tail, and stores up nuts for winter?"

"Well," the boy muttered, "I guess the answer is Jesus, but it sure sounds like a squirrel to me."

I act like that. I try to say spiritual-sounding things, even when I don't know what I'm saying: "I guess the answer is Jesus. . . ."

2. Am I becoming judgmental or exclusive or proud?

"They love to have the place of honor at banquets and the best seats in the synagogues."

Pride is a potential problem for anyone who takes spiritual growth seriously. As soon as we start to pursue virtue, we begin to wonder why others aren't as virtuous as we are. The great mystic St. John of the Cross wrote:

When beginners become aware of their own fervor and diligence in their spiritual works and devotional exercises, this prosperity of theirs gives rise to secret pride. . . . they conceive a certain satisfaction in the contemplation of their works and of themselves. . . . They condemn others in their heart when they see that they are not devout in their way.

Lee Strobel, my colleague at Willow Creek Community Church, is fond of quoting the reply Homer Simpson's fundamentalist neighbors gave when Homer asked them where they'd been: "We went away to a Christian camp. We were learning how to be more judgmental."

Where is that camp, and why is it so well attended?

I was in a small group with people I had just met, and immediately I found a little voice inside me categorizing everyone: "This one is needy and dependent—stay away. That one is bright and has much to offer try to connect." Why do I constantly find myself *rating* people as if they were Olympic contestants and someone appointed me judge? Why do I so often compare myself with them as if we were in some kind of competition?

This tendency is one reason why God sometimes graciously hides our own growth from our eyes. Jean Caussade said that while God is always at work in us, many times his work "is formed, grows, and is accomplished *secretly* in souls *without their knowledge*."

3. Am I becoming more approachable, or less?

"They love . . . to have people call them rabbi."

In Jesus' day, lepers and prostitutes and tax collectors were especially careful to steer clear of the rabbis, who were considered especially close to God. The rabbis' had the mistaken notion that their spirituality required them to distance themselves from people. The irony is that the only rabbi the outcasts could touch turned out to be God himself.

Jesus was the most approachable person they had ever seen. The religious leaders had a kind of differentness that pushed people away. Jesus had a kind of differentness that drew people to him. True spirituality is that way.

4. Am I growing weary of pursuing spiritual growth?

> "They tie up heavy burdens, hard to bear, and lay them on the shoulders of others."

The pursuit of righteousness is always an exhausting pursuit when it seeks a distorted goal. Steven Mosley speaks of how we trivialize goodness, becoming

> a "peculiar people" set at odd angles to the world rather than being an attractive light illuminating it. As a result, our morality calls out rather feebly. It whines from the corner of a sanctuary; it awkwardly interrupts pleasures; it mumbles excuses at parties; it shuffles along out of step and slightly behind the times. . . . It's often regarded by our secular contemporaries as a narrow, even trivial, pursuit.

He captures the dynamic of the boundary-marker quest: "Tragically, conventional religious goodness manages to be both *intimidating* and *unchallenging* at the same time."

"Both intimidating and unchallenging at the same time." This is the hallmark of spiritual life defined in terms of boundary markers.

The pursuit of righteousness is always an exhausting pursuit when it seeks a distorted goal.

Intimidating—because it may involve thirty-nine separate rules about Sabbath keeping alone. Unchallenging—because we may devote our lives to observing all the rules and yet never open the heart to love or joy.

This is why people inside the church so often get weary. Observing boundary markers, conforming to a religious subculture, is simply not a compelling enough vision to captivate the human spirit. It was not intended to be.

5. Am I measuring my spiritual life in superficial ways?

> "You blind guides! You strain out a gnat but swallow a camel!"

Suppose someone were to ask you, "How is your spiritual life going these days?" Quick—what's the first thing that comes to your mind?

For many years I thought about this only in terms of a few special activities. If someone asked me how my spiritual life was going, my first thought would be how I was doing at having a quiet time—praying and reading the Bible each day. If I had prayed and read the Bible for several consecutive prior days, I was likely to say that my spiritual life was going well. If not, I was likely to feel guilty and downcast. So prayer and Bible study became the gauge of my spiritual condition. As long as I did those two things I could go through the day confident of God's approval.

I often use a journal in these quiet times. But I discovered that sometimes when I was in a hurry and didn't really want to take time to be with God, I would still get out my journal and scribble a few sentences simply so I had an entry in it for that day (I'm not sure why I did this. Did I think I was going to have to hand it in?) I found myself measuring my spiritual life by the regularity of journal entries. I even devised a strategy in case there was an embarrassingly long gap between entry dates: I could keep two journals and merely write in one: "See other journal."

But God's primary assessment of our lives is not going to be measured by the number of journal entries. I recently received a book of which the stated goal was to enable the reader to get up to "340 or 350 quiet times a year"—as if that were the point.

I suspect that if someone had asked the apostle Paul or the apostle John about his spiritual life, his first question would have been, "Am I growing in love for God and people?" The real issue is what kind of people we are becoming. Practices such as reading Scripture and praying are important   not because they prove how spiritual we are—but because God can use them to lead us into life. We are called to do nothing less than to experience day by day what Paul wrote to the church at Ephesus: "But God, who is rich in mercy, out of the great love with which he loved us even when we were dead through our trespasses, made us alive together with Christ."

Many years ago I took one of my daughters to see her first movie: *Snow White and the Seven Dwarfs*. For an hour and a half we lived in another world. I had forgotten how dark movies can be for a two-year-old. My daughter cried at the wicked stepmother, at the bite of the apple, at the coming of the curse.

My tears came at another place. Snow White was cleaning out the cottage and singing, "Someday, my prince will come." Suddenly it was as if it were my little girl on the screen, and I was thinking about the day when her "prince"—whoever that was to be—would come and she would go away and they would be together.

In that moment I had new empathy for the dwarfs. In this story they give their home and risk their lives for this foolish girl who eats the forbidden fruit and falls asleep and breaks their heart. And then the prince comes and awakens her with a kiss, and she runs off with him without a regret. But of course that is how it must be. That is her destiny.

And that is ours, too.

Each of us has tasted the forbidden fruit. We have all eaten the apple. We have all fallen under the curse. We are all, on our own, in a kind of living death.

But still the Prince comes, to bring freedom from the curse, life from death. Still the Prince comes, to kiss his bride. And every once in a while, somebody, somewhere, wakes up. And when that happens—that's life.

> "Sleeper, awake!
> Rise from the dead,
> and Christ will shine on you."

CHAPTER 3

TRAINING VS. TRYING
The Truth About Spiritual Disciplines

*Christianity without discipleship is always
Christianity without Christ.*
DIETRICH BONHOEFFER

Imagine a group of people coming to your home and interrupting your Twinkie-eating, TV-watching routine with an urgent message: "Good news! We're from the United States Olympic Committee. We have been looking for someone to run the marathon in the next Olympics. We have statistics on every person in the entire nation on computer. We have checked everybody's records—their performance in the president's physical fitness test in grade school, body type, bone structure, right down to their current percentage of body fat. We have determined that out of two hundred million people, *you* are the one person in America with a chance to bring home the gold medal in the marathon. So you are on the squad. You will run the race. This is the chance of a lifetime."

You are surprised by this because the farthest you have ever run is from the couch to the refrigerator. But after the first shock passes, you are gripped by the realization of what's happening in your life. You picture yourself mingling with the elite athletes of the world.

You allow yourself to imagine that maybe you do have what it takes. At night you dream about standing on the podium after the race and hearing the national anthem, seeing the flag raised, and bending low to receive the gold medal.

You begin to feel a sense of urgency. It will be your body wearing those little racing togs, with a billion people watching on television. But greater than any external pressure is the internal drive that says, "This is the race I was created to run. This is my destiny. This is why I was born. *Here's my chance!*"

> **Trying hard can accomplish only so much. If you are serious, . . . you will have to enter into a life of training.**

This race becomes the great passion of your life. It dominates your mind. It occupies every waking moment. To run the race well—to win it if you can—becomes the central focus of your existence. It is what gets you out of bed in the morning. It is what you live for. It is the chance of a lifetime.

Then it dawns on you: Right now you cannot run a marathon. More to the point, you cannot run a marathon *even if you try really, really hard*. Trying hard can accomplish only so much. If you are serious about seizing this chance of a lifetime, you will have to enter into a life of training. You must arrange your life around certain practices that will enable you to do what you cannot do now by willpower alone. When it comes to running a marathon, you must train, not merely try.

This need for training is not confined only to athletics. Training is required for people who want to play a musical instrument or learn a new language or run a business. Indeed, it is required for any significant challenge in life—including spiritual growth.

Training Vs. Trying to Be Like Jesus

I devote this chapter to the single most helpful principle I know regarding spiritual transformation. It is by no means original with me. People who are wise in the ways of spiritual growth have understood it for centuries. I came across it at a time when I felt frustrated and stagnant in my own life with God, and through it I gained a firm hope that I really could grow. Through it—in a way I didn't recognize at the time—God was speaking to me. Here is the principle: *There is an immense difference between* training *to do something and* trying *to do something.*

I wish I could describe the hope I felt when I first came to understand this truth. I found it in Dallas Willard's book *The Spirit of the Disciplines*, and most of this chapter flows from the spirit of understanding that underlies his work. For much of my life, when I heard messages about following Jesus, I thought in terms of *trying hard* to be like him. So after hearing (or preaching, for that matter) a sermon on patience on Sunday, I would wake up Monday morning determined to be a more patient person. Have you ever tried hard to be patient with a three-year-old? I have— and it generally didn't work any better than would my trying hard to run a marathon for which I had not trained. I would end up exhausted and defeated. Given the way we are prone to describe "following Jesus," it's a wonder anyone wants to do it at all.

> Given the way we are prone to describe "following Jesus," it's a wonder anyone wants to do it at all.

Spiritual transformation is not a matter of trying harder, but of training wisely. This is what the apostle Paul means when he encourages his young protégé Timothy to "*train* yourself in godliness." This thought also lies behind his advice to the church at Corinth: "Everyone who competes in the games goes into *strict training*. They do it to get a crown that will not last; but we do it to get a crown that will last forever."

Athletics was familiar imagery to Paul's audience. Corinth was the site of the Isthmian Games, second only to the Olympics in prominence in ancient Greece. Paul himself had probably been in Corinth during the games of A.D. 51 and, according to Gordon Fee, may even have made tents for the visitors and contestants needing accommodations. That a competitor would strive for the crown by simply "trying really hard" apart from training was unthinkable. In fact, any athlete who entered the games was required to undergo ten months of strict training and could be disqualified for failing to do so. Paul said he, too, had entered a life of training, "so that after proclaiming to others I myself should not be disqualified."

Respecting the distinction between training and merely trying is the key to transformation in every aspect of life. People sometimes think that learning how to play Bach at the keyboard by spending years practicing scales and chord progressions is the "hard" way. The truth is the other way around. Spending years practicing scales is the easy way to learn to play Bach. Imagine sitting down at a grand piano in front of a packed concert hall and having never practiced a moment in your life. That's the hard way.

This need for preparation, or training, does not stop when it comes to learning the art of forgiveness, or joy, or courage. In other words, it applies to a healthy and vibrant spiritual life just as it does to physical and intellectual activity. Learning to think, feel, and act like Jesus is at least as demanding as learning to run a marathon or play the piano.

For me, this truth brought light to the darkness. For the first time as an adult, I found the notion of following Jesus a real, concrete, tangible possibility. I could do it. Following Jesus simply means learning from him how to arrange my life around activities that enable me to live in the fruit of the Spirit.

Following Jesus simply means learning from him how to arrange my life around activities that enable me to live in the fruit of the Spirit.

The traditional term for such activities is "spiritual disciplines." But for many people, that term carries associations of legalism, or attemptimg to earn God's goodwill, or something like New Year's resolutions—good intentions that are neither practical nor world-changing. Richard Foster's book, *Celebration of Discipline*, discusses twelve such activities for spiritual growth. When I read that book years ago, my immediate response was, "I already feel guilty about not reading the Bible and praying enough; the last thing in the world I want is ten other things to feel guilty about not doing."

My next response was to draw up a very ambitious plan for spiritual advancement that would immediately incorporate all twelve practices into my life so I could feel good about my spiritual growth. I tried this strategy for a few weeks, but I soon felt overwhelmed and exhausted by it. And my response after that was to give the whole project up as something practical only for monks and saints.

So before getting into what spiritual disciplines are, let's consider a few things spiritual disciplines are *not*:

1 Spiritual disciplines are not a barometer of spirituality.

Many people become burdened because they think God measures their spiritual performance on the basis of certain disciplines. The truth is both challenging and liberating.

Martin Luther begins his book *The Freedom of the Christian* with this paradox:

"A Christian is a perfectly free lord of all, subject to none."
"A Christian is a perfectly dutiful servant of all, subject to all."

Nowhere is this more true than with spiritual disciplines.

As we have seen, the true indicator of spiritual well-being is growth in the ability to love God and people. If we can do this without the practice of any particular spiritual disciplines, then we should by all means skip them. We are free of having to impress God or anyone else with our spiritual commitment. *Spiritual disciplines are to life what calisthenics are to a game.* Once the game starts, basketball players get no bonus points based on how many free throws they shot in practice. The only reason to practice them is to be able to make them in a game.

It is possible to spend every waking moment "practicing spiritual disciplines" but doing them in such a way as to make us less rather than more loving. In that case, of course, we would be better off if we did none at all.

2. Spiritual disciplines are not necessarily unpleasant.

What makes something a discipline depends on what we are training for. If we are training for a triathalon, we will pursue one set of practices. But if we are training for a pie-eating contest, our preparation will look like something else—mostly, consuming vast amounts of pie. If we keep at it long enough, we will be amazed at how much pie we can eventually put away compared with what we can now. What counts as "training" can only be determined when we know what it is we are training for.

Many of us got the impression somewhere that for an activity to count as a spiritual discipline, it must be something we would rather not do. However, if we are in training for a life characterized by joy, peace, and affection, we should assume that some of the practices are going to be downright enjoyable. Many of us need to discover "disciplines" such as celebration that will regularly produce in us rivers of wonder and gratitude.

3. Spiritual disciplines are not a way to earn favor with God.

Spiritual disciplines are not about trying to be good enough to merit God's forgiveness and goodwill. They are not ways to get extra credit, or to demonstrate to God how deeply we are committed to him. They exist for our sake, not God's. They have value only insofar as they help us morph.

> **Spiritual disciplines ... are not ways to get extra credit, or to demonstrate to God how deeply we are committed to him.**

In particular, spiritual disciplines don't oppose or exist in tension with grace. People who live under the bondage of legalism and then hear the message of grace are sometimes leery that talk of disciplines might lead to another form of religious oppression.

But spiritual disciplines are simply a means of appropriating or growing toward the life that God graciously offers. This is why they are sometimes called a "means of grace." Dietrich Bonhoeffer seemed to have this thought in mind when he wrote,

> We must therefore attempt to recover a true understanding of the mutual relation between grace and discipleship. . . . *Happy are they who know that discipleship simply means the life which springs from grace, and that grace simply means discipleship.* Happy are they who have become Christians in this sense of the word. For them the word of grace has proved a fount of mercy.

A Few Key Questions

What makes something a discipline?

Discipline: Any activity I can do by direct effort that will help me do what I cannot now do by direct effort.

People will sometimes speak of the "discipline of humility" or the "discipline of patience." Strictly speaking, however, such things are not really disciplines; they are the objects of the disciplines, the things we want to acquire through the disciplines.

In the children's book *Frog and Toad Together*, the two central characters discover the limits of mere trying when Frog bakes a batch of cookies. "We ought to stop eating," they say, as they keep eating. "We *must* stop," they resolve, as they eat some more. "We need willpower," Frog finally says, grabbing another cookie.

> Spiritual discipline: Any activity that can help me gain power to live life as Jesus taught and modeled it.

"What is willpower?" asks Toad, swallowing another mouthful.

"Willpower is trying very hard not to do something you want to do very much," Frog says.

Frog discusses a variety of ways to help with willpower—putting the cookies in a box, tying the box shut, putting it high up in a tree—but each time Toad points out (in between bites) that they could climb the tree and untie the box. In desperation, Frog finally dumps the remaining cookies outside on the ground: "Hey, birds!" he calls. "Here's cookies!"

"Now we have no more cookies," says Toad sadly.

"Yes," says Frog, "but we have lots and lots of willpower."

"You may keep it all," Toad replies. "I'm going home to bake a cake."

Disciplines are valuable simply because they allow us to do what we cannot do by willpower alone. This insight lies at the heart of Alcoholics Anonymous. The first of the Twelve Steps is to acknowledge that I cannot stop drinking by *willpower* alone ("trying really hard to stop drinking"). Then I must arrange my life around certain disciplines or practices—such as taking a ruthless moral inventory and confessing my faults—that will enable me to do what willpower can't. I must enter a life of *training* for sobriety.

What makes something a spiritual discipline?

Disciplines that are *spiritual* are simply those that help me live in the fruit of the Spirit.

Spiritual discipline: Any activity that can help me gain power to live life as Jesus taught and modeled it.

How many spiritual disciplines are there? As many as we can think of. Certain practices are basic, such as solitude, servanthood, confession, and meditation on Scripture. We will look at all these in the remaining chapters of this book. But we can turn almost any activity into a "training exercise" for spiritual life.

How do we know what spiritual disciplines to practice?

In a sense, the answer comes from thinking backward:

First, we must understand clearly what it means to live in the kingdom of God. Jesus spent much of his time helping people see what true spirituality looks like.

Second, we must learn what particular barriers keep us from living this kind of life.

Third, we must discover what particular practices, experiences, or relationships can help us overcome these barriers.

For instance, we know that we are called to be loving. One thing I discovered when I spent a day trying to live in a loving fashion is that love requires an enormous amount of energy. And I was just too tired to give it. So I realized that—as unspiritual as it sounds—if I was serious about becoming a more loving person, I was going to have to get more sleep.

I have discovered I have a very hard time thinking and feeling and acting like Jesus when I lack sleep. An article in *Time* magazine suggested that America has a sleep deficit that is worse than the national budget deficit, and it results in everything from increased irritability to fatal car accidents.

I was surprised to find that the Bible has much to say about what John Baillie called the theology of sleep. Sleep is a gift from God:

I will both lie down and sleep in peace;
for you alone, O LORD, make me lie down in safety.

It is an act of trust: I am reminded when I go to sleep that the world is in God's hands, not mine. The world will get along very well even though I am not awake to try to control things. At the appropriate time, my eyes will open and I will receive the gift of wakefulness once again.

I lie down and sleep;
I wake again, for the LORD sustains me.

Have you ever tried to pray when you are lacking sleep? Before Elijah was to spend a prolonged time in solitude and prayer at Mount Horeb, the angel of the Lord had him take not one, but two long naps. Contrast this with the disciples at Gethsemane, who could not pray because they kept falling asleep. Sleep is a gift from God.

It is in vain that you rise up early
and go late to rest,
eating the bread of anxious toil;
for he gives sleep to his beloved.

For some of you reading this book, perhaps the single most spiritual thing you could do right now is to put it down and take a nap.

What is a disciplined person?

The link between *disciple* and *discipline* is obvious. But getting the definitions right is very important, lest discipleship become rigid and mechanical.

A disciplined person is someone who can do the right thing at the right time in the right way with the right spirit.

Notice what a disciplined person is *not*. A disciplined person is not simply someone who exercises many disciplines. A disciplined person is not a highly systematic, rigidly scheduled, chart-making, gold-star-loving early riser. The Pharisees were rigid and organized, but they were not *disciplined persons* in the sense required by true discipleship.

Disciplined people can do what is called for at any given moment. They can do the right thing at the right time in the right way for the right reason.

This definition applies to artists and athletes and astronauts as well as to followers of Jesus. A disciplined follower of Jesus—a "disciple"—is not someone who has "mastered the disciplines" and never misses a daily regimen of spiritual exercises. *A disciplined follower of Jesus is someone who discerns when laughter, gentleness, silence, healing words, or prophetic indignation is called for, and offers it promptly, effectively, and lovingly.*

Signs of Wise Spiritual Training

Wise training respects the freedom of the Spirit.

At this point you may be wondering, *What about* God's *role in spiritual growth?* After all, the Bible speaks of transformation as the work of God. It's always a miracle when it happens. To speak of spiritual growth only as the product of training could make it sound like something *we* can engineer. Anytime a frog is turned into a prince—or even just a gentler, kinder frog—there is always something mysterious and awesome at work. In spiritual growth that "something mysterious" is the work of the Spirit. So another analogy from Scripture is helpful. "The wind blows where it chooses," Jesus said, "and you hear the sound of it, but you do not know where it comes from or where it goes. So it is with everyone who is born of the Spirit."

> **Disciplined people can do the right thing at the right time in the right way for the right reason.**

Consider the difference between piloting a motorboat or a sailboat. We can run a motorboat all by ourselves. We can fill the tank and start the engine. We are in control. But a sailboat is a different story. We can hoist the sails and steer the rudder, but we are utterly dependent on the wind. The wind does the work. If the wind doesn't blow—and sometimes it doesn't—we sit still in the water no matter how frantic we act. Our task is to do whatever enables us to catch the wind.

Spiritual transformation is that way. We may be aggressively pursuing it, but we cannot turn it on and off. We can open ourselves to transformation through certain practices, but we cannot engineer it. We can take no credit for it.

It is profitable to see this. This truth saves us from pride and misdirected effort. Fist-clenching, teeth-gritting exertion is usually not productive. Indeed, feeling a constant sense of strain or burden probably indicates that we are off course. Jesus offered his yoke—his way of life—to tired people because he said his way of life involved ease and lightness and "rest for your souls." This theme is echoed by many of his followers. Frank Laubach writes, "The sense of being led by an unseen hand which takes mine ... grows upon me daily. I do not need to strain at all to find opportunity. . . . strain does not seem to do good."

Another analogy from sailboating concerns the fact that wise sailors know that their main task is being able to "read" the wind—to practice discernment. An experienced sailor can simply look at a lake and tell where the wind is blowing strongest, or look at the sky and give a weather forecast. A wise sailor knows when to raise and lower which sails to catch the wind most effectively.

Spiritual growth requires discernment. We must learn to respond to the fresh wind of the Spirit. Moses didn't ask or arrange for the burning bush. But once it was there, he had to make a choice: whether to turn aside and pay attention to the work of God.

God's responsibility is to provide the burning bush. Our responsibility is to turn aside. Often I forget this.

Sometime ago I bought a devotional book and set a goal of finishing it by the end of the year. Several times as I read, it was clear that something was happening in my heart; I felt I should stop and study a certain passage for a while. But such delays would have kept me from my goal for finishing the book. So I kept going.

I should have realized that getting through the book "on time" was not, as I thought, the way to demonstrate my devotion. The purpose was to put myself in a place where transformation could happen. If God should speak to me through one passage—if I am being convicted or healed or challenged—then my role is to stay there until the wind dies down. Then it's time to move on. I was motorboating instead of sailing. I failed to turn aside.

Take another example. A friend of mine was at a retreat center recently where a group of people were spending a day in the practice of silence. One of them, not watching where she was walking, bumped into my friend and nearly knocked her over. But because the woman was engaged in silence, she didn't say a word, not even a simple "Excuse me." Yet, the whole purpose of practicing silence is not to see how long we can go without speaking; the goal is to make space for Jesus in our lives so we learn to live like him. Living like him in part involves responding with grace and civility when we bump into people.

Our primary task is not to calculate how many verses of Scripture we read or how many minutes we spend in prayer. Our task is to use these activities to create opportunities for God to work. Then what happens is up to him. We just put up sails: "The wind blows where it chooses. . . ."

Wise training respects our unique temperament and gifts.

There is good news here: Whatever your natural temperament may be, it is not a barrier to your spiritual growth.

Do you tend to be spontaneous, or are you a well-organized-plan-ahead type of person? Often people who are highly spontaneous think they are at a disadvantage for spiritual growth because living according to a predictable routine is difficult for them. (If you are still trying to decide which type you are, you can pretty much eliminate spontaneous.) In many ways, however, people with a gift for spontaneity have a great advantage in being able to give a good response promptly

> **Whatever your natural temperament may be, it is not a barrier to your spiritual growth.**

The particular combination of practices, relationships, and experiences needed for growth will be different for everyone. The life of Abraham Lincoln is by most accounts an amazing study in character formation. Yet he was notoriously disorganized; he even had a file in his law office labeled "If you can't find it anywhere else, try looking here."

We need the freedom to discover how God wants us to grow, for his design will not look quite the same for everyone. Perhaps God speaks to us in special ways through nature. Perhaps he made us to be formed by music. We may have an above-average capacity for silence and prayer. Or we might respond most strongly to images, symbols, and the fine arts. C. S. Lewis once surmised that each person is created to see a different facet of God's beauty   something no one else can see in quite the same way—and then to bless all worshipers through all eternity with an aspect of God they could not otherwise see.

Wise training will take into account our season of life.

There is more good news in that our season of life is not a barrier to spiritual growth.

A mother in our small group suggested that it was easier for her to "work on her spiritual life" before she became a mom. As we talked, it became clear what she meant. To her, reading the Bible and praying were the only two activities that counted spiritually. As a mother she felt that "time alone" was an oxymoron.

In this the church had failed her. She had never been taught to see that caring for two young children, offered daily with expressions of gratitude and prayers for help and patient acceptance of trials, might become a kind of school for transformation into powerful servanthood beyond anything she had ever known. Somehow having a "quiet time" *counted* toward spiritual devotion, and caring for two children did not.

It took creative effort for this mother to carve out time for solitude and stillness, and even then she could not free up the amount of time she had in college. But as a mother she had new opportunities for growth she did not have back then.

Our season of life—whatever it is—is no barrier to having Christ formed in us. Not in the least.

Whatever our season of life, it offers its own opportunities and challenges for spiritual growth. Instead of wishing we were in another season, we ought to find out what this one offers.

Life counts—all of it. Every moment is potentially an opportunity to be guided by God into his way of living. Every moment is a chance to learn from Jesus how to live in the kingdom of God.

Wise training respects the inevitability of troughs and peaks.

One of the most basic laws of life is rhythm. Night follows day, winter follows summer, we wake and we sleep.

In spiritual life, the traditional language for this is rhythm. There will be times of consolation and times of desolation. In times of consolation we like to pray because God seems close, the Bible seems alive, sin looks bad, and stoplights all seem green. Times of desolation are just the opposite: The Bible seems dry, prayer grows hard, and God is far away.

C. S. Lewis noted that at times God will send us a strong sense of his presence, a desire to be with him, the ability to withstand temptations with ease.

But He never allows this state of affairs to last long. Sooner or later He withdraws, if not in fact, at least from their conscious experience, all those supports and incentives. He leaves the creature to stand up on its own legs—to carry out from the will alone duties which have lost all relish. It is during such trough periods, much more than during the peak periods, that it is growing into the sort of creature He wants it to be.

When we forget the law of rhythm, we assume that whatever phase is current will last forever. In times of consolation I mistakenly think that I now have spiritual life mastered. In times of desolation I assume I must have done something wrong, or perhaps God is punishing me. In truth, both seasons are inevitable, and both seasons can bring unique growth.

Several years ago I was in a group devoted to learning how to pray. We all agreed we would pray for a long time (at least it was long to me) each day. We learned how to use Scripture when we prayed. We agreed to wake up at times to pray in the middle of the night, just to experience the stillness. We agreed to spend time reflecting on our prayers to learn how to recognize when God was speaking to us.

After the group disbanded, I was chagrined to realize that I was praying much less than I had when we were together. I really thought I had the prayer thing pretty much figured out. Then a wise friend explained that after you get stretched pretty hard, you generally have to rest for a while in order to "catch up." Sure enough—after a time of "resting," I found I had a new hunger for prayer.

This law of nature means it is probably a mistake to assume that one "spiritual routine" is adequate to cover us for the rest of our lives. We will have times of great growth, spending enormous amounts of time in prayer or service. We will have times of desolation when prayer comes hard. Perhaps during these latter times we will need more rest.

Wise training begins with a clear decision.

When I came to understand the idea of training to be like Jesus, I was faced with a choice. People do not just drift into a life of training.

Every year a few human beings approach their full physical potential of strength and conditioning; they show us what the body can become in body-builder competitions. They have devoted themselves to developing their bodies. Their habits of life—eating, exercise, rest, and so on—are arranged around a single task so that people can look at them and say, "So that's what a human body can be. I had no idea!"

This kind of conditioning does not come about by accident. Sometime ago my wife and I were watching a movie featuring a contemporary action star famous for his chiseled physique. For some reason, the poor guy had a terrible time keeping his shirt on, even though the story took place on a snowy mountain and everyone else was wearing parkas. At one point, as his rippling torso again filled the screen, Nancy looked at him, then took a long look at me—I was six-foot-one and 130 pounds as a freshman in high school, and what weight I've put on since then is mostly in the wrong places—looked back at him, then back at me, and finally said, "You know, I'm just not attracted to well-built men."

It is probably a mistake to assume that one "spiritual routine" is adequate to cover us for the rest of our lives.

I turned this comment over and over in my mind, looking for the compliment that I was certain lurked somewhere beneath the surface of what she said, but apparently it lurked too deep, for I could never find it. I wouldn't mind looking like the guy in the movie, but it is not likely to happen: I have never decided to order my life around that goal.

A newspaper in Los Angeles quoted a physical trainer and former Mr. Missouri contestant: "The guys you see on TV and in magazines that have that look—that look is what they do for a living. *The maintenance of that look is what their entire lives are based on— it's a lifestyle. It's 24 hours a day, 7 days a week.* We're such a now society. Guys come in thinking that in three months or by swimsuit season they can be looking all ripped and hard. And that's, um, pretty unrealistic."

Whether "looking all ripped and hard" is worth devoting your life to is, of course, another question. But it doesn't happen in a day. It is "what their entire lives are based on."

Jesus confronted people directly about the choice to become a follower. He came with the gracious announcement that it is now possible to live in the presence and under the reign of God—that was his Good News. It is possible to live in such a way that when people see us, they will say to themselves, "Wow! I didn't know that a life could look like that." It indeed happens. It has happened for many who have followed Christ, and it really is possible for us. This is the "pearl of great value" of which Jesus spoke, for which any sensible person would sell everything. This is the race for which we were born. But we will not drift into such a life. We must decide.

Final Preparations

Each of the remaining chapters in this book deals with a spiritual discipline. But before we turn to them, I want to say a word about how you can learn which practices might be most helpful in your own life. After all, offering people sound advice about their souls has often been compared to the wisdom a doctor gives a patient, and what a doctor prescribes will depend a great deal on the diagnosis.

On the diagnostic side, sin can be divided into two general categories: sins of omission and sins of commission. Sins of omission involve not doing those things we ought to do; sins of commission consist of things we do that we ought to avoid.

Similarly, Dallas Willard notes that spiritual disciplines can be placed in two categories—disciplines of engagement and disciplines of abstinence. Disciplines of engagement involve my intentionally *doing*

> If my problem is that I am *doing* something I ought not to do, I need to practice a discipline that strengthens my *not-doing* muscles.

certain things. Worship, study, fellowship, and giving are all disciplines of engagement. By contrast, disciplines of abstinence involve my intentionally *refraining* from doing things. These include practices such as fasting, solitude, and silence.

Here's the connection: If I struggle with a sin of *commission*, I will generally be helped by practicing a discipline of *abstinence*. In other words, if my problem is that I am *doing* something I ought not to do, I need to practice a discipline that strengthens my *not-doing* muscles. So if you have a problem with boasting (a sin of commission), what disciplines are likely to help? If you said silence or secrecy (both disciplines of abstinence), you're right—but don't tell anybody!

If I struggle with a sin of *omission*, I will usually be most helped by a discipline of *engagement*. That is, if my sin involves a failure to love or encourage or serve, I need practices that will help my *doing* muscles. If, for example, you ever wrestle with joylessness, you will want to immerse yourself in my favorite discipline of all—the discipline of celebration. So read on. The next chapter is just for you.

CHAPTER 4

A "DEE DAH DAY"
The Practice of Celebration

Joy is the serious business of heaven.
C. S. LEWIS

Sometime ago I was giving a bath to our three children. I had a custom of bathing them together, more to save time than anything else. I knew that eventually I would have to stop the group bathing, but for the time being it seemed efficient.

Johnny was still in the tub, Laura was out and safely in her pajamas, and I was trying to get Mallory dried off. Mallory was out of the water, but was doing what has come to be known in our family as the Dee Dah Day dance. This consists of her running around and around in circles, singing over and over again, "Dee dah day, dee dah day." It is a relatively simple dance expressing great joy. When she is too happy to hold it in any longer, when words are inadequate to give voice to her euphoria, she has to dance to release her joy. So she does the Dee Dah Day.

On this particular occasion, I was irritated. "Mallory, hurry!" I prodded. So she did—she began running in circles faster and faster and chanting "dee dah day" more rapidly. "No, Mallory, that's not what I mean! Stop with the dee dah day stuff, and get over here so I can dry you off. Hurry!"

Then she asked a profound question: "Why?"

I had no answer. I had nowhere to go, nothing to do, no meetings to attend, no sermons to write. I was just so used to hurrying, so preoccupied with my own little agenda, so trapped in this rut of moving from one task to another, that here was life, here was joy, here was an invitation to the dance right in front of me—and I was missing it.

So I got up, and Mallory and I did the Dee Dah Day dance together. She said I was pretty good at it, too, for a man my age.

> **Most of life is spent in transit: trying to get somewhere, waiting to begin, standing in line....**

Reflecting on this afterward, I realized that I tend to divide my minutes into two categories: living, and waiting to live. Most of my life is spent in transit: trying to get somewhere, waiting to begin, driving someplace, standing in line, waiting for a meeting to end, trying to get a task completed, worrying about something bad that might happen, or being angry about something that did happen. These are all moments when I am not likely to be fully present, not to be aware of the voice and purpose of God. I am impatient. I am, almost literally, killing time. And that is just another way of saying I am killing myself. Drying off the kids was just something I was trying to get through.

Ironically, often the thing that keeps me from experiencing joy is my preoccupation with *self*. The very selfishness that keeps me from pouring myself out for the joy of others also keeps me from noticing and delighting in the myriad small gifts God offers each day. This is why Walker Percy describes boredom as "the self *stuffed with the self*."

Life is not that way for Mallory. Her self is unstuffed. She just lives. While she's taking a bath, it's a dee dah day moment. And when it is time to get dried, that's another one. After she's dry, it will be time for another. Life is a series of dee dah day moments. Not every moment of life is happy, of course. There are still occasions that call for tears—skinned knees and cranky towel-bearers. But each moment is pregnant with possibility. Mallory doesn't miss many of them. She is teaching me about joy.

And I need to learn. Joy is at the heart of God's plan for human beings. The reason for this is worth pondering awhile: Joy is at the heart of God himself. We will never understand the significance of joy in human life until we understand its importance to God. I suspect that most of us seriously underestimate God's capacity for joy.

Our Joyful God

In respect to joy at least, G. K. Chesterton would insist that Mallory is a good deal more like God than I am. Chesterton's writings are filled with the centrality of joy in the character of God and his plans for humankind.

Jesus came as the Joy-bringer. The joy we see in the happiest child is but a fraction of the joy that resides in the heart of God. Chesterton speaks of this in a memorable passage:

> Because children have abounding vitality, because they are in spirit fierce and free, therefore they want things repeated and unchanged. They always say, "Do it again"; and the grown-up person does it again until he is nearly dead. For grown-up people are not strong enough to exult in monotony. But perhaps God is strong enough to exult in monotony. It is possible that God says every morning, "Do it again" to the sun; and every evening, "Do it again" to the moon. It may not be automatic necessity that makes all daisies alike; it may be that God makes every daisy separately, but has never got tired of making them. It may be that He has the eternal appetite of infancy; *for we have sinned and grown old, and our Father is younger than we.*

As an exercise in contrast, imagine for a moment how the opening sentences of the Bible might read if God were not a supremely joyful being. Imagine Genesis if God approached his work as we so often do:

In the beginning, it was nine o'clock, so God had to go to work. He filled out a requisition to separate light from darkness. He considered making stars to beautify the night, and planets to fill the skies, but thought it sounded like too much work; and besides, thought God, "That's not my job." So he decided to knock off early and call it a day. And he looked at what he had done and he said, "It'll have to do."

On the second day God separated the waters from the dry land. And he made all the dry land flat, plain, and functional, so that—behold—the whole earth looked like Idaho. He thought about making mountains and valleys and glaciers and jungles and forests, but he decided it wouldn't be worth the effort. And God looked at what he had done that day and said, "It'll have to do."

And God made a pigeon to fly in the air, and a carp to swim in the waters, and a cat to creep upon dry ground. And God thought about making millions of other species of all sizes and shapes and colors, but he couldn't drum up any enthusiasm for any other animals—in fact, he wasn't too crazy about the cat. Besides, it was almost time for the Late Show. So God looked at all he had done, and God said, "It'll have to do."

And at the end of the week, God was seriously burned out. So he breathed a big sigh of relief and said, "Thank Me, it's Friday."

Of course, Genesis looks nothing like that. Instead it throbs with the refrain "God said, . . . And it was so. . . . and indeed, it was very good."

On the first day, "God said, 'Let there be light'; and there was light. And God saw that the light was good." The first day was a Dee Dah Day. And God did a little dance. And the next day God said to the light, "Do it again." And the light did it again, and God danced once again. And so it has gone every day down to this one—down to the morning of the day you were born; down to the morning of this day in which you read these words.

So it is with God, but not with us. *"For we have sinned and grown old, and our Father is younger than we."*

We will not understand God until we understand this about him: "God is the happiest being in the universe." God also knows sorrow. Jesus is remembered, among other things, as "a man of sorrows, and acquainted with grief." But the sorrow of God, like the anger of God, is his temporary response to a fallen world. That sorrow will be banished forever from his heart on the day the world is set right. Joy is God's basic character. Joy is his eternal destiny. God is the happiest being in the universe.

And God's intent was that his creation would mirror his joy. The psalmist speaks of the sun, "which comes out like a bridegroom from his wedding canopy, and like a strong man runs its course with joy." This is not merely picturesque language; this is creation expressing God's own unwearying joy at simply being, at existing and knowing existence to be good. As products of God's creation, creatures made in his image, we are to reflect God's fierce joy in life.

Imagine Genesis if God approached his work as we so often do.

This is why the Bible speaks not just about our need for joy in general, but a particular kind of joy that characterizes God.

After teaching on the need for obedience, Jesus told his friends that his aim was that they should be filled with joy, but not just any *kind* of joy: "I have said these things to you so that *my* joy may be in you, and that your joy may be complete."

The problem with people, according to Jesus, is not that we are too happy for God's taste, but that we are not happy enough.

Lewis Smedes puts it this way: "To miss out on joy is to miss out on the reason for your existence."

C. S. Lewis said, "Joy is the serious business of heaven."

The apostle Paul wrote, "Rejoice in the Lord always; again I will say, Rejoice."

The Bible puts joy in the nonoptional category. Joy is a command. Joylessness is a serious sin, one that religious people are particularly prone to indulge in. It may be the sin most readily tolerated by the church. It is rarely the object of church discipline. Televangelists don't get canceled for displaying too much of it.

But how much damage have joyless Christians done to the cause of Christ? James Joyce writes in *A Portrait of the Artist as a Young Man* of his hero's decision not to become a priest. Stephen Dedalus has a vision of what would happen to his face, how it would become like the faces of other religious people he knew: "a mirthless mask reflecting a sunken day . . . sourfavored and devout, shot with pink tinges of suffocated anger." How often have people misunderstood God because they attributed to him the grim, judgmental, defensive, soul-wearying spirit of many who claim to be his followers?

The problem with people . . . is not that we are too happy for God's taste, but that we are not happy enough.

There is a being in this universe who wants you to live in sorrow, but it is not God. Francis de Sales wrote, "The evil one is pleased with sadness and melancholy because he himself is sad and melancholy, and will be so for all eternity. Hence he desires that everyone should be like himself."

Joy and Gratitude

We are invited to rejoice in every moment of life because every moment of life is a gift. Every once in a while the veil is lifted, and we see this.

The first close friendship I ever had began when I was fifteen years old. Chuck and I went through high school and college together; we double-dated together (and got rejected together); we were confidants and counselors and chums through every important event of life.

Several years ago Chuck called to tell me he had cancer. The initial prognosis was very good, although he did have to undergo difficult treatment. In typical fashion Chuck shaved his head before the chemotherapy began, covered it with glue, sprinkled it with gold glitter, and walked around the house in his underwear, calling himself "Chemo-Man."

Chuck and I lived more than two thousand miles apart at this time, but we talked every Saturday morning during the time he was undergoing treatment. The chemotherapy destroyed his appetite; he was unable to keep food down; he became so gaunt and emaciated that he was almost unrecognizable even to his children. At one point an infection set in, and his condition was briefly touch-and-go because the chemotherapy had so weakened his immune system. But Chuck pulled through, and eventually he completed treatment. Chemo-Man had prevailed.

A month later, Chuck had his first posttreatment checkup. He called me that night. The cancer was back, the doctor told him, at levels as high as they had been before treatment. Being a doctor himself, he knew that the return of the cancer this strongly, this quickly, meant that he was going to die. It was a death sentence.

I was numb. When I went to bed that night, I couldn't even pray. "It's some mistake," I protested. "They'll find out it's okay." I marveled at how quickly denial sets in.

At 6:30 the next morning, Chuck called again. "You won't believe this," he said. Someone in the lab had mistakenly switched his results with those of another patient, who had not yet even been through treatment. It turned out that Chuck's cancer was gone—and has not reappeared, these many years later.

"I'm going to live," my friend said. "I'm going to see my kids grow up. I'm going to grow old with my wife. I'm going to live."

For a few moments we just wept on the phone like a couple of characters out of a Hallmark commercial. Chuck told me he was filled with a gratitude he had never known. He couldn't stop touching his kids or hugging his wife. Things that had bothered him before faded into utter insignificance. He was going to live—and suddenly he did not just know intellectually but actually experienced the truth that life is a gift. We don't earn it, can't control it, can't take a moment of it for granted. Every tick of the clock is a gift from God. Every day is a Dee Dah Day.

The Necessity of Joy for Spiritual Life

We have greatly underestimated the necessity of joy. Nehemiah said to his grieving congregation, "This day is holy to the LORD your God; do not mourn or weep.... Go your way, eat the fat and drink sweet wine and send portions of them to those for whom nothing is prepared, for this day is holy to our LORD; and do not be grieved, for *the joy of the LORD is your strength.*"

Joy is strength. Its absence will create weakness. Or, in the words of Dallas Willard,

> failure to attain a deeply satisfying life always has the effect of making sinful actions seem good. Here lies the strength of temptation.... Normally, our success in overcoming temptation will be easier if we are basically happy in our lives. To cut off the joys and pleasures associated with our bodily lives and social existence as "unspiritual," then, can actually have the effect of *weakening* us in our efforts to do what is right.

Here is a key task for spiritual vitality: *We must arrange life so that sin no longer looks good to us.* One gets the sense that when Mother Teresa drove in congested traffic, she didn't have a hard time keeping herself from making rude gestures or calling other drivers bad names. Why? Such actions no longer looked appealing to her. She found a better way to live. The joy of the Lord brought strength.

I think the time has come, strange as it sounds, for us to take joy seriously.

You can become a joyful person. With God's help, it really is possible. The biblical writers would not command it if it were not so. But joyfulness is a learned skill. You must take responsibility for your joy. Not your friend, not your parent, not your spouse, not your kids, not your boss—your joy is your responsibility. For some of us, this does not come easily. You may be joy-impaired. You will have to fight for it. But it can be done.

Strategic Celebration

People who want to pursue joy especially need to practice the discipline of celebration. This is a primary reason that we see much emphasis placed on feast days in the Old Testament. Times of feasting were to be transforming experiences—just as times of meditating or fasting were. Celebration generally involves activities that bring pleasure—gathering with people we love, eating and drinking, singing and dancing. Spiritual celebration means doing them while reflecting on the wonderful God who has given us such wonderful gifts.

> **We must arrange life so that sin no longer looks good to us.**

The words of Nehemiah express this spirit of celebration. Our word *holiday* comes from the practice of "holy days." We often think of "discipline" as abstinence from pleasurable things, but Nehemiah commanded the people to set aside a time to revel in them *as a discipline for personal transformation*. "Eating the fat"—in other translations called "choice food"—can be every bit as much a discipline as fasting. We expect a prophet to tell us to eat locusts and brussel sprouts, or maybe nothing at all, but here we see Nehemiah handing out the equivalent of Twinkies and Fritos.

True celebration is the inverse of hedonism. Hedonism is the demand for more and more pleasure for personal gratification. It always follows the law of diminishing returns, so that what produced joy in us yesterday no longer does today. Our capacity for joy diminishes. Celebration is not like that. When we celebrate, we exercise our ability to see and feel goodness in the simplest gifts of God. We are able to take delight today in something we wouldn't have even noticed yesterday. Our capacity for joy increases.

So how do we pursue joy?

Begin Now

The first step for pursuing joy is simply to begin now. The psalmist says, "*This* is the day that the LORD has made; let us rejoice and be glad in *it*." He doesn't say, "Yesterday was God's day—how happy I was then." Nor does he say, "Tomorrow will be the great day—I'll just endure until then." *This* day, with all its shortcomings, is the great Dee Dah Day.

We all live with the illusion that joy will come someday when conditions change. We go to school and think we will be happy when we graduate. We are single and are convinced we will be happy when we get married. We get married and decide we will be happy someday when we have children. We have children and decide we will be happy when they grow up and leave the nest—then they do, and we think we were happier when they were still at home.

"This is God's day," the psalmist says. It is the day God made, a day that Christ's death has redeemed. If we are going to know joy, it must be in this day—today.

But this raises a question. How can I embrace joy amid all the pain and suffering in the world? Is it right to be joyful in a world of hunger and violence and injustice?

It is precisely here that we make one of the most surprising discoveries: Often it is the people closest to suffering who have the most powerful joy. Friends of Mother Teresa say that instead of being overwhelmed by the suffering around her, she fairly glowed with joy as she went about her ministry of mercy. One of the English officers imprisoned at Flossenburg with Dietrich Bonhoeffer said of him, "Bonhoeffer always seemed to me to spread an atmosphere of happiness and joy over the least incident and profound gratitude for the mere fact that he was alive."

Often it is the people closest to suffering who have the most powerful joy.

True joy, as it turns out, comes only to those who have devoted their lives to something greater than personal happiness. This is most visible in extraordinary lives, in saints and martyrs. But it is no less true for ordinary people like us.

One test of authentic joy is its compatibility with pain. Joy in this world is always joy "in spite of" something. Joy is, as Karl Barth put it, a "defiant nevertheless" set at a full stop against bitterness and resentment.

If we don't rejoice today, we will not rejoice at all. If we wait until conditions are perfect, we will still be waiting when we die. If we are going to rejoice, it must be in *this* day. This is the day that the Lord has made. This is the Dee Dah Day.

Find a "Joy Mentor"

Each of us knows a few people who are joy-carriers. When we are around them, they breathe life into us. Prize them. Thank them. Above all, get intentional about being with them. That is important, because there are other people in our lives also—people who have rejected joy, who have decided to be victims. They don't want us to be joyful either. They are like the black holes of outer space: If we allow it, they will suck the joy right out of us.

A farmer had a neighbor, a constant complainer, a wet blanket in the linen closet of life. The farmer decided to impress this man for once in his existence, so he bought the world's greatest hunting dog, trained it thoroughly, and invited his joyless friend to go hunting. He showed the neighbor how his dog could stand motionless for an hour and pick up a scent a mile away. No response. From the blind the farmer shot a duck, which landed in the middle of the pond. Upon command, the dog trotted out, *walked on the surface of the water*, retrieved the bird, and dropped him at the feet of his master. "What do you think of that?" the farmer challenged his neighbor. To which his friend responded, "Your dog can't swim, can he?"

We all know people like that. We all have to endure a few joy-destroying people in life. We need to love them as best we can, but we also have to be very careful not to let them shape us. We may need to limit the time we spend with them. We certainly need to restrain their ability to sway our hearts.

Perhaps the least surprising statement in Scripture is found in Proverbs: "Smiling faces make us feel happy." We need to identify a few people who play this role in our lives—especially if we tend to be joy-challenged. Make a joy appointment to spend some time with such a person this week. We need to spend regular and significant amounts of time around life-enhancing, joy-producing people.

We could take this one step further and ask someone to be our "joy mentor." Find a person who demonstrates this joy and tell her or him that you are trying to break out of your joy-impaired condition. Begin to pray together that the Spirit will produce this fruit in your life in greater abundance.

Set Aside a Day a Week

If joy does not come easily for us, we may have to designate one day a week to be our personal Dee Dah Day, filled with pleasant things. These include things that appear to be trivial: Bonhoeffer wrote that his meals in prison made an opportunity to exercise the discipline of joy.

> God cannot endure that unfestive, mirthless attitude of ours in which we eat our bread in sorrow, with pretentious, busy haste, or even with shame. Through our daily meals He is calling us to rejoice, to keep holiday in the midst of our working day.

Devote a specific day to acts of celebration so that eventually joy will infuse your entire life. One day a week eat foods you love to eat, listen to music that moves your soul, play a sport that stretches and challenges you, read books that refresh your spirit, wear clothes that make you happy, surround yourself with beauty—and as you do these things, give thanks to God for his wonderful goodness. Reflect on what a gracious God he is to have thought of these gifts. Take the time to experience and savor joy, then direct your heart toward God so that you come to *know* he is the giver of "*every* good and perfect gift." Nothing is too small if it produces true joy in us and causes us to turn toward God in gratitude and delight.

In general, I believe we have underestimated the importance of pleasure in spiritual formation.

In general, I believe we have underestimated the importance of pleasure in spiritual formation. In his fictional classic *Screwtape Letters*, C. S. Lewis has a senior demon giving advice to a nephew demon on how to tempt humans. Uncle Screwtape writes,

> Never forget that when we are dealing with any pleasure in its healthy and normal and satisfying form we are, in a sense, on the Enemy's ground. I know we have won many a soul through pleasure. All the same, it is His invention, not ours. He made the pleasures; all our research so far has not enabled us to produce one. All we can do is to encourage the humans to take the pleasures which our Enemy has produced, at times, or ways, or in degrees, which He has forbidden.... An ever-increasing craving for an ever diminishing pleasure is the formula.... To get the man's soul and give him *nothing* in return—that is what really gladdens our Father's heart.

Unplug for a Week

The Scriptures record many instances of people fasting from food, Jesus among them. I suspect that were he bodily with us today, Jesus might also talk about fasting of a different sort. Instead of an empty refrigerator, this fast would involve an unplugged home entertainment center.

The statistics are common knowledge: Nielsen reports that television sets in the United States are turned on an average of six hours a day. More than a decade ago, a Detroit newspaper offered 120 families five hundred dollars apiece to endure a month without watching TV; 93 families turned the offer down. (The other 27 families reported their lives significantly improved during the month without television, but then they promptly returned to their former viewing habits.)

One irony in this is that many people watch television because they are tired and want rest for the mind and body. But how often do we hear someone at work say something like this: "I watched TV from the evening news to late-night talk shows, and I am feeling rejuvenated, renewed, revitalized, and refreshed! What a tremendous, memorable evening that was! I'm so grateful for the gift of television in my life."

The worst thing about TV is not what it puts into our mind so much as what it prevents us from doing. Watching television kills intimacy and conversation and disrupts sustained thought. Therapist Dolores Curren asked a family to write down the phrases most heard around the house over a two-week period. The two chart-toppers stunned the family: "What's on?" and "Move."

Depression is generally as prevalent inside the church as outside.

So try something radical. Engage in the spiritual discipline of unplugging for a week. Commit to a one-week, cold-turkey, television fast: no *Oprah, Dave, Guiding Light, American Gladiators,* or Disease Movie of the Week.

Literally remove the plug from the socket and leave it out for one week. Ask for God's help in declaring a "Week of Jubilee." Use the freed-up time to do things you have needed or have been planning to do. Get more sleep. Read something. Have a really good conversation.

We live in an age of melancholy. Depression has replaced anxiety as "the common cold of emotional life." Suicide has skyrocketed as a cause of death particularly among young people.

More sobering is the fact that depression is generally as prevalent inside the church as outside. There is at least one notable exception: Janice Egeland has done research among the Amish in Lancaster County, Pennsylvania, since the 1970s. Her findings show that the Amish have a significantly lower rate of depression than the general population in America. (The exception is manic-depression, which seems to be genetically influenced in great measure.)

How ironic it is that in a day when we rely so heavily on the entertainment industry to give us relief from both the demands and boredom of everyday life, the least-depressed group in our society is the one that disdains electronics of any kind. In fact, even diagnosing the manic phase of manic-depression was difficult because of the Amish lifestyle. Typical examples were "racing one's horse and carriage too hard, excessive use of a public telephone, and planning vacations during the wrong seasons."

Here is the great challenge: Is it possible for the church to help people become thoroughly transformed while remaining engaged in what Robert Hughes has called a "Culture of Complaint"? Can we be truly in the world but not of it, as Christ admonished us? The reality of conditions such as depression suggest it may be far harder than we think.

Discipline Your Mind to View Life from a Biblical Perspective

To a large extent, joy flows from a certain kind of thinking. Cognitive psychologists remind us that always between the events that happen to us and our responses to them lie our *beliefs* or *interpretations* of those events. This thought helps us to understand the irrepressible theme of joy in the New Testament. The New Testament writers were engaged not so much in some form of positive thinking as in what might be called "eschatological thinking." That is, they viewed all events in light of the Resurrection and the ultimate triumph of the risen Christ.

It takes a certain kind of heroism to continue to celebrate what deserves to be celebrated even when all the details go disastrously wrong. A favorite story of mine expressing this kind of spirit is told by Robert Fulghum, about a wedding that was produced on an epic scale by an unhinged character known only as the Mother of the Bride (MOTB). The logistics—from an eighteen-piece brass-and-wind ensemble to gift registries spreading across most of the continental United States to twenty-four bridesmaids, groomsmen, flower-petal-throwers, and ringbearers—were of a scale usually seen only during the military invasion of a sizable country. But the plans were all working—until the climactic moment of the processional:

> Ah, the bride. She had been dressed for hours if not days. No adrenaline was left in her body. Left alone with her father in the reception hall of the church while the march of the maidens went on and on, she had walked along the tables

laden with gourmet goodies and absentmindedly sampled first the little pink and yellow and green mints. Then she picked through the silver bowls of mixed nuts and ate the pecans. Followed by a cheeseball or two, some black olives, a handful of glazed almonds, a little sausage with a frilly toothpick stuck in it, a couple of shrimps blanketed in bacon, and a cracker piled with liver pate. To wash this down—a glass of pink champagne. Her father gave it to her. To calm her nerves.

What you noticed as the bride stood in the doorway was not her dress, but her face. White. For what was coming down the aisle was a living grenade with the pin pulled out.

The bride threw up.

Just as she walked by her mother.

And by "threw up," I don't mean a polite little ladylike *urp* into her handkerchief. She puked. There's just no nice word for it. I mean, she hosed the front of the chancel—hitting two bridesmaids, the groom, a ringbearer, and me. . . .

Only two people were seen smiling. One was the mother of the groom. And the other was the father of the bride.

Fulghum explains how they pulled themselves together for a much quieter, gentler ceremony in the reception hall. And how "everybody cried, as people are supposed to do at weddings, mostly because the groom held the bride in his arms through the whole ceremony. And no groom ever kissed a bride more tenderly than he."

But the best part of the story is that, ten years later, everybody was invited back for another party to celebrate this disaster. They watched the whole thing on three TV sets—the MOTB had had three video cameras going at once during the wedding. And this party was thrown by the Mother of the Bride herself.

How could all these people rejoice when everything had gone wrong? Because, in spite of all the mess, the bride still got the groom. At the end of the day, that was all that mattered. The bride got the groom. It was a Dee Dah Day.

How is it possible to become a joyful person in a pain-filled world? Look at the promise that comes right near the very end of the Bible:

> Let us rejoice and exult
>> and give him the glory,
> for the marriage of the Lamb has come,
>> and his bride has made herself ready.

Heaven's groom gets the bride.

The joy that is in store for God's people is so great that the only image that can do it justice is the joy between a lover and his beloved. Then we will see the wedding of which the greatest weddings on this earth have only been a dim foreshadowing.

Then God will dance with his people. Then joy will reign undiminished and uninterrupted. Then will be fulfilled the words of the prophet, who was trying to express the inexpressible:

> You shall go out in joy
>> and be led back in peace;
> the mountains and the hills before you
>> shall burst into song,
>> and all the trees of the field shall clap their hands.

The apostle John tried to say them, too.

> He will dwell with them as their God;
> they will be his peoples,
> and God himself will be with them;
> he will wipe every tear from their eyes.
> Death will be no more;
> mourning and crying and pain will be no more.

Then will dawn that great Dee Dah Day that will never end.

CHAPTER 5

AN UNHURRIED LIFE
The Practice of "Slowing"

People nowadays take time
far more seriously than eternity.
THOMAS KELLY

Not long after moving to Chicago, I called a wise friend to ask for some spiritual direction. I described the pace at which things tend to move in my current setting. I told him about the rhythms of our family life and about the present condition of my heart, as best I could discern it. What did I need to do, I asked him, to be spiritually healthy?

Long pause.

"You must ruthlessly eliminate hurry from your life," he said at last. Another long pause.

"Okay, I've written that one down," I told him, a little impatiently. "That's a good one. Now what else is there?" I had many things to do, and this was a long-distance conversation, so I was anxious to cram as many units of spiritual wisdom into the least amount of time possible.

Another long pause.

"There is nothing else," he said.

He is the wisest spiritual mentor I have known. And while he doesn't know every detail about every grain of sin in my life, he knows quite a bit. And from an immense quiver of spiritual sagacity, he drew only one arrow. "There is nothing else," he said. "You must ruthlessly eliminate hurry from your life."

Imagine for a moment that someone gave you this prescription, with the warning that your life depends on it. Consider the possibility that perhaps your life *does* depend on it. Hurry is the great enemy of spiritual life in our day. Hurry can destroy our souls. Hurry can keep us from living well. As Carl Jung wrote, "Hurry is not *of* the devil; hurry *is* the devil."

Again and again, as we pursue spiritual life, we must do battle with hurry. For many of us the great danger is not that we will renounce our faith. It is that we will become so distracted and rushed and preoccupied that we will settle for a mediocre version of it. We will just skim our lives instead of actually living them.

> The great danger is not that we will renounce our faith, but settle for a mediocre version of it.

The Disease: Hurry Sickness

We suffer from what has come to be known as "hurry sickness." One of the great illusions of our day is that hurrying will buy us more time. I pulled into a service station recently where the advertising slogan read, "We help you move faster." But what if my primary need is not moving faster?

Time magazine noted that back in the 1960s, expert testimony was given to a subcommittee of the Senate on time management. The essence of it was that because of advances in technology, within twenty years or so people would have to radically cut back on how many hours a week they worked, or how many weeks a year they worked, or else they would have to start retiring sooner. The great challenge, they said, was what people would do with all their free time. Yet thirty years later, not many of us would say that our primary challenge in regard to time is what to do with all the excess.

We will buy anything that promises to help us hurry. The best-selling shampoo in America rose to the top because it combines shampoo and conditioner in one step, eliminating the need for all the time-consuming rinsing people used to have to do. Domino's became the No. 1 name in pizza because the company promised to deliver in thirty minutes or less. ("We don't sell pizza," said their CEO, "We sell delivery.") *USA Today* reports, "Taking a cue from Domino's Pizza, a Detroit hospital guarantees that emergency-room patients will be seen within 20 minutes—or treatment is free." The paper notes that since the offer was made, business has been up 30 percent at the hospital.

We worship at the shrine of the Golden Arches, not because they sell "good food," or even "cheap food," but because it is "fast food." Even after fast food was introduced, people still had to park their cars, go inside, order, and take their food to a table, all of which took time. So we invented the Drive-Thru Lane to enable families to eat in vans, as nature intended.

Our world has become the world of the Red Queen in *Alice in Wonderland*: "Now *here*, you see, it takes all the running *you* can do, to keep in the same place. If you want to get somewhere else, you must run at least twice as fast as that!"

Ironically, all our efforts have not produced what we're after: a sense of what we might call "timefulness," a sense of having enough time. We often experience the opposite. Robert Banks notes that while American society is rich in goods, it is extremely time-poor. Many societies in the two-thirds world, by contrast, are poor in material possessions, by our standards, but they are rich in time. They are not driven or hurried. They live with a sense that there is adequate time to do what needs to be done each day.

Meyer Friedman defines hurry sickness as "above all, a continuous struggle and unremitting attempt to accomplish or achieve more and more things or participate in more and more events in less and less time, frequently in the face of opposition, real or imagined, from other persons." Hurry will keep us consumed by "the cares and riches and pleasures of life," as Jesus put it, and prevent his way from taking root in our hearts.

Jesus was quite aware of this kind of problem in his day. As we will see, he repeatedly withdrew from crowds and activities. He taught his followers to do likewise. When the disciples returned, their adrenaline pumping, from a busy time of ministry, Jesus told them, "Come away to a deserted place all by yourselves and rest a while." Mark explains that "many were coming and going, and they had no leisure even to eat." That could be the motto for some people today. Some people imagine this to be a good thing that perhaps God will reward one day: "What a life you had! You were even too busy to eat. Well done!"

But Mark did not mean this statement as a commendation. Jesus urged his disciples to take time out. Following Jesus cannot be done at a sprint. If we want to follow someone, we can't go faster than the one who is leading.

We must ruthlessly eliminate hurry from our lives. This does not mean we will never be busy. Jesus often had much to do, but he never did it in a way that severed the life-giving connection between him and his Father. He never did it in a way that interfered with his ability to give love when love was called for. He observed a regular practice of withdrawing from activity for the sake of solitude and prayer. Jesus was often busy, but never hurried.

Hurry is not just a disordered schedule. Hurry is a disordered heart.

Let's do a brief diagnostic exercise. How do we know if we are suffering from this hurry sickness? Here are some symptoms.

Constantly Speeding Up Daily Activities

If we have hurry sickness, we are haunted by the fear that there are just not enough hours in the day to do what needs to be done. We will read faster, talk faster, and when listening, nod faster to encourage the talker to accelerate. We will find ourselves chafing whenever we have to wait. At a stoplight, if there are two lanes and each contains one car, we will find ourselves guessing—based on the year, make, and model of each car—which one will pull away the fastest.

At a grocery store, if we have a choice between two check-out lines, we find ourselves counting how many people are in each line, multiplying this number by the number of items per cart. If we have a really bad case of hurry sickness, then even after we get in line we keep track of the person who *would have been me in the other line*. If we get through and the person who would have been me is still waiting, we are elated. We've won. But if the alter-me is walking out of the store and we're still in line, we feel depressed. We have hurry sickness.

"Multiple-Tasking"

Despite all this rushing around, the hurry-sick person is still not satisfied. So out of the desperate need to hurry, we find ourselves doing or thinking more than one thing at a time. Psychologists speak of this as polyphasic activity; the more hopeful euphemism is multiple-tasking. (It could be called "doing more than one thing at a time," but that takes too long to say.) The car is a favorite place for this. Hurry-sick people may drive, eat, drink coffee, monitor the radio, shave or apply make-up, talk on the car phone, and make gestures—all at the same time. Or they may try to watch television, read, eat dinner, and carry on a conversation simultaneously.

Clutter

The lives of the hurry-sick lack simplicity. These people often carry around a time organizer the size of Montana. They keep acquiring stacks of books and magazines and then feel guilty for not reading them. They buy time-saving gadgets and don't have the time or patience to read the instructions and figure out how to use them.

Paul Pearsall writes that many of these types cannot seem to get rid of their "stuff." He advises,

> You may require a "closet exorcist" experienced in dealing with the demons of closet clutter. . . . A trusted friend can also prevent the "restuffing phenomenon." Restuffing

happens when, in the process of cleaning out closets and drawers, we somehow are stimulated to acquire new stuff.

There are other, less material forms of clutter. Life is cluttered when we are weighed down by the burden of all the things we have failed to say no to. Then comes the clutter of forgetting important dates, of missing appointments, of not following through.

Superficiality

"Superficiality is the curse of our age," writes Richard Foster. If Superficiality is our curse, then Hurry pronounces the spell. Depth always comes slowly.

This is simply a truth about human formation. Perhaps one reason that Abraham Lincoln achieved the depth of thought he did is that he grew up with so *little* to read. David Donald notes in his biography that Lincoln grew up with access to very few books: the Bible, Aesop's Fables (which he virtually memorized), and a few others. "He must understand everything—even to the smallest thing—minutely and exactly," his stepmother remembered. "He would then repeat it over to himself again and again . . . and *when it was fixed in his mind to suit him he never lost that fact or the understanding of it.*"

> we have largely traded wisdom for information, depth for breadth. We want to microwave maturity.

Lincoln himself often spoke of how slowly his mind worked, how even as an adult he read laboriously and out loud. His law partner and biographer William Herndon claimed that "Lincoln read less and thought more than any man in his sphere in America."

But today we have largely traded wisdom for information. We have exchanged depth for breadth. We want to microwave maturity.

An Inability to Love

The most serious sign of hurry sickness is a diminished capacity to love. Love and hurry are fundamentally incompatible. Love always takes time, and time is one thing hurried people don't have.

A pilot once told me his favorite airline story. An elderly couple were flying first class, sitting behind a businessman who was enormously frustrated with them. They had been just ahead of him in line at the gate, and again boarding the plane, and they moved slowly, but he was in a hurry. When the meal was served, they delayed the businessman again by having to get some pills from the overhead storage, inadvertently dropping a battered duffel bag. "What's the matter with you people?" he exploded, loudly enough for the whole cabin to hear. "I'm amazed you ever get anywhere. Why can't you just stay home?"

To register his anger, the man sat down and reclined his seat back as hard as he could—so hard that the elderly husband's tray of food spilled all over him and his wife. The flight attendant apologized to the couple profusely: "Is there anything we can do?" she asked. The husband explained it was their fiftieth wedding anniversary and they were flying for the first time. "Let me at least bring you a bottle of wine," the flight attendant offered.

She did so. When it was uncorked, the old husband stood up, proposed a toast—and poured the bottle over the head of the impatient businessman sitting in front of them.

And, the pilot told me, everybody in the cabin cheered.

Sunset Fatigue

Hurried people cannot love. Lewis Grant suggests we are afflicted with what he calls "sunset fatigue." When we come home at the end of a day's work, those who need our love the most, those to whom we are most committed, end up getting the leftovers. Sunset fatigue is when we are just too tired, or too drained, or too preoccupied, to love the people to whom we have made the deepest promises. Sunset fatigue has set in, Grant says, when

— you find yourself rushing even when there's no reason to;
— there is an underlying tension that causes sharp words or sibling quarrels;
— you set up mock races ("OK, kids, let's see who can take a bath fastest") that are really about your own need to get through it;

— you sense a loss of gratitude and wonder;
— you indulge in self-destructive escapes from fatigue: abusing alcohol, watching too much TV, listening to country western music [okay, the last one is mine, not Grant's].

It is because it kills love that hurry is the great enemy of spiritual life. Hurry lies behind much of the anger and frustration of modern life. Hurry prevents us from receiving love from the Father or giving it to his children. That's why Jesus never hurried. If we are to follow Jesus, we must ruthlessly eliminate hurry from our lives—because, by definition, we can't move faster than the one we are following.

We can do this: We can become unhurried people. We can become patient people.

Curing the Hurry Sickness

But we will not become unhurried on our own. We cannot achieve this alone. We will have to enter a life of training. So let's look at practices for the hurry-sick.

"Slowing"

The first practice is one we might call "slowing." This involves cultivating patience by deliberately choosing to place ourselves in positions where we simply have to wait. (This practice has a definite "gamelike" quality, although we may not like it much, at least at first.)

Over the next month deliberately drive in the slow lane on the expressway. It may be that not swerving from lane to lane will cause you to arrive five minutes or so later than you usually would. But you will find that you don't get nearly so angry at other drivers. Instead of trying to pass them, say a little prayer as they go by, asking God to bless them.

Declare a fast from honking. Put your horn under a vow of silence.

For a week, eat your food slowly. Force yourself to chew at least fifteen times before each swallow.

For the next month, when you are at the grocery store, look carefully to see which check-out line is the longest. Get in it. Let one person go ahead of you.

Go through one day without wearing a watch.

The list could go on, but you get the idea. We must find ways to deliberately choose waiting, ways that make hurry impossible. As we practice them, we should tell God we are trusting him to enable us to accomplish all we need to get done.

Often people worry that if they don't rush, they will accomplish less. In fact, researchers have found that there is simply no correlation between hurry or Type-A behavior and productivity.

We will discover we can survive without hurry. If we practice these ways diligently enough, we will become unhurried people.

The Need for Solitude

A more traditional practice is solitude. Jesus engaged in it frequently. At the beginning of his ministry, Jesus went to the wilderness for an extended period of fasting and prayer. He also went into solitude when he heard of the death of John the Baptist, when he was going to choose his disciples, after he had been involved in healing a leper, and after his followers had engaged in ministry. This pattern continued into the final days of his life, when again he withdrew into the solitude of the garden of Gethsemane to pray. He ended his ministry, as he began it, with the practice of solitude.

Jesus taught his followers to do the same. And as he said to them, "Come away to a deserted place," he says to us still. Wise followers of Christ's way have always understood the necessity and benefit of solitude. It is, to quote an old phrase, the "furnace of transformation."

What makes solitude so important? *Solitude is the one place where we can gain freedom from the forces of society that will otherwise relentlessly mold us.*

According to a much-traveled analogy, if we put a frog in a pot of boiling water, it will immediately hop out. But put the frog in water that's at room temperature and heat it slowly, and the creature will stay there until it boils to death. Put him in a lethal environment suddenly, and he will escape. But introduce the danger gradually, and he will never notice.

The truth is that the dangers to which we are most vulnerable are generally not the sudden, dramatic, obvious ones. They are the ones that creep up on us, that are so much a part of our environment that we don't even notice them.

The deeper truth is that we live in a lethal environment. American society is filled with ideas and values and pressures and temptations about success and security and comfort and happiness that we will not even notice unless we withdraw on occasion. Thomas Merton wrote that the early church fathers placed such a premium on solitude because they considered society to be a shipwreck from which any sane person must swim for his life. These people believed that to let oneself drift along, passively accepting the tenets and values of what they knew as society, was purely and simply a disaster. The apostle Paul put it this way: "Don't let the world around squeeze you into its own mold."

One writer notes an experiment done with mice a few years ago. A researcher found that it takes a high dose of amphetamines to kill a mouse living in solitude. But a group of mice will start hopping around and hyping each other up so much that a dosage *twenty times smaller* will be lethal—so great is the effect of "the world" on mice. In fact, a mouse that had been given no amphetamines at all, placed in a group on the drug, will get so hopped up that in ten minutes or so it will be dead. "In groups they go off like popcorn or firecrackers," the writer observed.

We might guess that only a mouse would be so foolish as to hang out with a bunch of other mice that were so hopped up, going at such a frantic pace in such mindless activity for no discernible purpose, that they would put their own well-being and even lives at risk. It would be wrong to think so. The messages come at us in a continual stream:

"We'll help you move faster. . . . Act now, don't delay!. . . You can buy it now if you'll just stretch—no money down, easy monthly payments. . . . You can earn it if you run a little faster, stay a little longer, work a little harder. . . . It's okay to get old as long as you don't get wrinkled or gray or liver spots or bald—as long as you don't *look* old. . . . It's okay to be frantic and stressed and empty and exhausted— that's the way *everybody* is. . . . We'll help you move faster."

"The press of busyness is like a charm," Kierkegaard wrote. "Its power swells. . . . it reaches out seeking always to lay hold of ever-younger victims so that childhood or youth are scarcely allowed the quiet and the retirement in which the Eternal may unfold a divine growth." The truth is, as much as we complain about it, we are drawn to hurry. It makes us feel important. It keeps the adrenaline pumping. It means we don't have to look too closely at the heart or life. It keeps us from feeling our loneliness.

Solitude is the remedy for the busyness that charms. But what exactly *is* solitude? What do we *do* when we practice solitude? What should we bring along to that quiet place?

The primary answer, of course, is "nothing." A man recently told me about preparing for his first extended period of solitude. He took books, message tapes, CDs, and a VCR—some of the very things we would think of trying to get away from.

At its heart, solitude is primarily about *not* doing something. Just as fasting means to refrain from eating, so solitude means to refrain from society. When we go into solitude, we withdraw from conversation, from the presence of others, from noise, from the constant barrage of stimulation.

> **At its heart, solitude is primarily about not doing something.**

"In solitude," Henri Nouwen wrote, "I get rid of my scaffolding." Scaffolding is all the stuff we use to keep ourselves propped up, to convince ourselves that we are important or okay. In solitude we have no friends to talk with, no phone calls or meetings, no television sets, no music or books or newspapers to occupy and distract the mind. Each of us would be, in the words of the old hymn, "just as I am." Neither accomplishments nor résumés nor possessions nor networks would define me—just me and my sinfulness, my desire or lack of desire for God.

Practicing Solitude

Solitude requires relentless perseverance. I find that unless I pull my calendar out and write down well in advance the times when I am committed to times of solitude, it won't happen.

I find it helpful to think about solitude in two categories. We need brief periods of solitude on a regular basis—preferably each day, even at intervals during the day. But we also need, at great intervals, extended periods of solitude—half a day, a day, or a few days.

We may want to begin a particular day by praying over the day's schedule—meetings to attend, tasks to perform, people we will be with—and placing it in God's hands. Through the day we could take five-minute breaks if that is possible, close the door to the office, and remind ourselves that one day the office and the building will be gone—but we will still belong to God.

At the end of the day it can be helpful to review the day with God: to go over the events that took place, to see what he might want to say to us through them, and to hand any anxieties or regrets over to him. The next page has a format that I find helpful.

For most, the best time to review a day is at bedtime, but if you are a confirmed morning person, you may want to do it when you first get up the next morning. A great benefit of this exercise is that we begin to *learn* from our days. When I was in athletics in school

---

Reviewing the Day with God

1. Be still for a moment and quiet your mind.
2. Acknowledge that Jesus is present. Invite him to teach you.
3. Go back in your mind to when you first woke up. Watch that scene, as if on video. This may lead you to pray for patience, greater love, courage, forgiveness, or other virtues.
4. Continue through the day, going from scene to scene. As you reflect on them, some scenes may fill you with gratitude, others with regret. Speak directly to the Lord about this. You may also be led to pray for some of the people you were interacting with during the day.
5. End with a prayer of thanksgiving for God's mercy and love. Ask him to refresh you as you sleep.

---

we used to watch videotapes of our performance. Watching the tapes was sometimes painful, yet worth it to be spared our making the same mistakes over and over.

The same idea holds here. When I began to practice solitude with this exercise, I discovered I experienced much more anger than I would ever have thought. I began to be aware of the attitudes and responses that were guiding my life.

Extended Solitude

I also need extended times alone. I try to withdraw for a day once a month or so, and sometime during the year I try to have a retreat for a couple of days. Retreat centers designed for such experiences are becoming more and more common, although any place where you can be undisturbed suffices.

Francis de Sales used the image of a clock to express his need for extended solitude.

> There is no clock, no matter how good it may be, that doesn't need resetting and rewinding twice a day, once in the morning and once in the evening. In addition, at least once a year it must be taken apart to remove the dirt clogging it, straighten out bent parts, and repair those worn out. In like manner, every morning and evening a man who really takes care of his heart must rewind it for God's service. . . . Moreover, he must often reflect on his condition in order to reform and improve it. Finally, at least once a year he must take it apart and examine every piece in detail, that is every affection and passion, in order to repair whatever defects there may be.

One of the great obstacles to extended solitude is that frequently it may feel like a waste of time. This may happen partly because we are conditioned to feel that our existence is justified only when we are *doing* something. But I believe this feeling comes also because our minds tend to wander. I used to think that if I devoted a large block of time to praying, I should be able to engage

Extended Solitude

1. Find a place where you can be uninterrupted and alone, such as a park or a retreat center.
2. Spend a brief time the night before to get ready, to ask God to bless the day, and to tell him you want to devote the day to him. This day is your gift to God, but even more, it is a gift God wants to give you. What do you need from the Lord: a sense of healing and forgiveness? Conviction for an apathetic heart? Compassion? A renewed sense of mission? Ask him for this.
3. Arrange the day around listening to God. The following format is adapted from Glandion Carney's book *The Spiritual Formation Toolkit*.

8:00–9:00	Prepare your mind and heart, take a walk, or do whatever will help you set aside concerns over tasks and responsibilities. Try to arrange your morning so you can remain in silence from the time you awaken.
9:00–11:00	Read and meditate on Scripture, taking time to stop to reflect when God seems to be speaking to you through the text.
11:00–12:00	Write down responses to what you have read. Speak to God about them.
12:00–1:00	Eat lunch and take a walk, reflecting on the morning.
1:00–2:00	Take a nap.
2:00–3:00	Set goals that emerge from the day's reflection.
3:00–4:00	Write down these goals and other thoughts in a journal. You may want to do this in the form of a letter to God. Prepare to reenter society.

in solid, uninterrupted, focused prayer. But I can't. The first time I tried extended solitude, my mind wandered like a tourist with a Eurail pass. I would start praying, and the next thing I knew, I was immersed in an anger fantasy. In this fantasy someone who had hurt me was being deeply wounded by the wrong they had done me as I was righteously vindicated. Another time, after beginning to pray, I found myself the object of a success fantasy so grandiose that it would make Narcissus blush with modesty.

What I have come to realize, over time, is that brief times of focused prayer interspersed with these wanderings is all my mind is capable of at this point. One day I hope to do better. But for now, I find consolation in the words of Brother Lawrence: "For many years I was bothered by the thought that I was a failure at prayer. Then one day I realized I would always be a failure at prayer; and I've gotten along much better ever since."

You may be ready to try spending an extended period of time alone with God—perhaps a day. The first attempt at extended solitude can feel intimidating so some structure such as that described on the previous page may help.

Defeating Hurry Sickness

Sometime ago a newspaper in Tacoma, Washington, carried the story of Tattoo the basset hound. Tattoo didn't intend to go for an evening run, but when his owner shut his leash in the car door and took off for a drive, Tattoo had no choice. A motorcycle officer named Terry Filbert noticed a passing vehicle with something that appeared to be dragging behind it. As he passed the vehicle, he saw Tattoo. Officer Filbert finally chased the car to a stop, and Tattoo was rescued—but not before the dog reached a speed of twenty to thirty miles per hour and rolled over several times. He has not asked to go out for an evening walk for a long time.

There is too much Tattoo behavior going on in American society. There are too many people who spend their days going from one task to another. It is time to enter training for another way to live.

We must ruthlessly eliminate hurry from our lives.

CHAPTER 6

INTERRUPTING HEAVEN
The Practice of Prayer

Prayer unites the soul to God.
JULIAN OF NORWICH

There is only one play I can think of in football with an overtly religious name. I saw it recently at a Chicago Bears game. The Bears were a touchdown behind, the clock was ticking off the final few seconds, and the goal line was many yards away. So the Bears ran all their receivers to one corner of the end zone, and their quarterback heaved a desperate toss against impossible odds. The ball bounced off a few people and fell into the hands of James Allen, a diving running back, and the Bears won the game. This particular kind of play picked up a name—originating with Doug Flutie's last-minute touchdown against Miami in 1984—that is used by Protestants, Catholics, and atheists alike: the hail Mary pass. The rationale is that a pass thrown under such desperate circumstances could only be completed with the help of divine intervention. People sometimes say a quarterback in that situation "threw up a prayer."

The phrase comes, of course, from the Catholic prayer based on the angel's greetings to Mary recorded in the first chapter of Luke's gospel: "Hail Mary, full of grace. . . ."

Why is only that one play named after prayer? There are no "hail Mary kick-off returns" to start games or, to use a more common evangelical prayer, no "Lord, I just want to ask you . . ." draw plays in the first quarter.

I believe Mary is brought in for the last play of the game because prayer is something we generally associate with desperation. The idea behind this terminology is that for the majority of the game I can rely on my own resources. I will depend on my game plan and my personnel. However, at a moment of crisis and desperation when I've run out of time and opportunity, when human cleverness and mortal strength have failed me, and when all other options are gone, that's the time to throw up a prayer. "Hail Mary . . ."

Desperate people pray. They pray without thinking about it; they pray even if they are not sure who they're praying to or if anyone out there is listening at all. People in foxholes pray. So do people who go through divorce, have children that run away, or hear from a doctor that the lab results say the growth is malignant. When we reach the limit of our resources, we pray instinctively, reflexively —like the way a man lacking oxygen gasps for breath and the way a man who is falling reaches out for something to grab.

It is not bad to pray in a time of crisis. One of God's most amazing attributes is that he is humble enough to accept people when they turn to him in sheer desperation, even when they have been ignoring him for years.

Desperation prayers have been the beginning of spiritual life for many people. But by themselves such prayers are not sufficient to sustain spiritual life. Many of us fall into a pattern where the only times we pray are the times when we are prompted by crisis or pain; the rest of the time we rely on our own strength and cleverness.

This pattern points to what we really believe regarding prayer. In most ordinary moments we are not convinced that prayer *really* changes things. Many people believe that their prayers won't change God's actions, so they ask themselves what the point is of praying. As Dallas Willard puts it, "The idea that everything would happen exactly as it does regardless of whether we pray or not is a specter that haunts the minds of many who sincerely profess belief in God. It makes prayer psychologically impossible, replacing it with dead ritual at best."

Prayers to Heaven

Let's look at how seriously the writers of Scripture viewed prayer. In the eighth chapter of the book of Revelation, John describes a scene in heaven after the seals have been broken on the scrolls that tell the story of human sin and violence and God's judgment.

Then a remarkable thing happens. John writes that "there was silence in heaven for about half an hour." During this time an angel with a golden censer comes to the altar and offers much incense, which is a representation of prayers arising from earth: "The smoke of the incense, together with the prayers of the saints, went up before God from the angel's hand." Following this come great acts of judgment on the earth—pictured by rumbles of thunder, flashes of lightning, and great earthquakes. But what is most striking is that these acts come *in response to the prayers of the saints*.

> All of heaven stops so the prayers of the saints can rise before God.

Usually we think of events on earth being interrupted because of actions taken in heaven. However, here it is the other way around. All of heaven comes to a standstill. The endless songs and praises of heavenly hosts suddenly stop. Why? Because someone is praying. All of heaven stops so the prayers of the saints—your prayers and mine, every one of them—can rise before God. They are heard. They matter. Prayers of real human beings—like you and me—interrupt heaven.

And what happens next on earth happens because people pray.

Walter Wink says that this is the message of John's text: "History belongs to the intercessors—those who believe and pray the future into being."

History does not belong to the powerful, or the wealthy, or the rulers, or the armies, or the corporations, or the global media empires. What they do on their own, apart from God, may look impressive for a time. But the day will come when all merely human actions will be tossed, forgotten, on the ash heap of the dead past.

History belongs to the intercessors—to those who believe and pray the future into being. Interceding is what Jesus is doing now: "It is Christ Jesus, who died, yes, who was raised, who is at the right hand of God, who indeed intercedes for us." His teaching ministry lasted three years. His intercessory ministry has been going on for two thousand.

The Power of Prayer

The Bible's teaching on prayer leads overwhelmingly to one conclusion: Prayer changes things. The first extended prayer recorded in Scripture takes place when Abraham finds out Yahweh is about to destroy the town of Sodom. What is striking about the conversation is the care with which Abraham marshals his argument and states his case—clearly he feels he is talking to a person whose course of action really can be affected by what he says: "Will you indeed sweep away the righteous with the wicked? Suppose there are fifty righteous within the city; will you then sweep away the place and not forgive it for the fifty righteous who are in it? . . . Far be that from you! Shall not the judge of the earth do what is right?"

God says okay, he will spare the city for the sake of fifty righteous people. You can almost hear the wheels turning in Abraham's head: *Do I dare keep going?*

He dares. "Let me take it on myself to speak to the Lord, I who am but dust and ashes. Could I negotiate you down to forty-five?"

God agrees to that request too. Abraham keeps whittling the number down—forty, thirty, twenty; then one last shot: "Oh, do not let the Lord be angry if I speak just once more. Suppose ten are found there."

God nods his head once more and says yes. And in the end he spares Lot and his family, even though there are only four of them and Lot is an immigrant to boot. The moral of the story, according to Walter Wink, is that it pays to haggle with God. "The fawning etiquette of unctuous prayer is utterly foreign to the Bible. Biblical prayer is impertinent, persistent, shameless, indecorous. It is more like haggling in an oriental bazaar than the polite monologues of the churches."

Prayer changes things. Thomas Merton, then a young man pursuing great success in a career in literature, felt drawn for reasons he did not understand to spend some time in a religious community with men who devoted much of their days to prayer. He wrote that when he left he was struck by the haste and anxiety of "normal" life: "My heart sank within me. I thought: 'What am I getting into? Is this the sort of thing I myself have been living in all these years?'" The thought occurred to him that in some real way these few men devoted to prayer "are doing for their land what no army, no congress, no president could ever do as such: they are winning for it the grace and the protection and the friendship of God."

You don't know how many people have been strengthened because you asked God to encourage them; how many people have been healed because you prayed for their bodies; how many spiritual runaways have come home because you prayed for their souls. None of us may ever know the true effects of our prayers this side of death. But we do know this: History belongs to the intercessors.

> We may never know the true effects of prayer this side of death. But we do know this: History belongs to the intercessors.

However, prayer does not happen automatically. My hunch is that of all spiritual disciplines, prayer is the one that people feel most guilty about. Somehow it seems that if we really love God prayer should flow out of us without effort or discipline. In fact, this was not the case even with Jesus' first followers.

They had a front row seat to watch the greatest pray-er who ever prayed. And they noticed that things happened when he prayed.

Once, he took Peter, James, and John with him and went up a mountain to pray. "As he was praying, the appearance of his face changed, and his clothes became as bright as a flash of lightning." Does that ever happen to you when you pray?

Jesus' followers wanted to know God like that. So one day one of them had an idea. What if Jesus would show them how to do it? Could they pray like that?

Finally he got his courage up and made the request: "Lord, teach us to pray."

This is a startling request because as Jews the disciples would have known all about prayers. They would have grown up with prayers offered through the day, before meals, at the beginning of Sabbath, and when they went to synagogue. They weren't just asking what words to say.

Prayer is learned behavior. Nobody is born an expert at it. No one ever masters prayer.

The disciples noticed Jesus looked forward to prayer and actually hungered for it. They saw that somehow prayer fed Jesus' soul the way food fed their stomachs. They observed a richly interactive life between Jesus and his Father. They noticed that at crisis points—when Jesus was grieving over the death of John the Baptist, when he experienced need, when he was tired from ministry—his consistent response was to pray. They wanted to be nourished by prayer the way that Jesus was. So they asked him to teach them.

Here's the lesson: *Prayer is learned behavior.* Nobody is born an expert at it. No one ever *masters* prayer. As Thomas Merton put it in his book *Contemplative Prayer:* "We do not want to be beginners. But let us be convinced of the fact that we will never be anything else but beginners all our life!"

So let's roll up our sleeves. How do we learn to pray?

Prayer Patterns

Let's start at the very beginning. To learn how to pray we need two things: a time and a place. Linette Martin writes about the single most important rule when it comes to establishing a regular time of prayer:

The way to begin is slowly. I advise five minutes a day. This may feel impossibly short, but it is better to get a short time established than to begin with a longer one that you give up later as being impractical. It should not be longer on one day because it feels nice and shorter on another as the mood takes you. Even if you feel great enthusiasm and want to go longer on one day, please restrict yourself to only five minutes. Set aside the same small block of time day after day. It can be done.

So choose one time each day to have a focused time of prayer. Make it the same time each day. We are busy people, and I know for many it may seem impossible. But if you allow the time to vary, it has a way of evaporating altogether.

Many people get stuck on a kind of prayer treadmill. They go too long without praying, then they feel guilty so they resolve to change their prayer habits. They decide they will pray for vast stretches of time and try to go far longer than they are capable. When they can't sustain it any longer, they give up until the next time they feel guilty. So break the cycle. Keep it to five minutes every day. We want to become masters of prayer overnight, but it doesn't usually work that way.

After some days or weeks—assuming you're human—you will be tempted to quit. You may get discouraged or bored. When this happens, don't play games with your pattern. Don't say, "I'll skip today and do ten minutes tomorrow"—or there's a good chance you'll end up on the weekend needing to pray thirty-five minutes. And if you do miss a day, don't waste time feeling guilty. Go back to five minutes the next day.

Also, it helps to pay some attention to the *setting* where you're going to pray. The Gospels tell us that Jesus did this: "Very early in the morning, while it was still dark, Jesus got up, left the house and went off to a solitary place where he prayed." And he taught this to his followers as well: "'Come with me by yourselves to a quiet place and get some rest.' So they went away by themselves in a boat to a solitary place."

Jesus took care to find places that would be free of distractions. The first chapter of Mark's gospel describes Peter looking for Jesus when he was praying. When he finally found Jesus, Peter said, "Everyone is looking for you." There seems to be a slight criticism behind his words: *You have no pager, no cell phone, left us no fax number—what were you thinking?* It apparently did not occur to Peter (at least then) that being inaccessible was precisely Jesus' goal. When I'm praying I can get distracted by noises that normally are inaudible to the human ear, so finding a quiet setting is important to me.

It is interesting that the Gospels record Jesus mostly praying outdoors in places of beauty—up in the mountainside, for instance, or at the sea of Galilee. Contemporary writers sometimes speak of people having different spiritual pathways to God. Jesus apparently had the nature pathway, which is not surprising since he created nature.

Somehow I grew up with the idea that you ought to have a "prayer closet," and a closet is not often a setting of great beauty. So I have learned over the years the importance of finding a place that supports my attempts at prayer. At home, I have a window that I will sit in front of because of the view it offers. I will sometimes draw up another chair to remind me that prayer is not simply me thinking thoughts on my own, that Jesus really is present. During times of longer prayer I will often try to go outside to a lake or (if I'm lucky) to the ocean. Sometimes I'll simply light a candle, which reminds me of the frequent teaching of Scripture that the light of God's presence and wisdom is available to guide me.

Over time, a space that is used again and again for prayer becomes sacred. Just as couples often have favorite restaurants or friends have one particular booth at a restaurant where they always gather, having one place where you have met God in prayer over the years becomes a gift to your soul. I know of a woman who has what she calls a "prayer chair" that has been bathed with tears over decades; another friend of mine has a corner of his office that contains "relics" like a crown of thorns and a shepherd's staff that he often holds while making requests. These places and objects help people enter deeply into prayer.

As for what time of day this should happen, the best idea is to pray when you are at your best. Some people have been taught that it *has* to be in the morning. After all, the passage in Mark I mentioned earlier said Jesus got up "very early in the morning, while it was still dark." "Give God the best time of the day," people will say.

But what if morning is your worst time of the day? You may be the kind of person even Jesus doesn't want to talk to in the morning. Give him *your* best time. God created all kinds of people. Not all of them are morning pray-ers. "God made many other birds beside the larks."

Like any other demanding activity, prayer requires a certain level of preparation. This is especially true in our day. I think it is more difficult for us to pray than for people in past centuries. The pace of our lives causes our minds to race at fast levels. Then our leisure often involves TV or movies, which use external stimulation and noise to keep us from becoming bored. And if we do get bored, we have the remote control ready. All day long we are flooded with noise. In addition most of us are so sleep-deprived that if we do get quiet and still for more than a few minutes, we fall

> Like any other demanding activity, prayer requires a certain level of preparation.

to sleep. (Quite seriously, when I hold prayer retreats that last a half-day or day, the biggest single barrier to prayer people struggle with is their inability to stay awake.) So our ability to give sustained, focused, quiet attention is probably at an all-time low.

This means we need a little help to get started. Henri Nouwen once said that when we go to pray, thoughts jump around in our minds like monkeys jumping around on banana trees. So at the beginning of prayer it is important to take a few moments to allow the monkeys to settle down. You may want to do this simply by taking a few deep breaths and allowing your mind to slow down. You may want a physical object to focus your eyes on, like a flower or a lit candle. You may simply want to whisper "Heavenly Father" a few times, until your mind is composed enough to go further.

Simple Prayer

What should we pray about? Whole books have been written on that subject, but this chapter is for beginners, so I want to focus on what Richard Foster calls "simple prayer."

The problem is that my mind has a steady stream of thoughts: will I get a year-end bonus, will the meeting I'm supposed to lead come off all right, what's for dinner—but none of these things seem spiritual. So I force myself to pray for things that seem nobler—missionaries and world peace. But there is a gap between what I am supposed to pray for and what I am really thinking about.

Removing this gap is what simple prayer is about. In simple prayer, I pray about what is really on my heart, not what I wish was on my heart. As Foster put it, "We bring ourselves before God just as we are, warts and all. Like children before a loving father, we open our hearts and make our requests. We do not try to sort out the good from the bad. . . . We tell God, for example, how frustrated we are with the co-worker at the office or the neighbor down the street. We ask for food, favorable weather, and good health."

You may wonder at offering God prayer that seems so trivial—even selfish. However, nothing kills prayer faster than when I pretend in prayer to be more noble than I really am. Dallas Willard sees this:

> Prayer simply *dies* from efforts to pray about "good things" that honestly do not matter to us. The way to get to meaningful prayer for those good things is to start by praying for what we are truly interested in. The circles of our interests will inevitably grow in the largeness of God's love. . . . Many people have found prayer impossible because they thought they should only pray for wonderful but remote needs they actually had little or no interest in or even knowledge of.

Simple prayer is the most common type of prayer in Scripture. Jesus himself teaches it when he tells us to pray for our daily bread. Sometimes it looks amazingly non-spiritual, as when Gideon asks God to give a few more reasons why he should trust him or when

Moses complains about his job description. ("Did I conceive all this people? Did I give birth to them, that you should say to me, 'Carry them in your bosom, as a nurse carries a sucking child,' to the land that you promised on oath to their ancestors?") Or,

> **Simple prayer is the most common type of prayer in Scripture.**

in a truly remarkable example, when Elijah prays to complain about a group of youths calling him "baldy" (take a look at 2 Kings 2:24). This doesn't seem like the prayer of a spiritual giant.

Of course, I'd like to grow so that my concerns become increasingly less selfish. But prayer—like any other relationship—must begin in honesty if it is to grow. C. S. Lewis wrote that in prayer we must "lay before Him what is in us, not what ought to be in us."

Learning to Be Fully Present

It is time to be honest: Does your mind ever wander when you pray?

Mine does. I used to think the day would come when I would be capable of vast stretches of purely focused prayer, but so far it has not happened. Something about praying often seems to push my mind into a kind of Spiritual Attention Deficit Disorder.

For a long time I felt guilty about this. I thought it involved a kind of failure. And of course, sometimes it does indicate a need to pause and refocus my attention, as we discussed earlier. But over time I have learned that if my mind keeps returning to a particular topic during prayer, it is probably an indication that this is the topic that is of most concern to me and I need to talk to God about.

I remember one day sitting down to pray and noticing that I was in the middle of an anger fantasy involving a leader from a church I used to serve. In my anger fantasies I rarely lash out at someone overtly—that wouldn't seem very pastoral. Instead, I made this person I was angry at realize how miserably he had behaved by heaping coals of reproach on his head.

It occurred to me that I might have some issues around resentment and forgiveness to deal with. And I understood that rather than try to repress this thought and return to my original prayer agenda, I needed to stop and talk with God about my anger.

Sometimes I will be praying and notice that I am having a fantasy about achieving some grandiose accomplishment or doing something that requires great courage (I'm not going to give any examples—this is embarrassing enough already). At those times what I need to talk to God about is my need to feel important and inappropriate ways I feed that need. I may need to pause during prayer to be reminded by God that I am loved simply because he made me and has redeemed me.

Talking to God directly about what is happening has made prayer become a much more lively experience.

It may well be that when your mind wanders, it is wandering to what your heart most needs to speak with God about. A friend once told me that it may be far better to think of these wandering thoughts as stepping stones to prayer rather than as barriers.

This is a part of learning to be *fully present* when praying. We all know what it is like to have a conversation with someone when they are distracted or preoccupied and are with us in body only. The same thing can easily happen in prayer. So I have had to learn to become aware of and speak with God about what is actually happening within me during prayer.

I learned this through conversations with a spiritual director—someone I met with on a regular basis solely for the purpose of learning more about prayer. I would write down in a journal a review of what had taken place each time I prayed. Often in talking with my spiritual director afterward I would say something like: "I was quite tired while I prayed Monday." And she would ask me: "Did you speak to the Lord about this?"

—"No."

—"Do you think it would be a good idea to do that?"

—"Yes."

I was humbled by how long it took to learn this one lesson. To be aware of what is happening within me when I pray—whether I

A Review of Prayer

Sometimes people fail to learn more about prayer because they don't reflect on what actually happens when they pray. This is an exercise to help us learn to pray.

Think of this as what we might do after a visit with a good friend. We spend a few moments alone and think about our time together. We recall moments when we felt especially close, or perhaps moments when there was conflict or confusion. We remember saying something that feels unfinished or needs to be resolved. We are grateful for the time we were able to spend with that friend.

Here is how you might review your prayer:

- Take three or four minutes after you have finished praying to reflect on the prayer. This is not part of the prayer, but a separate exercise.
- How did the prayer get started? Were you aware of God's presence, or was there a sense that you were simply thinking by yourself?
- Did any parts of the prayer seem especially "alive" as you prayed? Did you have times of strong convictions or emotion, and if so, what were they? Did they seem to be moving you closer to God, or farther away?
- What difficulties did you encounter? Did you feel tired or bored or experience other barriers? Did you find your mind wandering, and if so, to what? What were you praying over when this happened? How did you respond?
- Did you have any sense of being called to respond or carry out some action? If so, what was it?
- What was the general "tone" of your prayer: warm and loving? difficult or painful? dark? reassuring? sobering? foggy?

Write down the results of this review, as that can help you learn from your prayers over time.

am tired, or bored, or excited, or distracted—and then *talking to God directly about what is happening* has made prayer become a much more lively experience in my life.

Interceding for Others

While simple prayer may be the type most commonly *practiced* in Scripture, intercession is perhaps the kind of prayer most commonly *commanded* in Scripture. Dietrich Bonhoeffer wrote that "intercessory prayer is the purifying bath into which the individual and the fellowship must enter every day." When I intercede for others, the circle of my concern becomes expanded a little beyond myself. More than that, when I intercede for others, God is at work in ways I do not understand.

One of my favorite stories about intercessory prayer comes from Tony Campolo. A prayer meeting was held for him just before he spoke at a Pentecostal college chapel service. Eight men took Tony to a back room of the chapel, had him kneel, laid their hands on his head, and began to pray. That's a good thing, Tony wrote, except that they prayed a long time, and the longer they prayed, the more tired they got, and the more tired they got, the more they leaned on his head. "I want to tell you that when eight guys are leaning on your head, it doesn't feel so good."

To make matters worse, one of the men was not even praying for Tony. He went on and on praying for somebody named Charlie Stoltzfus: "Dear Lord, you know Charlie Stoltzfus. He lives in that silver trailer down the road a mile. You know the trailer, Lord, just down the road on the right-hand side." (Tony said he wanted to inform the pray-er that it was not necessary to furnish God with directional material.) "Lord, Charlie told me this morning he's going to leave his wife and three kids. Step in and do something, God. Bring that family back together."

Tony writes that he finally got the Pentecostal preachers off his head, delivered his message, and got in his car to drive home. As he drove onto the Pennsylvania Turnpike, he noticed a hitchhiker. I'll let him tell it from there:

We drove a few minutes and I said: "Hi, my name's Tony Campolo. What's yours?" He said, "My name is Charlie Stoltzfus." I couldn't believe it!

I got off the turnpike at the next exit and headed back. He got a bit uneasy with that and after a few minutes he said, "Hey mister, where are you taking me?" I said, "I'm taking you home." He narrowed his eyes and asked, "Why?"

I said, "Because you just left your wife and three kids, right?" That blew him away. "Yeah! Yeah, that's right." With shock written all over his face, he plastered himself against the car door and never took his eyes off me.

Then I really did him in as I drove right to his silver trailer. When I pulled up, his eyes seemed to bulge as he asked, "How did you know that I lived here?" I said, "God told me." (I believe God did tell me.) . . .

When he opened the trailer door his wife exclaimed, "You're back! You're back!" He whispered in her ear and the more he talked, the bigger her eyes got.

Then I said with real authority, "The two of you sit down. I'm going to talk and you two are going to listen!" Man, did they listen! . . . That afternoon I led those two young people to Jesus Christ.

Of course, it is not often (at least in my experience) to have prayers answered in such a dramatic fashion. But that is not the point. Jesus often taught about intercessory prayer, and if his teachings could be summarized by a single word it would probably be "persistence." He told parables about people who would not stop requesting—stubborn widows who had no power except the power to nag a corrupt judge, needy neighbors who wouldn't stop banging on the door to get some food, small children who were quite adamant that their father would answer their requests. All these stories pointed in the same direction—if persistence pays off even on the human level where we have to overcome resistance and apathy on the part of those we approach, how much more should we continue to persist when we approach a heavenly Father whose love and wisdom exceed our wildest imaginings.

Prayer As Relationship

Prayer, perhaps more than any other activity, is the concrete expression of the fact that we are invited into a relationship with God. Prayer is "talking with God about what we are doing together," as Dallas Willard puts it. In addition to all the other work that gets done through prayer, perhaps the greatest work of all is the knitting of the human heart together with the heart of God. I have sat by the bedside of many people who have reached the end of their lives, and have heard them express regrets about many activities—years wasted in obsessions over work, time thrown away in pursuit of more money. I have never yet heard a person at the end of their life regret time they had spent in prayer. For where there is much prayer there is much love.

Richard Foster writes of a friend walking through a shopping mall with his two-year-old son. The boy was cranky and out of sorts, and nothing the father did would settle him down.

When nothing else works the father finally picks his son up, holds him in his arms, and begins to sing to him a song that he makes up as he goes along: "I love you. I love the way you laugh. I'm glad I get to be your dad."

Suddenly this song does what nothing else could. His son's eyes get wide, his mouth closes and grins, he nestles into his father's chest and listens all the way out to the car.

When his father puts him into the car seat and buckles him in, his son throws out his arms and says, "Sing it to me again, Daddy. Sing it again."

Prayer is like that. With simplicity of heart we allow ourselves to be gathered up into the arms of the Father and let him sing his love song over us.

Sing it again.

CHAPTER 7

"APPROPRIATE SMALLNESS"
The Practice of Servanthood

We are all worms. But I do believe
that I am a glowworm
WINSTON CHURCHILL

Leon, Joseph, and Clyde all suffered from a messiah complex. It was not just a touch of narcissism or a dash of grandiosity. They were three chronic psychiatric patients at a hospital in Ypsilanti, Michigan, all diagnosed with psychotic delusional disorder, grandiose type. Each one maintained he was the reincarnation of Jesus Christ. Each one believed he was the central figure around whom the world revolved: the three little messiahs.

Psychologist Milton Rokeach wrote *The Three Christs of Ypsilanti* about his attempts to help these men come to grips with the truth about themselves and learn to be just Leon, Joseph, and Clyde.

Rokeach spent two years working with the men, but change came hard. It was as if they were not sure they could bear to live if they weren't who they thought they were. They could be very rational in other aspects of life but, as Rokeach put it, they would hold onto messianic delusions "even though they are grotesque, ego-defensive distortions of reality."

With little to lose, Rokeach decided to try an experiment. He put the three men into one small group. For two years the three delusional messiahs were assigned adjacent beds, ate every meal together, worked together at the same job, and met daily for group discussions. Rokeach wanted to see if rubbing up against other would-be messiahs might diminish their delusion—a kind of messianic twelve-step recovery group.

The experiment led to some interesting conversations. One of the men would claim, "I'm the messiah, the Son of God. I am on a mission. I was sent here to save the earth."

"How do you know?" Rokeach would ask.

"God told me."

And one of the other patients would counter, "I never told you any such thing."

Aim for the Three Messiahs and you end up playing the Three Stooges—Larry, Moe, and Curly arguing over their place in the Trinity. As we read about this, we don't know whether to laugh or cry.

The bitter irony is, the very delusion to which they clung so tenaciously is what cut them off from life. To stop being the messiah sounded terrifying. But it would have been their salvation, if they could only have tried. If Leon and Joseph and Clyde could have stopped competing to see who gets to be the messiah, they could have become Leon and Joseph and Clyde. ("Now, with God's help, I shall become myself.")

Every once in a while, one of the men would get a glimmer of reality. Leon eventually decided that he wasn't actually married to the Virgin Mary after all—she was his sister-in-law. What little progress they made resulted from their togetherness. But that change was only a glimmer, and the light of reality never shone very bright or lasted very long.

To maintain the illusion that you are the messiah, you must shut out any evidence to the contrary. If you want to be your own god, you have to settle for living in a tiny universe where there is room for only one person. Your world could grow infinitely bigger if you were only willing to become, in the words of a friend of mine, "appropriately small."

The Oldest Sin

I have my own share of a messiah complex. It is not the kind that would get me sent to Ypsilanti. But in its own way, it is just as serious and irrational as the dilemma of Leon, Joseph, and Clyde.

You have a share as well. In fact, the sin of pride is the oldest one in the Book. The writer of Genesis states that it was through pride that the serpent tempted Eve to eat the forbidden fruit in the Garden of Eden: "For God knows that when you eat of it your eyes will be opened, and *you will be like God.*"

> We have all, in our own way, been trying to take God's place ever since Eden.

And we have all, in our own way, been trying to take God's place ever since. We have all been inmates in the same asylum.

How do we recognize pride in ourselves? Let us look at its features, starting with the milder forms.

Vanity

Vanity involves a preoccupation with my appearance or image. If we exercise in spandex—ever—there's a good chance we have this problem. If we work out at a gym where there are mirrors on the wall and we watch, that's a strong sign also. If, when we get new photographs developed, we pretend we are looking at the other people in the picture while secretly looking only at ourselves, we might very well have this problem. If you wear makeup, there's a good chance you're married to someone with this problem.

Vanity is perhaps the most common form of pride. It can be irritating and silly, but it is fortunately not the most dangerous.

Stubbornness

"One who is often reproved, yet remains stubborn, will suddenly be broken beyond healing," says the writer of Proverbs. Stubbornness is the pride that causes us to shun correction. It renders us unable to stop defending ourselves. When someone points out an error or flaw, we evade or deny or blame someone else. (This is difficult to penetrate. Defensive people rarely thank us for pointing out their defensiveness.)

Exclusion

At the deepest level, pride is the choice to exclude both God and other people from their rightful place in our hearts. Jesus said that the essence of spiritual life is to love God and to love people. *Pride destroys our capacity to love.* The greedy and the gluttonous may still be capable of at least a certain kind of love, but pride is a form of antilove. Pride moves us to exclude instead of to embrace. Pride moves us to bow down before a mirror rather than before God. Pride moves us to judge rather than to serve.

At the deepest level, pride is the choice to exclude both God and other people from their rightful place in our hearts.

Pride means not only that we want to be smart and wealthy, but also that we will not be satisfied until we are smarter and wealthier than those around us. Pride is essentially comparative in nature.

Jesus himself made this connection when he told a story about two men at prayer. The sins of the tax collector were obvious to all: greed, dishonesty, corruption. The Pharisee thanked God that he was in a different category: "I am not like other people: thieves, rogues, adulterers, or even like this tax collector. I fast twice a week; I give a tenth of all my income." (The Pharisee appeared to be seeking "extra credit"—fasting was commanded for only one day a year.) The Pharisee was right about two categories, but he was mistaken about which one was okay. He was noxious in the sight of God because he failed at the first command to love and didn't even recognize his need for God's help. He did not embrace sinners. He did not recognize that his own sin was greater than the tax collector's. He didn't realize that he was the biggest sinner in the room. Luke says Jesus told this story to some "who were confident of their own righteousness *and looked down on everybody else*." Pride and lovelessness always go together.

That Confusing Thing Called Humility

Where once pride was recognized as a fatal flaw, in our day it comes close to being celebrated. We live in what Christopher Lasch has called "the Culture of Narcissism." Muhammad Ali's signature line expressed the quest of the rest of us: "I am the greatest." Boxing promoter Don King was quoted in the *Los Angeles Times* as saying, "I never cease to amaze my own self"—and then added, "I say that humbly." How would that come out if he were to say it with pride?

In place of pride, Jesus invites us to a life of humility: "All who humble themselves will be exalted." But we have become badly confused about humility. We know we ought to become humble, but we're not sure it is all that desirable. We're not even sure what a humble person is like.

What does it mean to "humble yourself" in everyday life? Let's say we take this seriously. Someone compliments us on the way we look. We are trying to live in God's kingdom and respond as Jesus would if he were in our place. What do we do?

- Look down at the ground, shuffle our feet, and say, "I'm not really attractive. It's just that the light in here is pretty dim."
- Boldly speak the truth by saying, "I'm terribly interested in what you say. Tell me more, and let us celebrate this good news together."
- Quote Proverbs 11:22 in order to correct the other person's superficial focus on physical appearance: "Like a gold ring in a pig's snout is a beautiful woman without good sense." (This will pretty much remove any problem of receiving too many compliments.)
- Be direct and to the point: "You are giving me a swelled head. Get behind me, Satan."
- Smile, say "thank-you," then be quiet.

Humility is not about convincing ourselves—or others— that we are unattractive or incompetent. It is not about "beating ourselves up" or trying to make ourselves nothing. If God wanted to make us nothing, he could have done it.

Humility has to do with submitted willingness. It involves a healthy self-forgetfulness. We will know we have begun to make progress in humility when we find that we get so enabled by the Holy Spirit to live in the moment that we cease to be preoccupied with ourselves, one way or the other. When we are with others, we are truly *with* them, not wondering how they can be of benefit to us.

> **Humility involves a Copernican revolution of the soul, the realization that the universe does not revolve around us.**

Indeed, humility involves a Copernican revolution of the soul, the realization that the universe does not revolve around us. Humility always brings a kind of relief.

A friend named Gwen Bird was teaching a Sunday school class and decided to have the children "reenact" the Creation. This required children to portray animals and plant life. One six-year-old, whom we will call Jonathan, was assigned to stand on a ladder and shine a flashlight on the whole proceedings. He was supposed to represent God. Just about the time the creeping things were starting to creep over to where the swimming things were supposed to swim, Gwen felt a tug on her skirt. It was "God." He wanted out. "I'm just feeling too crazy to be God today," said Jonathan. "Could you get somebody else?"

Humility, if ever we could grow into it, would not be a burden. It would be an immense gift. Humility is the freedom to stop trying to be what we're not, or pretending to be what we're not, and accepting our "appropriate smallness." In Luther's words, humility is the decision to "let God be God."

The Elusive Pursuit

But right here we meet a difficulty. How on earth can we pursue humility? Pride is a persistent problem for people who strive for spiritual growth.

Once in a while I go on a diet. At those times, if I am in a restaurant, watching people eat, I find certain thoughts involuntarily running through my mind. *How can people eat this stuff? How can they treat their bodies this way? Don't they know this junk is lethal? Have they no discipline, no self-restraint? Are these the ones, then, of whom St. Paul wrote, "Their end is destruction; their god is the belly"?*

I get these thoughts even though—or perhaps more precisely, because—these people are eating the same things I ate yesterday before my diet began and will be eating again next week after I have given it up.

Here is the problem: When I try to do something good, I am intensely aware of it. And I tend to be aware of other people who aren't putting forth the same effort. Then I tend to think they should: I start to compare my effort with their sloth. The result is pride, comparison, judgmentalism, and a lack of love. (Ironically, these people may be more virtuous than I in a thousand other ways; they may have received much less support and encouragement and teaching than I—but these thoughts are less likely to occur to me.)

One of the hardest things in the world is to stop being the prodigal son without turning into the elder brother. So how can humility be pursued?

Following Jesus in the Practice of Servanthood

Richard Foster writes,

> More than any other single way the grace of humility is worked into our lives through the Discipline of service.... Nothing *disciplines* the inordinate desires of the flesh like service, and nothing *transforms* the desires of the flesh like serving in hiddenness. The flesh whines against service but screams against hidden service. It strains and pulls for honor and recognition.

Here, as elsewhere in regard to spiritual life, our teacher is Jesus. The Lord said that he had come "not to be served but to serve." Many people think of this as a temporary interruption of Jesus' normal experience, which would be to *receive* service. In fact, serving is God's business.

The idea of divine servanthood is beautifully expressed in Gerald Hawthorne's translation of the great tribute to Christ expressed in Philippians 2:6–11. Many biblical scholars believe this passage existed originally as a hymn—one of the oldest confessions of the early church. The text says we should have the same attitude, or mindset, as Christ, who "being in very nature God, did not consider equality with God to be grounds for grasping, but poured himself out, taking the very nature of a servant."

The participle *being* is known in Greek as a circumstantial participle. How we are to translate such a participle depends on the context—the "circumstances" surrounding it. Circumstantial participles may be used to express purpose, result, duration, or several other qualities. Consider a couple of examples:

Being Chicago Bulls fans, we predict our team will win the title.

In this sentence we observe that *being* expresses cause, and therefore we might translate it this way: "*Because we are* Chicago Bulls fans, we predict our team will win the title."

Being Chicago Cubs fans, we predict our team will win the title.

The Cubs can't quite equal the Bulls' record in recent years, not having won the World Series since 1908. Therefore we would probably consider this instance of *being* concessive and might translate the sentence thus: "*Despite the fact that we are* Cubs fans, we predict our team will win the title."

With all this in mind, how are we to understand the meaning of Paul's hymn to the servanthood of Christ?

It is possible to translate *being* as a concessive. In that case Paul would be saying we should have a mindset like Christ

who, *although* or *in spite of the fact that he was in nature God*, did not consider equality with God something to be grasped, but poured himself out, taking on the very nature of a servant.

From a human standpoint, this makes perfect sense. This is just the sort of way we would think about the statement. Jesus became a servant *in spite of the fact* that he was God. Several Bible translations take it just this way.

But Hawthorne writes that this is to miss the essential point Paul is making about Christ. The correct way to understand Paul's thinking, Hawthorne says, is to take that little verb as the *cause* of Christ's action. In other words:

> Your attitude should be the same as that of Christ Jesus, who—*precisely because he was in very nature God*—did not consider equality with God to be grounds for grasping, but poured himself out, taking the very nature of a servant.

We perceive here the sheer goodness of God.

In an ancient Greek myth, Zeus and Hermes came down to earth for a brief time disguised as poor slaves. They did this to fool human beings, to get a reading on the level of homage people pay to the gods. When Zeus and Hermes found out what they wanted to know, they threw off their rags and revealed themselves in all their Olympian splendor. It was Clark Kent and Superman all over again. They took on the outward form of a servant, but that was just a disguise.

> **When Jesus came in the form of a servant, he was not disguising who God is. He was revealing who God is.**

Jesus did not take on the "outward form" of a servant. Paul uses the same term to describe both Jesus' servanthood and his Godhood. (It is the word *morphe*—our little morphing word again.) When Jesus came in the form of a servant, he was not *disguising* who God is. He was *revealing* who God is.

I remember hearing a Christian speaker say once that pride is forbidden to human beings, but is okay in God because, after all, he is God. This is wrong. God is the Infinite Servant. God is the most humble being in all the universe. Jesus did not come as a servant *in spite of* the fact that he is God; he came *precisely because of* the fact that he is God.

Jesus' Plan for His Followers

Jesus knew that his own followers would wrestle with the messiah complex, so he decided to put them in a small group together. For two years they ate meals together, met together daily for group discussions, went everywhere together. And sure enough, one day they "argued with one another who was the greatest." It will happen in any gathering of human beings: Hang out with a group of people long enough, and the messiah complex will rear its ugly head.

Dietrich Bonhoeffer put it like this:

> We know who it is that sows this thought in the Christian community. But perhaps we do not bear in mind enough that no Christian community ever comes together without this thought immediately emerging as a seed of discord. Thus at the very beginning of Christian fellowship there is engendered an invisible, often unconscious, life-and-death contest. "There arose a reasoning among them"; this is enough to destroy a fellowship.

So Jesus took a little child, and had his Leons and Clydes and Josephs gather around. He told them their job was to welcome, to receive, to serve this little child. They needed to do this, not just for the child's sake, but for their own. It is through servanthood that they will come to see the truth about themselves.

I'm Not Superman

Growing up, I loved Superman because he was so strong. Clark Kent fooled people sometimes, but his vulnerability was just an act. Underneath was the man of steel. Superman came to help people who were weak and needy; but he himself was never afraid, never confused. Superman never joined a twelve-step recovery group, even though he had lost both his biological parents and the planet he had called home. He never joined a lonely hearts club, although he was always alone. He never got into therapy, even though he wore blue tights and a cape beneath his regular clothes.

I wanted to be Superman. I wanted his X-ray vision, wanted to bend steel with my bare hands, and most of all wanted his chest, with that giant red S on it. I never had the kind of chest that could accommodate a red S—a less curvy letter, perhaps, a lowercase *l* or *i*.

Sometimes we adults try to be Superman. We try to look smarter or more successful or more spiritual than we are. We try to answer questions we don't understand. But it is a heavy burden, trying to be Superman when we're grown up.

There is another way to help people out instead of trying to be the Superpeople we aren't. The primary reason Jesus calls us to servanthood is not just because other people need our service. It is because of what happens to us when we serve.

This has to do with the nature of the relationship between authentic helping and healing. We discover this difference in Ernest Kurtz's excellent book *Not-God: A History of Alcoholics Anonymous.*

Not long after he found sobriety, Bill Wilson—known in AA lore as "Bill W"—realized he was about to get drunk. In desperation, he sought and found the name of another alcoholic, Dr. Bob, to whom he could tell his story. Ultimately, Dr. Bob also became sober and with Bill W became the cofounder of Alcoholics Anonymous. But Bill W understood that the main reason for telling his story was not to save Dr. Bob; rather, if he didn't give away what he had, he would get drunk again.

Bill W knew that it was not because he was strong and Dr. Bob was weak that he was able to help Dr. Bob. Bill W could help because he was weak, and in helping, he received strength.

This truth went deep. As AA became known, Bill W began giving interviews and became known as the "founder" of the organization. Gradually he grew too busy and began to neglect his family, but he told himself that all those alcoholics needed him. Friends pulled him aside and spoke truth to him: "You are on a road to death. You are thinking of yourself as unique; exceptional—and this is typical alcoholic thinking."

Like Bill W, we have to realize that we are not Superpeople or messiahs. We must embrace limitations. That is whence strength comes. God is not chewing his fingernails over whether or not we can save alcoholics.

We must minister out of weakness. The reason we help others is not because we are strong and they need us; it is because if we don't help them, we will end up a hopeless relic.

Why does AA insist on anonymity? The purpose is not only that people can attend AA meetings without being exposed to the outside world as alcoholics; there is the added reason that no one is allowed to use AA as a vehicle to fame. The founders realized the fatal lure of celebrity. The only way to life was to remain a fellowship of drunks helping each other.

That is the kind of servanthood Jesus calls us to—a society of sinners helping each other.

A Life of Servanthood

How do we enter a life of servanthood?

1. The Ministry of the Mundane

Jesus took a little child in his arms and said, in effect, "Here's your ministry. Give yourselves to those who can bring you no status or clout. Just help people. You need this little child. You need to help this little child, not just for her sake, but more for your sake. For if you don't, your whole life will be thrown away on an idiotic contest to see who is the greatest. But if you serve her—often and well and cheerfully and out of the limelight—then the day may come when you do it without thinking, 'What a wonderful thing I've done.' Then you will begin serving naturally, effortlessly, for the joy of it. Then you will begin to understand how life in the kingdom works."

This might be called "the ministry of the mundane." The opportunity is offered to us countless times a day. A colleague asks for help with a project at work. Someone's car stalls by the side of the road.

This ministry can happen at home, in the middle of the night when one of the children cries. I could fake being asleep and then, as my wife is leaving the room, say a few words very groggily, as if I would have tended the child but I'm just a heavier sleeper so it's too late now. This way I get both the credit for wanting to help and the luxury of staying in bed.

But here's what can happen. I could get up and take care of her. Instead of being resentful, I could be thankful she's alive. During the day, instead of focusing on all the "ministry tasks" she is keeping me from, I could just focus on being there to help her. If I do this, I become a little less addicted to having to have my own way. I become freer to serve someone else without thinking, "Wow, what a wonderful husband and father I am!"

This kind of servanthood can even be fun. In fact, it is almost impossible to serve without creating a greater sense of intimacy and community. I remember that in the early days of parenthood, Nancy would tell me that few things created within her a greater feeling of closeness to me than when I did acts of service. She said that my vacuuming the carpet felt like an act of valuing her. When I cleaned the garage, she felt a strong sense of oneness and connectedness between us. She said that when she saw me bathing our kids, she felt a physical attraction toward me.

Families can be wonderful places to pursue the practice of servanthood. This is the theme of Ernest Boyer's book A Way in the World. The idea for the book came to him while he was at a seminar on spiritual life that looked at the importance of the desert—for spending vast amounts of time in isolation—in the history of spirituality. When he contrasted this with his life, he was moved to ask, "Is there child care in the desert?"

Of course, child care is not something we have to be excused from to pursue spiritual formation. Caring for children in and of itself—when it is bathed in prayer and offered with as much grace and energy as we can muster—is one of the most powerful tools for transformation available to us.

Let me issue one note of caution: It is generally easier to hear about serving than to actually *serve*. I know of a woman who, when she was facing an important operation, asked her husband to look after the children over the weekend. He said no, he was going to attend a huge rally for men that would teach them how to live as

Christian husbands and fathers. He refused to serve his wife on the grounds that he had to attend a conference where he would be taught and inspired to serve his wife!

Authentic community is characterized perhaps more than anything else by mutual servanthood and submission. When Jesus said the last shall be first, and the least shall be great, and the slave the greatest of all, he wasn't giving orders. He was simply describing the truth about God's kind of community and how different it looks from the way things generally work in our world.

2. The Ministry of Being Interrupted

Another form of service might be called the ministry of availability. In the Russian church certain people called *poustinikki* would devote themselves to a life of prayer. They would withdraw to the desert (*poustinia*) and live in solitude, but not in isolation. (The Russian word for solitude means "being with everybody.") By custom, "the latch was always off the door" as a sign of availability, according to Tilden Edwards. "The *poustinik's* priority at any time was his neighbor's need (which might stretch beyond prayer and counsel to physical labor, as at harvest time)."

Sometimes in our work we must be interruptible for tasks that are not on our agenda. Sometimes we must live with the "latch off the door." Sometimes we need to be available to talk or pray with troubled people—people whom we will not be able to "cure" and who can't contribute to our career success.

So that I can practice this, occasionally I will set aside a day off at home to be a "day of secret service," when I am simply available to my family and have no agenda of projects or tasks of my own. The idea is that when my only task is to be available, it is impossible to be interrupted. The goal of the day is simply to serve. But it is always humbling to see how quickly my need to create my own personal agenda arises.

Sometimes service involves delays and interruptions that come from following the rules everybody else follows. Muhammad ("the Greatest") Ali once allegedly refused to fasten his seat belt on an airplane. After repeated requests by the flight attendant to buckle up, Ali finally said, "Superman don't need no seat belt." To which the attendant is said to have replied, "Superman don't need no airplane."

We are all of us would-be Supermen. If we can't fly on our own, we would at least like to think we're special enough to be exempt from the rules. When we patiently wait our turn in a traffic jam when we're tempted to swerve from lane to lane and go faster at someone else's expense, it can be a tiny reminder that contrary to the bumper sticker, the road doesn't belong to us. The other people on it are just as important.

Sometimes service means doing routine tasks even if we could have someone else do them. There is a story about Abraham Lincoln—possibly apocryphal but certainly in character—that a cabinet member once saw him shining his shoes. The cabinet member expressed surprise that the president of the United States was blacking his own boots. Lincoln responded, "Whose boots do you expect me to black?"

> If we can't fly on our own, we would at least like to think we're special enough to be exempt from the rules.

Service does not mean we do nothing but mundane tasks. Nor does it mean our day should be filled with nothing but interruptions. Knowing when to be available for "the ministry of the mundane" takes discernment and wisdom. Generally speaking, the higher our grandiosity quotient, the greater our need for this ministry.

The ministry of the mundane will, it is hoped, be helpful to others, but it is also a ministry *to* us ourselves—a grandiosity buster. Dietrich Bonhoeffer wrote of this as the ministry of "active helpfulness." This means, initially, simple assistance in trifling, external matters. We can find a multitude of such things wherever people live together. Nobody is too good to perform the lowliest task. People who worry about the loss of time that such petty, outward acts of helpfulness might entail are probably taking themselves and their careers too seriously. Considering the fact that Bonhoeffer himself was a brilliant theologian, author, teacher, pastor, seminary president, and leader in the anti-Nazi underground movement who would ultimately be martyred for his witness, this is a sobering thought.

3. Embracing Our Weaknesses and Limitations

Sometime ago, I had a run of too much travel, too many meetings, and too many talks, and I was fatigued. I had a standing commitment to a friend who was also involved in church work, and weekly we would talk about ministry and spiritual life. I was complaining to him about my schedule, looking for some sympathy, when he surprised me by asking *why* I chose to live like this. I was not used to thinking about my schedule as a choice. It was more tempting to think of my level of busyiness simply as a given, like living with air pollution or being a Cubs fan—which no one would choose, of course, but which if that were your lot in life you would simply cope with as best you could.

"*Why* do you choose to be so busy?" he persisted, which made me uncomfortable because then I had to think about it. The only honest answer was that, more than anything else, I was running on grandiosity. I was afraid that if I declined opportunities, they would stop coming, and if opportunities stopped coming I would be less important, and if I were less important, that would be terrible. Obviously, then I could cover my schedule over with a veneer of spirituality; I could try to convince myself that it was all about service—but it was grandiosity all the same. I didn't want to have to admit I have severe limitations. I didn't want to acknowledge my need for things like rest. I didn't want to admit I wasn't Superman.

As a result of this encounter I developed a small "personal schedule group," with a covenant that we would not take on any added commitments in life without discussing them with each other and with our families first. The covenant also gave us full permission to talk not only about our schedules but also the motives behind our activities.

It is dangerous to live without this kind of accountability. The father of one of my friends has been involved in evangelical ministry for nearly fifty years. His dad recently told him, "Well, son, we'll have to get together soon, as soon as I can get my schedule under control." His son's comment to me: "For all thirty-nine years of my life my dad has talked about what we're going to do as soon as he gets his schedule 'under control.' He actually seems to believe that someday his schedule will somehow come under control. What is worse, he refuses to talk about or even acknowledge to himself the *real reason why* his schedule is out of control."

4. The Ministry of "Holding Your Tongue"

Perhaps the least-practiced form of servanthood today is what Bonhoeffer called "the ministry of holding one's tongue."

> Often we combat our evil thoughts most effectively if we absolutely refuse to allow them to be expressed in words.... It must be a decisive rule of every Christian fellowship that each individual is prohibited from saying much that occurs to him.

This behavior flies in the face of the conventional wisdom today, when saying "everything that occurs to you" is taken as an essential component of mental health. But sometimes this "ministry of the closed mouth" is a victory for the kingdom.

Victory may come about this way: We are in a meeting at work. As the conversation unfolds, we become aware of a subtext: "Here is a chance to let everybody discover how much I know. This is a chance to tell a story in a way that subtly underscores my importance around here. I have a chance to correct someone and show my competence."

Recently some staff were discussing a relatively minor decision, and I found myself sitting on the edge of my seat, gesturing animatedly, while a voice that sounded suspiciously like mine kept rising higher and higher. I realized that I wasn't all that concerned about this decision; instead, I had locked myself into a contest to see whose decision was going to prevail.

Sometimes this ministry involves our holding our tongues about the spiritual progress we think we are making. Francis de Sales writes,

> We often say that we are nothing, that we are misery itself and the refuse of the world, but we would be very sorry if anyone took us at our word or told others that we are really such as we say.... We pretend to want to be last in the company and to be seated at the foot of the table, but it is with a view to moving more easily to the upper end. True humility does not make a show of itself and hardly speaks in a humble way. It not only wants to conceal all other virtues but most of all it wants to conceal itself.

This ministry can also mean holding loosely the tasks in our care. Lewis Smedes tells a wonderful story about Pope John XXIII. A member of the curia was continually nagging him to fix this or that problem; this official lived as though he alone saw the severity of the problems facing the church and the world, and as if without his warnings everything would collapse. Finally the pope had had enough, so he took his hyperconscientious advisor aside and confessed that he, too, was sometimes tempted to live as though the fate of the world rested on him. He was helped, he said, by an angel who would sometimes appear by the side of his bed and say, "Hey there, Johnny boy, don't take yourself so seriously." We need angels to remind us that we are not the messiah. We're not even the pope.

5. The Ministry of "Bearing"

We are called to bear each other's burdens. Sometimes this may involve praying for another's need, or trying to comfort someone in pain. But at times it may feel as if an entire relationship is burdensome. I may need to "bear with" people until I learn to love them.

I was in a prayer group of about ten people, most of them involved in church ministry. The stated goal of our meetings was to report on and learn from our experiences in prayer during the past week. The leader of the group gave some thoughtful advice. She said we should set aside any tendency we might have to evaluate the people and their comments and simply let God speak through them.

I realized that I tend to approach things the other way. As a reflex I had started sizing up the group from our first meeting. *Here* is a troubled, whining, recovery junkie type, I thought as one person spoke. And here is a traditional, hyperrational, old-school character who will not discover or reveal his heart. And here is a wise, high-functioning person whom I can really learn from. On I went, putting people on a kind of maturity continuum, ready to listen to and try to connect with those who seemed advanced and to endure those who seemed to lag behind.

> **The ministry of bearing with one another is learning to hear God speak through difficult people.**

The leader's directive—to let go of evaluations and allow God to speak—was, unknown to her, a gentle indictment of my whole way of listening. I realized that my evaluations, while perhaps not totally off-base, had more to do with me than with the people I was evaluating. More important, they kept me from listening to what God might want to say to me through people. They kept me from seeing the truth that all of us are somewhere on a journey to God, and the gap between least and most advanced is infinitely smaller than the gap between the most advanced and God himself.

The ministry of bearing with one another is more than simply tolerating difficult people. It is also learning to hear God speak through them. It is learning to be "for" them. It is learning that the difficult person I have most to deal with is *me*.

This means that a part of the ministry to which I am called is to free people—repeatedly if necessary—from the little mental prisons to which I consign them. It may be a person who criticizes the way I teach, whether justly or unjustly, lovingly or spitefully. It may be the most difficult kind of person of all—one in whom I see the same struggles that rage inside me.

"Bearing with them" does not require becoming best friends, but means learning to wish them well, releasing our right to hurt them back, coming to experience our common standing before the Cross.

It turns out that the life we have always wanted—when our wants are purified and true—is a life of humility. We see this most clearly in Jesus himself.

There was no grandiosity in Jesus at all. That is one reason that people had such a hard time recognizing him. The oldest Christo-logical heresy—Docetism—arose because people could not absorb the notion that God himself might enter into vulnerability and suf-fering. They believed that Jesus had only the appearance of humanness, not its reality. The apostle John said it is no less than the spirit of the antichrist that denies that Jesus came "in the flesh."

Every human being who has ever lived has suffered from a messiah complex—except one.

Jesus was no Superman. He did not defy his enemies with hands on his hips and bullets bouncing harmlessly off his chest. The whip of the Roman soldiers drew real blood, the thorns pressed real flesh, the nails caused mind-numbing pain, the cross led to actual death. And through it all, he bore with them, forgave them, and loved them to the end.

God's great, holy joke about the messiah complex is this: Every human being who has ever lived has suffered from it—except one.

And he was the Messiah.

CHAPTER 8

LIFE BEYOND REGRET
The Practice of Confession

Many Christians are unthinkably horrified when a real
sinner is suddenly discovered among the righteous. So we
remain alone with our sin, living in lies and hypocrisy. . . .
He who is alone with his sins is utterly alone.

DIETRICH BONHOEFFER

Some years ago we traded in my old Volkswagen Super Beetle for
our first piece of new furniture: a mauve sofa. It was roughly the
shade of Pepto-Bismol, but because it represented to us a substantial investment, we thought "mauve" sounded better.

The man at the furniture store warned us not to get it when he
found out we had small children. "You don't want a mauve sofa,"
he advised. "Get something the color of dirt." But we had the naive
optimism of young parenthood. "We know how to handle our children," we said. "Give us the mauve sofa."

From that moment on, we all knew clearly the number one rule
in the house. Don't sit on the mauve sofa. Don't touch the mauve
sofa. Don't play around the mauve sofa. Don't eat on, breathe on,
look at, or think about the mauve sofa. Remember the forbidden tree
in the Garden of Eden? "On every other chair in the house you may

freely sit, but upon this sofa, the mauve sofa, you may not sit, for in the day you sit thereupon, you shall surely die."

Then came The Fall.

One day there appeared on the mauve sofa a stain. A red stain. A red jelly stain.

So my wife, who had chosen the mauve sofa and adored it, lined up our three children in front of it: Laura, age four, and Mallory, two and a half, and Johnny, six months.

"Do you see that, children?" she asked. "That's a stain. A red stain. A red jelly stain. The man at the sofa store says it is not coming out. Not forever. Do you know how long forever is, children? That's how long we're going to stand here until one of you tells me who put the stain on the mauve sofa."

Mallory was the first to break. With trembling lips and tear-filled eyes she said, "Laura did it." Laura passionately denied it. Then there was silence, for the longest time. No one said a word. I knew the children wouldn't, for they had never seen their mother so upset. I knew they wouldn't, because they knew that if they did, they would spend eternity in the time-out chair.

I knew they wouldn't, because *I* was the one who put the red jelly stain on the mauve sofa, and I knew I wasn't saying anything. I figured I would find a safe place to confess—such as in a book I was going to write, maybe.

The Stain of Sin

The truth is, of course, that we have all stained the sofa. Some of the stains are small and barely noticeable. But some of them bleed through the entire fabric of our lives. They are the stains we regret in the wee, cold hours of the night as we lie in bed staring at the ceiling, wishing we could go back and relive some moments and get things right this time.

They may be the stains that, if we don't regret, we ought to— and we would if our hearts were working right. We are all, to mimic the title of Cornelius Plantinga's remarkable book, "not the way we're supposed to be."

People do not talk a great deal about sin anymore. As Plantinga puts it,

The awareness of sin used to be our shadow. Christians hated sin, feared it, fled from it, grieved over it. Some of our grandparents agonized over their sins. A man who lost his temper might wonder whether he could still go to Holy Communion. A woman who for years envied her more attractive and intelligent sister might worry that this sin threatened her very salvation.... In today's group confessionals it is harder to tell. The newer language of Zion fudges: "Let us confess our problem with human relational adjustment dynamics, and especially our feebleness in networking." Or, "I'd just like to share that we just need to target holiness as a growth area." Where sin is concerned, people just mumble now.

> **Many of us struggle, not so much with understanding the message of forgiveness, but with living in the reality of it.**

All of us will have to log some time in front of the sofa.

I believe that what many of us are searching for is not simply another message reassuring us that God forgives freely. As wonderful as it is, that information alone is not enough to enable people to grow in their *experience* of God's liberating forgiveness. Many of us struggle at this point—not so much with understanding the message of forgiveness, but with living in the reality of it.

Confession: For Our Healing

This inability to accept the reality of forgiveness is the reason that God has given us the practice of confession. Sometimes people wonder, *If I'm a Christian and God has already forgiven me, why should I have to confess?* This is looking at confession the wrong way.

Confession is not primarily something God has us do because he needs it. God is not clutching tightly to his mercy, as if we have to pry it from his fingers like a child's last cookie. We need to confess in order to heal and be changed.

> **Confession that helps us experience the power of forgiveness is a process, not a single act.**

Nor is confession simply an accounting procedure: "That sin was on the debit side of God's ledger; now I have confessed it, and it got erased." Confession is not mechanical. It is a practice that, done wisely, will help us become transformed.

When we practice confession well, two things happen. The first is that we are liberated from guilt. The second is that we will be at least a little less likely to sin in the same way in the future than if we had not confessed. Sin will look and feel less attractive.

So how do we practice confession in a way that begins to heal our souls? What hope is there for stained people like us? Confession that helps us experience the power of forgiveness is a process, not a single act. Let us think about confession as a six-step process for spiritual stain removal.

Preparation

The first step is preparation. We begin by placing ourselves into the care of the Spirit and asking for help. Apart from this, confession is dangerous. If left to ourselves, we are prone to self-condemnation for things we ought not to feel guilty about, or alternatively prone to glossing over the truly ugly stains that demand attention. We need help.

Clifton Fadiman tells a wonderful story about Charles Steinmetz, a genius of an electrical engineer for General Electric in the early part of the twentieth century. On one occasion after his retirement, when the other engineers around GE were baffled by the breakdown of a complex of machines, they finally asked Steinmetz to come back to see if he could pinpoint the problem. Steinmetz spent several minutes walking around the machines, then took a piece of chalk out of his pocket and made a cross mark on one particular piece of one particular machine.

To their amazement, when the engineers disassembled that part of that machine, it turned out to be the precise location of the breakdown.

A few days later, the engineers received a bill from Steinmetz for $10,000—a staggering sum in those days. This seemed exorbitant, so they returned it to him with a request that he itemize it. After a few more days they received a second, itemized bill:

Making one cross mark: $1.00
Knowing where to put it: $9,999.00

The hard part of self-examination is knowing where to place the mark. "But who can detect their errors? Clear me from hidden faults," writes the psalmist. Confession always starts with our placing ourselves under the protection of God, asking him to put the cross mark on the right spot.

Self-Examination

The next step is self-examination. This entails taking time to reflect on our thoughts, words, and deeds and acknowledging that we have sinned. Historically this was known as the "prayer of examen," in which we examine the state of our conscience. This is so important that in many eras it could simply be taken for granted that followers of the Way knew how to pray the prayer of examen. Francis de Sales wrote, "As to the examination of conscience . . . everyone knows how it is to be performed."

A helpful approach to self-examination is to think through various categories of sin. Probably the list used most often is that of the seven deadly sins: pride, anger, lust, envy, greed, sloth, and gluttony. Where do we stand in regard to each of these? Martin Luther used the Ten Commandments as a form to help him examine his life.

Confession should be specific, concrete, and particular. One "I lied to my boss and said I was working when I wasn't because I wanted to avoid trouble" can bring about more honesty and change than twenty variations of "I haven't been truthful enough." It is this aspect of Christian confession that moved Bill W to speak of the fourth of the twelve steps of Alcoholics Anonymous as a "fearless" or "ruthless" moral inventory.

At the heart of it, confession involves taking appropriate responsibility for what we have done. This is not easy to do. We try to slip out of it. What starts as a confession often ends up an excuse: "I didn't mean to yell at you; I was having a bad day."

To confess means to own up to the fact that our behavior wasn't just the result of bad parenting, poor genes, jealous siblings, or a chemical imbalance from too many Twinkies. Any or all of those factors may be involved. Human behavior is a complex thing. But confession means saying that somewhere in the mix was a choice, and the choice was made by us, and it does not need to be excused, explained, or even understood. The choice needs to be forgiven. The slate has to be wiped clean.

Perception

We need a new way of looking at our sin; a new understanding of it. All sin involves denial. One of the worst things about sin is that it carries with it a certain moral myopia—nearsightedness. It distorts our ability to detect its presence.

A new perspective can be quite dramatic. Civil War historian James McPherson writes about a plantation-owner named James Hammond, who served as both congressman and governor. Besides being insatiably ambitious and an ardent defender of slavery, Hammond also indulged a voracious sexual appetite. In 1839 he purchased an eighteen-year-old slave named Sally and her infant daughter, Louisa. He made Sally his concubine and fathered several children by her; then when Louisa reached the age of twelve, he installed her in her mother's old role and fathered several more children. His political career was halted—but only temporarily—when his wealthy brother-in-law, Wade Hamilton, threatened to reveal publicly that Hammond had been sexually abusing Hamilton's four daughters, aged thirteen to eighteen.

> Sin carries with it a certain moral myopia. . . .
> It distorts our ability to detect its presence.

Most remarkable, though, are the reflections Hammond made in his diary when his wife left him and when epidemics took the lives of many of his slaves and livestock (whom he lumped together in the same category):

> It crushes me to the earth to see every thing of mine so blasted around me. Negroes, cattle, mules, hogs, every thing that has life around me seems to labour under some fated malediction. . . . Great God, what have I done. Never was a man so cursed. . . . what have I done or omitted to do to deserve this fate?. . . No one, *not one*, exercises the slight undulgence towards me. Nothing is overlooked, nothing forgiven.

We may not be monsters; we may not have enslaved or violated human beings as Hammond did. But in a smaller, quieter way, the same capacity for self-deception works within us. We can lie to avoid pain and hardly be aware we have done so. We can flatter or seek to manipulate almost without even being aware of it, as if functioning on autopilot. We can ignore injustice or human need for long stretches of time without any moral warning lights going on.

So in this step of confession, we ask for honest perception. We want to see our sins through a new lens. We begin to see them through the eyes of the person we sinned against. We struggle to see them through the eyes of God.

Jesus often spoke of the need for this different perspective. He warned religious leaders not to judge:

> Why do you see the speck in your neighbor's eye, but do not notice the log in your own eye? Or how can you say to your neighbor, "Let me take the speck out of your eye," while the log is in your own eye? You hypocrite, first take the log out of your own eye, and then you will see clearly to take the speck out of your neighbor's eye.

When we have a log in one eye—not a twig, but something the size of a canoe—our ability to perceive accurately is affected. This is what happened to Jesus' listeners. The people saw the sins of prostitutes and cheaters and had nothing to do with them. Jesus' listeners were proud of their spiritual superiority. But Jesus accused them of being in denial. They needed to have a radial keratotomy performed on the eyes of their soul. Then they would perceive their behavior in a new light.

Taking his words to heart, Jesus' followers would say, "Now I see the truth about my actions. When I was aloof and distant and superior to prostitutes and cheats, I wasn't holding up the banner for righteousness. I was feeding my smugness and pride. I can't even love. These 'gross sinners' are more loving than I am. They are more righteous than I. God help me."

We have to see our sin through new eyes. We need to see them through the eyes of those against whom we have sinned.

Two Questions: Why and What Happened?

Two questions in particular help us gain a new perception. The first one is, "Why did I do what I did?"

We may find that we lied so as to try to escape the consequences of what we have done: "I'm sorry, officer—the speedometer on my car must be broken. I am sure I was driving under the speed limit." We may discover that the reason we gossiped about someone is that we were feeling insignificant or jealous.

This question is critical because sin is usually tied to some need or another. Indeed, sin is often the attempt to meet a legitimate need in an illegitimate way. If we don't address that need in appropriate ways, we will go right on sinning. It may be that we need to learn to experience the love of God more fully so we can be liberated from petty jealousy that makes gossiping almost irresistible. Perhaps we simply need to decide we are willing to tolerate a higher level of emotional pain for the sake of speaking the truth when lying instead could get us out of a tight spot.

The second question is, "What happened as a result of my sin?"

Sometime ago I became painfully aware that I had lied to a good friend. This had several consequences: I walked around under a cloud of guilt; a silent breach opened up in our relationship because I had placed a barrier of untruth between us; I was a little more inclined to tell a lie the next time; I found myself avoiding God.

When I recognized all this, I knew I had to confess to my friend. Even then it took some time for me to face the embarrassment of identifying what I had done. However, when I had looked at the results of my actions as honestly as I could, a wonderful thing happened: I found myself not wanting to do that again.

Unraveling the knots of the motives and consequences of our sin requires a patient, quiet spirit. But what price wouldn't we pay to have a log taken out of our eye?

A New Feeling

After understanding comes a new way of feeling. True confession is not just an exchange of information; it also involves entering into the pain of the person we have hurt and entering into God's pain over sin.

The epistle of James says, "Cleanse your hands, you sinners, and purify your hearts, you double-minded. Lament and mourn and weep. Let your laughter be turned into mourning and your joy into dejection."

I used to consider this a depressing statement when, in fact, it speaks of a great gift. Many spiritual counselors have said that when we begin praying, we should ask God for what we want, even if, in confession, it means asking for the gift of tears. Contrition is as useful to the soul as pain is to the body.

Having said that, we must balance this with another statement: Confession is an act of grace.

Confession can safely be made only in the context of grace. Feelings of remorse are no guarantee of authentic repentance, and they can be highly destructive.

It helps to know what our tendencies are, whether we tend to beat ourselves up or let ourselves off the hook.

The apostle Paul made a distinction between two kinds of sorrow. There is what

> **True confession involves entering into the pain of the person we have hurt and entering into God's pain over sin.**

he called "godly sorrow," which is a fitting emotional response to our wrongdoing. It leads us to seek restitution and reconciliation; it compels us to change and grow; it leads us to grace. It is nontoxic. The other kind of sorrow is what Paul calls "worldly sorrow." Instead of leading toward life, it produces death.

I was leaving for work after a tense morning at home. I had snapped at the kids, I was feeling pushed for time, and I was preoccupied. As I was going out the door, my son Johnny asked whether I was coming to visit his class that day for the hour when parents were invited. I started to snap "no" and then felt a discernible tug. Something—Someone—invited me to think things over. I felt a stab of pain at my impatience that morning, at the needless hurt I had impetuously caused those I love. That pain, I believe, was part of the ministry of the Holy Spirit. So I apologized as best I could and told Johnny I would be at his school.

> "Godly sorrow" is a fitting response to our wrongdoing. "Worldly sorrow" produces death.

When I arrived at Johnny's class, I observed that all but two or three children had parents there. Johnny's face lit up. For the next half-hour he sat in my lap as we joined in the activities. We were each to draw a picture—not a task I enjoy, being unable to draw a straight line. What made it worse is that the dad next to me drew like Michelangelo. He sketched a hearthside scene, incorporating perspective, shading, and chiaroscuro.

"Use some blue, Daddy," his son said.

"No," said Michelangelo. "That would throw off my color scheme."

The teacher came by, looked at the man's drawing, then called the other parents just to observe it. She pointed out mine as a kind of study in contrast.

Now I felt another kind of guilt—the guilt of an inadequate artist. But that was the pain of creatureliness, not something that calls for repentance. I had to find another way to deal with my inadequacy. So I waited until the dad next to me wasn't looking, then marked on his picture with a blue crayon. Then I had something to confess.

I looked at Johnny's picture: clouds, snow, one tree, and what looked like Barney the dinosaur with a human face. Underneath my son had a caption: "I'm thankful for God, my dad, and snow." I felt pretty good about the sequence.

When it was time for the parents to leave, Johnny grabbed me and said, "I just can't let you go."

I left, but for a few moments I just stood in the doorway and looked at my son. It seemed like only a few years ago that I was a little boy in first grade. Now here he was. Now it was my son's day. That is his little world—his little turkey up on the chalkboard, his little desk, his slender little fingers determinedly gripping the pencil, his learning how to make letters. And in what will seem like only another few days, he will be the one standing in the doorway and it will be his little boy sitting at the desk.

"What if I hadn't come?" I mused. "What if he had sat here all alone while other kids were surrounded by their parents? How long will I carry in my heart that little picture that says, 'I'm thankful for God, my dad, and snow'?"

That little stab of pain that called me to think again, to decide differently, is spoken

> **Confession is not just naming what we have done in the past. It requires a kind of promise for the future.**

of in the church as the convicting power of the Holy Spirit. We can all experience that. It is the still small voice that nudges us and says, "You have spoken bitter words that have hurt someone. You need to go back and make things right."

"You cheated on your taxes. You need to make restitution." (One financial expert who works with an evangelical clientele estimates that 50 percent of his clients cheat on their tax returns.)

"You spoke deceit. You need to go back and tell the truth."

This is hopeful pain, the sorrow of wounds that heal.

A New Promise

But confession is not just naming what we have done in the past. It involves our intentions about the future as well. It requires a kind of promise.

As God does his work in us through the process of confession, we will feel a deep desire not to do this hurtful thing again. So we make a vow. We resolve that, with God's help, we will change. This will involve trying to set right what we did wrong, to the extent that such is possible.

This is what Zacchaeus determined to do. "I will repay anyone I've cheated four times over," he said, "and half of all my goods I will give to the poor."

The level of our promise helps us to know whether we are actually repenting or just attempting damage control. Is our desire to set things right, or merely to minimize painful consequences?

Lewis Smedes asks,

Why should you expect anyone to take your confession seriously unless you promise that you do not intend again to foul your relationship with still more of the same unfair pain? You can give no guarantee; the best of us go back on promises. But anyone who has been hurt should expect a sincere intention, at least.

The Summit: Healing Grace

The final step in confession—the top of the mountain—is grace. This is not just the idea of grace, but grace as a reality, being immersed in it, given life by it.

In the movie *The Mission*, Robert De Niro plays the role of Mendoza, a character so thoroughly vile, selfish, and brutal that there seems to be no hope for him. When he decides to repent, he is required, as an act of penance, to carry a heavy burden tied to his body everywhere he goes. Through this ordeal he begins to see life differently and discovers that everything he has built his life around has really been a burden—both to him and to those he has hurt. He comes to see his own helplessness and dependence.

One day, on a desperate climb up a mountain, Mendoza realizes that he is not going to make it and is imperiling the lives of those climbing with him. Suddenly, one of the tribesmen takes out a knife. Mendoza fears he will be killed, but instead the knife slashes the rope that has bound him to his burden. He is free. He will live. The burden has done its work.

The giving of the burden was an act of grace. It caused pain and hardship, but it was grace all the same. The release from the burden was an even greater act of grace. So it is with confession.

CHAPTER 9

THE GUIDED LIFE

Receiving Guidance from the Holy Spirit

> There is a way of ordering our mental life on more than
> one level at once. On one level we may be thinking,
> discussing, seeing, calculating, meeting all the demands
> of external affairs. But deep within, behind the scenes,
> at a profounder level, we may also be in prayer and
> adoration, song and worship and a gentle receptiveness
> to divine breathings.
>
> THOMAS KELLY

It is one thing to speak to God. It is another thing to listen. When we listen to God, we receive guidance from the Holy Spirit.

Sometime ago I woke up in the middle of the night. Dawn was hours away, but I could see quite clearly in our bedroom because moonlight was streaming through the window.

I looked at my wife, Nancy, sleeping beside me, and suddenly, instead of feeling groggy as one might expect, I was overwhelmed by the most intense sense of love. It was as if I saw our entire married life in one kaleidoscopic viewing. One scene after another replayed in my mind: the afternoon we met, our first private joke, the first time we ever laughed really hard together, secret nicknames and hidden traditions, the way she smiled at me when she walked down the aisle at our wedding. I saw all those kinds of events—some momentous, some trivial but for some reason unforgettable—that anyone who has ever loved will carry to the grave.

I thought what my life would be like without Nancy. I thought not just how empty it would be, but how that who I am now is somehow wrapped up in this one sleeping beside me.

For the longest time I just watched my wife in wonder as she slept. I studied her face. It was one of the most tender moments I have ever known.

Then something else happened that I did not expect. Propped up on one elbow and watching Nancy sleep, I thought, *While I lie in bed sleeping, God is watching me*. As the psalmist expressed it, "He who keeps you will not slumber. He who keeps Israel will neither slumber nor sleep."

And the thought came to me that God was saying something like this:

> I love you like that. While you lay sleeping, no one can see you, but I watch you. My heart is full of love for you. What your heart is feeling right now as you watch your wife, what a parent feels watching a child, is a little picture for you, a gift, so you can know—every night when you go to sleep—that this is my heart for you. I want you to reflect on this at night before you close your eyes. I'm watching you, and I'm full of love.

It was an overwhelming moment. I had the sense that God himself was somehow speaking to me. These were not just thoughts *about* God, but thoughts *from* God. I felt that God wanted to speak of his love to me—*personally*.

Learning to Listen to God

Was it the Holy Spirit speaking that night, or just a thought produced by my own mind? I do not know for sure. I certainly have no way to prove it was God speaking to me. A few friends have told me that early in life they were given a clear sense of when God was speaking to them. They learned to recognize certain movements of

> **If I am to have a relationship with God that is in any sense personal, I must be open to the possibility that sometimes God does speak directly to me.**

heart and mind as being the voice of God the way children learn to recognize the voice of their mother. This was such a natural part of life that my friends did not reflect much about it.

But that is not my experience. I have never heard an audible voice from God, and I did not grow up with an intuitive discernment as to when God was communicating with me. In fact, I have always tended to be suspicious of people who speak easily of such things.

I have come to believe that this suspicion is not altogether a good thing. I realize now that if I am to have a relationship with God that is in any sense personal, I must be open to the possibility that sometimes God does speak directly to me.

Therefore, in this chapter I look at the way we receive what might be called "leadings" or "promptings" from the Holy Spirit.

Through the centuries, Christians have given different names to this phenomenon. In his journal, George Fox wrote about the Lord's "opening" a truth to him—by which he meant that God had spoken directly, though not necessarily audibly, to his mind. John Calvin spoke of the "inner testimony" of the Holy Spirit. St. Ignatius talked of "movements" of the soul—thoughts, feelings, or desires that could in fact be gifts given directly to us by God to move us closer to him.

These promptings may come as conviction of sin, an assurance of God's love, or a call to action. But they are crucial to the Spirit-guided life. We must learn to listen for the still, small voice.

(I was so overwhelmed by my experience that I woke up Nancy from a deep sleep to tell her about it. This may not have been a leading.)

A Nonoptional Part of Transformation

Prayer involves an odd paradox in our day. Almost everyone talks to God. *Newsweek* magazine noted that in a recent survey more

Americans said they pray in a given week than work, exercise, or have sexual relations. Of the 13 percent of Americans who claim to be atheist or agnostic, one in five prays daily.

So why are we so often ambivalent about the notion of God talking to us? One recalls Lily Tomlin's line in the play *The Search for Signs of Intelligent Life in the Universe:* "Why is it that when we speak to God we are said to be praying, but when God speaks to us we are said to be schizophrenic?" Why should God's end of the line be equipped with a receiver but no mouthpiece?

Being open and receptive to the leadings of the Holy Spirit is a nonoptional part of transformation.

In fact, being open and receptive to the leadings of the Holy Spirit is a nonoptional part of transformation. Richard Foster makes this point:

> In our day heaven and earth are on tiptoe waiting for the emerging of a Spirit-led, Spirit-intoxicated, Spirit-empowered people. All of creation watches expectantly for the springing up of a disciplined, freely gathered, martyr people who know in this life the life and power of the kingdom of God. It has happened before. It can happen again. . . .
>
> Such a people will not emerge until there is among us a deeper, more profound experience of an Emmanuel of the Spirit—God with us, a knowledge that in the power of the Spirit Jesus has come to guide His people Himself, an experience of His leading that is as definite and as immediate as the cloud by day and fire by night.

I believe that the Holy Spirit really does offer to lead or guide or give direction to human beings—ordinary people. He wants to do this for all of us.

We can all learn how to be open to the promptings of the Spirit. They are not reserved for the elite or for leaders only or for "important people." They are not reserved for people who work as pastors or missionaries. They are not reserved for people who are "more spiritual" than you. The Holy Spirit can and will give direction to us if we desire it.

You may be right on the verge of experiencing this. Your adventure is about to begin.

"Spiritual Mindlessness": Missing God's Presence

In George Bernard Shaw's play *St. Joan*, one of the characters asks Joan of Arc why the voice of God never speaks to him as she claims it speaks constantly to her. "The voice speaks to you all the time," she says. "You just fail to listen." I believe that one reason why we fail to hear God speak is that we are not attentive. We suffer from what might be called "spiritual mindlessness."

Psychologists define mindlessness as a tendency toward mental drift. It is a failure to be fully present, a lack of attending to the present moment. In such a state, we go on autopilot. For instance, suppose you are reading a passage in a book—I trust, not this one—and as you reach the bottom of a page, you suddenly realize that you have no idea what you have just read.

> One reason why we fail to hear God speak is that we are not attentive. We suffer from what might be called "spiritual mindlessness."

I took a semester off from college to work full-time for a metal-fabricating company called W. A. Whitney. I was perhaps the most spectacularly incompetent person on the maintenance crew, so I was finally given the job of making deliveries, on the theory that I could do minimal damage to the company in that position. But even in making deliveries I found that my mind tended to wander and lack focus.

One morning I completed my last delivery, to Johnson Electrical Supply and was driving back to the plant in a white, nondescript pickup truck. I noticed some unusual things on my way. The gearshift indicator, which had been broken, had somehow been healed. The radio buttons were programmed to different stations than they were before. *This is odd*, I thought astutely.

I parked the truck at the plant, went in for lunch, then went out again to make a mail run to the post office. Then, as I emerged from the post office and looked around the parking lot, I realized that the Whitney truck was gone. "Someone has stolen our truck," I said to myself. Then I saw an amazing coincidence: There in the parking lot was a white, nondescript pickup truck from Johnson Electrical Supply.

Came the dawn.

I had stolen a truck.

And I hadn't even noticed.

Someone at Johnson's had left the keys in the ignition. When I came out of their shop, I got in the wrong truck without ever noticing such incidentals as the words JOHNSON ELECTRICAL SUPPLY written in very large blue letters on the side. I had stolen a truck.

I prayed, on the way back to Whitney's, that no one would have noticed yet. No such luck. Someone from Johnson's had called just about the time I had left for the post office.

That mistake occurred twenty years ago. To this day, I still can't show my face at Whitney's.

To quote Don King again: "I never cease to amaze my own self. I say that humbly." My capacity for mindlessness is staggering. Such a trait can be embarrassing in a job. But my capacity for spiritual mindlessness is much more serious: It can cripple my spiritual life.

Sometimes when I have problems, I don't even think to pray about them for long stretches at a time. I worry, I obsess or sweat a little, but I don't pray.

At a church service not long ago, I became dimly aware that I was not fully engaging in worship. I knew there was a matter of sin in a corner of my life that I wasn't quite ready to deal with. So I simply went through the motions of worship. I was not present to the Spirit. I was not listening.

I was feeling a little bit as Jacob must have felt at Bethel: "Surely the LORD is in this place, and I was not aware of it."

Jacob had never listened to God—or to anybody else, for that matter. He was what today we would call a "con man," guided only by his own guile. The name *Jacob* itself means "schemer."

One night while Jacob was sleeping, God spoke to him. Jacob saw a ladder, with angels ascending and descending—a vision of the kingdom of God. In that moment God himself promised to be present with Jacob, to guide him and protect him.

Jacob was shaken. "How awesome is this place! This is none other than the house of God, and this is the gate of heaven." Jacob was staggered by his spiritual mindlessness. God was right there, speaking, and Jacob had not even known it. Jacob named the place Bethel, the "house of God." He took the stone he had used as a pillow and set it up as a pillar, an altar, to help him remember how close God was and how much he needed to listen.

"Surely the LORD is in this place, and I was not aware of it." Those words can describe us. But we want to grow more sensitive to God's presence. We want to be able to say in more and more moments of life: "This is the house of God! This is the gateway to heaven!"

God can directly guide my thoughts without the aid of intervening sounds or images.

So we, too, need to be altar-builders. We need our own pillars to remind us to listen. Sometimes I will write the word *listen* on a piece of paper and tape it to the dashboard of the car or carry it around in my pocket, to remind me to be attentive. In my office I keep a few objects that, because of the profound experiences attached to them, serve as physical reminders of God's presence with me. I am so prone to spiritual mindlessness that I desperately need these altars to remind me that this very moment can be "the gateway to heaven."

How God Speaks to Us

To "speak" to someone is simply to direct their thoughts toward something. Because you are reading these words, you are thinking a series of thoughts that you would not be thinking otherwise. Your thoughts are being led by another person.

Because I am a finite human being, I have to use indirect means to guide your thoughts. I must express ideas in words so you can hear them or read them. I need to give them some physical form in order to communicate with you.

But God does not. *God can directly guide my thoughts without the aid of intervening sounds or images.*

C. S. Lewis was getting at this idea when he wrote,

> If your thoughts and passions were *directly present* to me, like my own, without any mark of externality or otherness, how should I distinguish them from mine? . . . You may reply, as a Christian, that God (and Satan) do, in fact, affect my consciousness in this direct way without signs of "externality." Yes: and the result is that most people remain ignorant of the existence of both.

Here is the vital point: God may be speaking to you—"affecting your consciousness," to use Lewis's words—while you "remain ignorant" of the fact that this very thought is coming from God.

So it is possible that God may speak to us and our thoughts may be guided by him without our knowing that it is God's guidance. This happened to Samuel when he was a boy. God spoke to him directly one night, but Samuel did not realize that it was God speaking. Samuel needed the help of Eli the priest to learn to recognize the voice of God.

Before we consider how to pursue guidance, let us clear up some misconceptions about it.

What Guidance Is Not

Guidance Is Not "Insider Information"

An old television show, *Let's Make a Deal,* reached its climax each week in what was called the Big Deal of the Day. Two contestants were given a choice: "You can have what's behind Door No. 1, Door No. 2, or Door No. 3." The contestants could give up what they had won so far for the chance at Really Big Money. But they might end up with nothing at all.

This choice was often an agonizing experience for the contestants. Behind one door might lie riches, and behind another, the show's announcer dressed as a toddler sitting in a giant rocking chair. What the contestants desperately wanted was inside information—some hint as to which door would lead to money and happiness.

> **How often do I seek God's guidance when I'm *not* facing trouble or a difficult decision?**

Many people give little thought to spiritual guidance until they face a major decision: whom to marry, which house to buy, where to go to school, what job to accept? What these people really want is not guidance, in any Christian sense of the term. They want "inside information" so they will know which door to choose. They want to know beforehand which choice will lead to money, happiness, and success.

A key test to know whether we really want God's guidance is to ask, How often do I seek God's guidance when I'm *not* facing trouble or a difficult decision?

A helpful way to learn to see guidance is at first to avoid seeking guidance for external decisions like taking a job or whom to marry. Start by seeking guidance for the growth of your soul.

What that means is to ask questions like these:

- How do I become a more truthful person?
- Whom do I know who can teach me to pray in a way that will nourish my soul?
- What practices will enable me to live in joy continually?

Guidance Is Not a Badge of Spirituality or Importance

Hearing God speak to us is no indication that we are unusually spiritual or mature or important. God is able to communicate with whomever he chooses.

The book of Numbers expresses this kind of communication almost at the level of comedy in the story of a prophet named

Balaam. Balaam was being enticed by Balak, king of Moab, to curse the people of Israel. God was naturally displeased about this and, as Balaam was traveling to Moab, sent an angel to block Balaam's way. Oddly enough, the angel was invisible to Balaam, but clearly perceived by his donkey. Three times the donkey turned aside when blocked by the angel, and each time the beast was beaten by the unperceiving Balaam. Finally "the LORD opened the mouth of the donkey, and it said to Balaam, 'What have I done to you . . .?'" The donkey told Balaam about the unseen visitor. At last Balaam's eyes were opened and he saw the angel, who told him that if indeed the donkey had not had the good sense to turn aside, the angel would have slain Balaam and saved the beast.

Now imagine that the donkey had responded to that event as many of us might be tempted to. Suppose the donkey had returned to its stable all puffed up because of its superior spiritual insight: "I was able to discern the angelic presence when even the prophet himself was ignorant!" What if the donkey had put on airs and considered itself in an exalted spiritual class above the other quadrupeds? It would have made an ass of itself.

"Seeking Guidance" Is Not the Same Thing as Being Passive

People will wonder whether they should pursue a new job. One man told me he decided not to *seek* a job he was interested in, on the grounds that it would be a sign of God's will if he got the job *without* trying.

The problem with this line of reasoning is that it assumes that whatever happens as a result of our passivity is God's will. This is obviously not true. Try going out and sitting in the middle of an expressway, saying, "I'm not going to move. I'll just sit right here, and if I don't get run over by a car, then I will know it is God's doing and not me acting in the flesh."

We would consider such action stupid.

Broadly speaking, God did not create people in his own image for passivity. He is not a passive God. When we face important decisions, we must pray, seek guidance, *and* exercise judgment, wisdom, initiative, choice, and responsibility.

Guidance Is Not a Way to Avoid Taking Risks

Sometimes we don't really want guidance so much as we want to avoid taking chances. Decision making can be lonely. Even small decisions can create anxiety. Watch an indecisive person with a large menu and an impatient waiter, and you'll see the tension that comes with choice and risk.

> **God's purpose in guidance is not to get us to perform the right actions. His purpose is to help us become the right kind of people.**

God does not intend that guidance be a shortcut to escape making decisions and taking risks. Indeed, God wants us to develop good judgment, and there is no way to develop it apart from a process that involves choices and risks. If we are parents, we want to raise our children to become mature, healthy, responsible, and decisive adults. How can that happen if, the whole time they are growing up, they never make a decision on their own and they are instructed precisely what to do in every situation—what to wear, what to eat, what classes to take, whom to date. *God's purpose in guidance is not to get us to perform the right actions. His purpose is to help us become the right kind of people.*

Personhood is formed through making decisions. We learn to think and weigh options, we discover what we truly value, we take responsibility for our choices. God wants us to be people, not robots, and that means we must make decisions.

Pursuing the Guidance of the Spirit

If all those things are what guidance is not, how do we, then, pursue the guidance of the Spirit?

Listen for the Spirit Continually

Thomas Kelly wrote,

> *There is a way of ordering our mental life on more than one level at once.* On one level we may be thinking, discussing, see-

ing, calculating, meeting all the demands of external affairs. But deep within, behind the scenes, at a profounder level, we may also be in prayer and adoration, song and worship and a gentle receptiveness to divine breathings.

This gentle receptiveness, this ordering our minds on more than one level at once, is a skill that can be learned. For instance, if we have a significant decision to make tomorrow, we can stop and ask for wisdom. If we have some discretionary time unexpectedly open up, we can pause and ask God, "Do you have anything for me to do?" Then we can "listen" for a moment, and if no prompting comes, we simply do what seems wisest. Each time we greet someone tomorrow, we can inwardly ask the Spirit, "How can I respond to this person? Do you want to speak or work through me?"

We can really do this. The church I serve has a large food court. One of my friends on the staff there was practicing this "ordering of the mind" as he talked to a person who had volunteered there a few times. On this particular night this volunteer had attended a church service and then was to help serve pizza afterward. But when the service was over, my friend on the food staff had a sense that he should ask this volunteer about her life with God.

"Let's sit down and talk about the service," he invited.

"Don't we have to go back and work in the food court?" she asked.

"Nah—let them get their own food," my friend replied.

He explained the gospel to this volunteer and told her what it means to be a Christ-follower.

"Does that make sense to you?" he asked.

"It's very helpful," she replied. "I understand much better now. Thanks very much."

My friend explained further that understanding isn't all there is to it, that it is possible to place her life in God's hands in that moment, commit her life to him. And she did.

Was it the guidance of the Holy Spirit that caused my friend to talk with this volunteer? That was certainly his impression. "To not talk to her would have been a sin of omission," is how my friend put it.

This kind of listening has been vital to Christ-followers throughout the centuries. So let us try an experiment. This week, as you are interacting with people, listen for the prompting of the Spirit. As you listen to people, listen also for what the Spirit is saying. The Holy Spirit will lead you to be with people as Jesus would be with them if he were in your place.

Be Relentlessly Responsive

Guidance only makes sense for people who are resolved to respond. Responding begins, of course, with obedience to God's clear guidance from Scripture. One of my college friends had been sexually involved with his girlfriend for two years. As we neared graduation, he wondered about marriage. "Is it God's will for me to marry this girl?" he asked.

My friend didn't really want guidance. He already had clear scriptural guidance about sexual behavior that he wasn't the least bit interested in. He just wanted to know if this girl was the Big Deal of the Day or if he should wait to see what's behind Door No. 2.

It only makes sense to ask God for guidance in the context of a life committed to "seeking first the kingdom." The only kind of guidance God gives is for living as Jesus would in our place. We may have a great map of Cleveland, but before we consult it, we had better decide whether Cleveland is where we want to go.

This truth makes us realize what is so sad about people seeking information from psychic hotlines and horoscopes. They are trying to locate the Big Deal of the Day apart from any concern for moral guidance. Rarely, for example, will a "psychic friend" tell a caller, "You need to repent of your racism and apathy toward those who live in the inner city."

Frank Laubach made his life an experiment in listening for the guiding voice of God. He played what he called "games with minutes" to see whether he could continually turn his mind back to the Spirit. He wrote about the connection between surrender and guidance:

> As for me, I never lived, I was half dead, I was a rotting tree, until I reached the place where I wholly, with utter honesty,

resolved and then re-resolved that I would find God's will, and I would do that will though every fiber in me said no, and I would win the battle in my thoughts. It was as though some deep artesian well had been struck in my soul. . . . Money, praise, poverty, opposition—these make no difference, for they will all alike be forgotten in a thousand years, but this spirit which comes to a mind set upon continuous surrender, this spirit is timeless life.

Sometimes we quench or stifle God's voice. A while ago I had what I think was a leading to help someone financially, and I did nothing. Not only did someone not receive help, but I diminished the likelihood of my hearing God in the future.

We should be determined that as best we can, we will be responsive to God's leadings. If we feel a prompting to write a note or make a call, we must follow through. If we have a sense that God wants us to encourage someone, we must say the word.

Listen for the Spirit's Voice in the Words of Others

God speaks not only *to* us, but *through* us. Scripture is full of accounts of God's message being pronounced through human agency. At times the speaker was even unaware of it. From Moses to Paul, God often said, "I will be with your mouth and teach you what you are to speak." Jesus promised his followers that in times of persecution they could trust that "the Holy Spirit will teach you at that very hour what you ought to say." Paul also said we are to speak to each other in Spirit-guided wisdom.

> God speaks not only *to* us, but *through* us.

God spoke to me one time, I believe, in most unusual circumstances through a friend named Lorraine.

Lorraine was well into her sixties when I met her, although her hair was the same auburn-shade it had been when she was a bride. Her great passion was learning. Her house was mostly a place to store her books, just as her body was mostly a place to store her mind. As much as she loved learning, she loved teaching even more, and she taught Bible classes that attracted several hundred people. Lorraine was the sort of teacher who was convinced she had unlocked the key to Revelation by studying an obscure commentary written by Isaac Newton in his later years.

This friend was one of the first people to insist to me that my true calling was to preach. "Now, honey," Lorraine would say— "honey" being her address of choice for just about everyone except her husband—"you mustn't let someone talk you into doing something else. God made you to preach, and you won't be happy doing anything else."

It took a while, but I gradually decided Lorraine was right. I eventually moved away to become a full-time preacher, and we drifted out of touch.

Some years later, my family and I came back to visit the church. Lorraine was not attending; she had suffered a stroke and was confined to her bed. Her husband, Don, had been devoted to her his whole life, and now, sadly, her life was slowly slipping away.

Our visit to Lorraine's home was a bittersweet thing. She lay in a hospital bed in the front room, Don seated next to her. The mind that had been the source of pleasure to so many people no longer responded properly to the will of its owner. The books sat on the shelves, useless except as ornaments. Nancy and I both tried to talk with her.

We could see Lorraine trying to bring forth memories that had become inaccessible, but she couldn't. She wasn't quite able to place who this couple were. She spoke only in the language of vague murmurs and uncertain nods. After talking as best we could, we got up to leave.

Nancy was already out the door and I was on the threshold when I heard Lorraine's voice—only *this* time it was *her* voice. It sounded like the Lorraine we used to know.

"John Ortberg," she called. "Are you happy?"

"Yes," I said, too surprised to do anything but answer the question. "Yes, I really am."

"Good," she said. "Because God made you to preach. You should be full of joy when you do it, honey." And then Lorraine sank back into the pillow, exhausted, and she was gone again.

Lorraine did not know that we were facing a major decision at that time, and her comments about joy became enormously helpful. It became clear that one option would lead to a much greater sense of joy, even though in some ways it was the more difficult choice. God was, as best as I can discern it, speaking to us through a friend who could hardly speak at all.

In the early church, believers would gather together and ask God to guide them in their choices—a practice that continues widely among Christians today. Members of the Church of the Savior in Washington, D.C., speak of "sounding the call"—calling a group of believers together to pray together for guidance when someone is facing an important decision. We can "sound the call" with those in our community of believers when we need wisdom for finances, relationships, or jobs.

Practice Listening in Small Matters

Much of the adventure of Christian living involves responsiveness to the guidance of the Holy Spirit. This guidance is not restricted to momentous decisions. It is learned mainly as we practice it on a continuing basis. This means that sometimes it may involve God's gracious attention to small details.

One day I was driving on the freeway when I realized I had lost my Day-Timer. Then I remembered I had put it on the roof of my car while I was putting away some packages, then I had driven off without retrieving the notebook. Since I rely heavily on the Day-Timer, I turned around and retraced my route to search for it. I found one little part of it—a part that contained a few addresses— by the side of the road about a mile from where I had parked my car. The rest of the notebook was gone.

As I stood there, feeling desperate, a car swerved over, the driver honking her horn and waving my Day-Timer. She rolled down the window, placed the Day-Timer in my eager hands, and said, "I found this here. I got a few blocks away, and I got this impression that I should drive back here and look for the owner. This may sound strange, but I'm a Christian, and I believe that thought came from God, from the Holy Spirit. Do you believe in the Holy Spirit?"

"Believe in him? Lady, I work for him!" I said.

Did the Holy Spirit really instruct her to do this? I don't know. Many people get very nervous when ordinary human beings speak about being spoken to by God. I get nervous about the idea myself. It has often been abused. When I was in college, it was not too unusual for a guy to tell a girl who had not been too receptive to his overtures: "I think it is the Lord's will that we should date each other." Pastors will sometimes use the ploy as a preemptive strike to discourage criticism of a career change or to encourage participation in a church building program. A tremendous temptation can exist to use the authority of "Thus saith the Lord" as a way to manipulate people in settings where such authority is unlikely to be questioned. That is a good reason to be cautious about claiming God's direct guidance too casually.

However, we cannot be transformed if we close ourselves off to the guiding power of the Holy Spirit. We must come to believe— mind-stretching as it sounds—that God really can and does personally attend to us. As long as we are going to pray to the God who spoke the creation into being, who communicated to prophets and priests and kings—and ordinary people, who wrote a thousand page book we know as the Bible—and who refers to his Son as "the Word made flesh," then surely we accept the possibility that sometimes he may want to get in a word or two with us.

CHAPTER 10

A LIFE OF
FREEDOM
The Practice of Secrecy

When you give to the needy, do not let your left
hand know what your right hand is doing, so
that your giving may be in secret.
MATTHEW 6:3–4 NIV

In general, the soul makes greater progress
when it least thinks so . . . most frequently when
it imagines that it is losing.
ST. JOHN OF THE CROSS

Mayor Richard J. Daley was as celebrated in Chicago for his mala-
propisms as for his ability to get votes from the unlikeliest sources.
Whole books have been devoted to chronicling these statements,
including this classic from the 1968 riots: "The police are not here
to *create* disorder. The police are here to *preserve* disorder."

Every once in a while, one of these statements carried so much
truth—even if unintentionally—that one had to stop and contemplate. One such statement was the occasion when Daley said about
his opponents, "They have vilified me, they have crucified me, yes,
they have even criticized me." As if to say, "Vilification and cruci-
fixion I can put up with, but criticism—that's hitting below the
belt." Another time Hizzoner expressed the same sentiment in an

unforgettable question: "Anybody can make allegations—but where are the alligators?" Mayor Daley did not like to have alligators.

He's not the only one.

Why is it we often respond so strongly to criticism? I believe it reveals a serious addiction in many of us. This addiction has nothing to do with chemical dependency or substance abuse. There are no twelve-step groups to help people fight it, nor any Betty Ford treatment centers in which to detoxify.

I refer to what might be called "approval addiction." Some people live in bondage to what others think of them. The addiction takes many forms. If we find ourselves often getting hurt by what others say about us, by people expressing other than glowing opinions about us, we probably have it. If we habitually compare ourselves with other people, if we find ourselves getting competitive in the most ordinary situations, we probably have it. If we live with a nagging sense that we aren't important enough or special enough, or we get envious of another's success, we probably have it. If we keep trying to impress important people, we probably have it. If we are worried that someone might think ill of us should he or she find out we are an approval addict, we probably are.

Like other addicts, we will go to great lengths to get a "fix" when we feel desperate. Yet, like other addicts, we find that no fix lasts forever, so we keep coming back for more.

Henri Nouwen puts this problem in perspective:

> At issue here is the question: "To whom do I belong? To God or to the world?" Many of my daily preoccupations suggest that I belong more to the world than to God. A little criticism makes me angry, and a little rejection makes me depressed. A little praise raises my spirits, and a little success excites me. . . . Often I am like a small boat on the ocean, completely at the mercy of its waves.

The Alternative: "Living Freely with Our Critics"

The alternative to this addiction—the life you've always wanted—is a life of freedom. Lewis Smedes writes,

One of the fine arts of gracious living is the art of living freely with our critics. When we have the grace to be free in the presence of those who judge our lives and evaluate our actions, we have Christian freedom.

This is the kind of freedom the apostle Paul described to some of his critics: "But with me it is a very small thing that I should be judged by you or by any human court. I do not even judge myself. . . . It is the Lord who judges me."

Paul considered it "a very small thing" in asking the Corinthians to back off. He did not say, "It is nothing." It still mattered to Paul what they thought of him—but it didn't matter too much. Criticism could no longer rock his boat. His balance and his sense of well-being rested on acceptance from a higher court: "It is the Lord who judges me." Paul was not overly concerned about the alligators.

> One of the fine arts of gracious living is the art of living freely with our critics.
> —Lewis Smedes

Imagine receiving criticism or judgment as "a very small thing." Imagine being liberated from the need to impress anyone. Imagine our sense of esteem no longer resting on whether someone notices how smart, or attractive, or successful we are. Imagine being able to actually feel love toward someone who expresses disapproval of us.

As approval addicts we are always at the mercy of others' opinions. Hence the old preacher's story: "I was leaving my last church, and a woman at the farewell reception was weeping. 'Don't be sad,' I said, 'I'm sure the next pastor will be better than me.' 'That's what they said last time,' she cried, 'but they keep getting worse.'"

This addiction has been around since Cain felt out-sacrificed by Abel. Cain killed his brother over who was doing best at being acceptable to God. (Thus we see that this disease can strike at the core of our efforts at spiritual living.) The primary symptom is the tendency to confuse our performance in some aspect of life with our worth as a person. The result is that we seek a kind of approval from people that can satisfy only when it comes from God.

> **When Jesus spoke, he was free from the need to create an impression. He was free to speak the truth in love.**

Paul rails against this addiction when he writes to the church at Galatia: "Am I now seeking human approval, or God's approval? Or am I trying to please people? If I were still pleasing people, I would not be a servant of Christ."

Even more disturbing are the words of the apostle John. Religious leaders were coming to believe Jesus because they thought his message made sense, but they would not "confess their faith." That is, they would not commit themselves to becoming Jesus' disciples. The reason is that "they loved praise from men more than praise from God."

I know what this drug tastes like, and I know how it feels when it gets withheld.

When I stand before the congregation to preach, the people hear my voice, but I hear another, more confusing voice in my head. It is also my voice. Sometimes it proclaims, "Thus saith the Lord." But at other times—more often than I like to admit—the voice is less prophetic.

"What will they think of me?" the voice wonders.

Sometimes I feel less like the prophet Amos and more like Sally Field at the Academy Awards. I find myself wanting to be able to say, as she did after winning her second Oscar: "You like me! You really like me!"

I do not like this Sally Field voice. I wish I had more of a Rhett Butler voice and could greet evaluations after the service with "Frankly, my dear . . ."

When Jesus spoke, he was free from the need to create an impression. He was free to speak the truth in love. He was free with the freedom of the Beloved of God. But the voice within us is not free. It is driven by ego and pride. It is ugly to us, and we would turn it off if we could, but turning it off proves not to be so simple. Where does this voice come from?

Our "Generalized Other"

Sociologist George Herbert Mead wrote about what he called the "generalized other," the mental representation we carry inside ourselves of that group of people in whose judgment we measure our success or failure. Our sense of esteem and worth is largely wrapped up in their appraisal of our worth.

Our "generalized other" is a composite of all the Siskels and Eberts in our life whose thumbs up or thumbs down signal carries emotional weight with us.

Think of the problem as a kind of mental jury box containing all the people who rate us like so many judges evaluating an Olympic skater. Almost certainly our parents are in that box. Probably some school teachers are there, too, and some significant members of our peer group, not to mention our boss, co-workers, neighbors, and perhaps other members of our profession. It gets pretty crowded, that jury box.

Of course, we never really know for sure the totality of what *any* other person is actually thinking about us. Part of the irony of the generalized other is that it is not really *other* at all—it's what we *think* others are thinking.

When you're in your twenties, someone once wrote, you live to please other people. When you're in your thirties, you get tired of trying to please others, so you get miffed with them for making you worry about it. When you're in your forties, you realize nobody was thinking about you anyway.

Unfortunately, even though we can tell ourselves others aren't thinking about us, that information alone does not bring true inner freedom. When our identity is wrapped up in whether or not we are perceived as successful, we are set up for the approval addiction. Our sense of self is on the line.

"Who am I?" Henri Nouwen asks. "I am the one who is liked, praised, admired, disliked, hated, or despised. Whether I am a pianist, a businessman, or a minister, what matters is how I am perceived by my world." If being busy is important to others, then I must be busy. If having money is a sign of real freedom, then I must claim my money. If knowing many people proves my importance, I will have to make the necessary contacts.

One Sunday morning as I was greeting people after church, a visitor handed me his card. "I usually attend Hollywood Presbyterian," he said, "but we're visiting here today. Give me a call sometime."

I looked at his card: SPEECH INSTRUCTOR.

The senior pastor at Hollywood Presbyterian Church at that time was Lloyd Ogilvie, who is now chaplain of the United States Senate. I feel that as a preacher, he comes about as close to perfection as a human being can come. His hair is perfect, his robe is perfect, his smile is perfect, but above all, his voice is perfect. Deep as the ocean, rich and resonant, Lloyd Ogilvie sounds like what I expect God will sound like on a good day.

Next to Ogilvie's voice, mine sounds as if I were trapped in perpetual adolescence. It is difficult to feel prophetic when you hear yourself chirping like Mickey Mouse: "Okay, now, let's repent."

When I catch myself comparing myself with others or thinking, *I could be happy if only I had what they have*, then I know I need to withdraw for a while and listen for another voice. Away from the winds, the earthquakes, and the fires of human recognition, I can hear again the still, small voice, posing the question it always asks of self-absorbed children: "What are you doing here?"

Too often I reply to the voice by whining about some of my own Ahabs and Jezebels. And the voice gently reminds me, as it has reminded thousands of Elijahs before me, that I am only a small part of a much larger movement and that at the end of the day there is only one King whose approval will matter: "It is the Lord who judges me."

The voice also whispers, *Do not despise your place, your gifts, or your voice, for you cannot have another's, and it would not fulfill you if you could.*

Approval Addiction and Our Beliefs

Psychiatrist David Burns notes that it is not another person's compliment or approval that makes us feel good; rather, it is *our belief* that there is validity to the compliment.

Suppose you were to visit the psychiatric ward of a hospital, Burns suggests, and a patient approaches you with this greeting: "You are wonderful. I had a vision from God. He told me the thirteenth person to walk through the door would be the special messenger. You are the thirteenth, so I know you are the chosen one, the holy one, the bringer of peace to the world; let me kiss your shoe."

Most likely your sense of self-esteem would not rise. Why not? When I was studying pyschology in college, I spent a summer internship at a place called the Spiro Agnew Mental Health Center in Dorchester County, Maryland. One woman there used to tell me regularly that she wanted to marry me because she could not stop thinking about my body. She was heavily medicated, had lived in the facility for twenty years, and would say the same thing to every other member of the staff. On her less lucid days she would say the same thing to plants and inanimate objects. It was an outrageous compliment that she "could not stop thinking about my body," but it did nothing to enhance my sense of value as a person.

> We are not the passive victim of others' opinions. Their opinions are powerless until we validate them.

For good reason. In between other people's opinions of us and our pleasure in them is our assessment of the validity of their approval.

We are not the passive victim of others' opinions. Their opinions are powerless until we validate them. No one's approval will affect us unless we grant it credibility and status. The same holds true for disapproval.

This explains why people can accomplish extraordinary things and still feel like a failure. Consider this life assessment:

> I have done nothing. I have no ability to do any thing that will live in the memory of mankind. My life has been spent in vain and idle aspirations, and in ceaseless rejected prayers that something should be the result of my existence beneficial to my own species.

These words were written, toward the end of his life, by John Quincy Adams—a former United States president, secretary of state, ambassador, and congressman.

Taking Thoughts Captive

The apostle Paul states that in our spiritual battle with the forces of darkness we must assess our thoughts and beliefs and reckon whether they are moving us closer to conformity to Christ or farther away from it. "We take every thought captive to obey Christ." This means, in part, refusing to allow other people's approval or disapproval to dominate our lives.

Of course, being addicted to approval is not the same as having a healthy appreciation for praise. Affirmation and encouragement are good things. C. S. Lewis wrote,

> The child who is patted on the back for doing a lesson well, the woman whose beauty is praised by her lover, the saved soul to whom Christ says, "Well done," are pleased and ought to be. For here the pleasure lies ... in the fact that you have pleased someone you wanted (and rightly wanted) to please.

What a sad world it would be if artists were never applauded, if home runs were never cheered, if children received no expressions of wonder and amazement at their first steps, if authors received no encouraging notes or (worse yet) no royalties.

I walked through a preschool playground recently, where thirty or so children were playing tag, kicking red rubber balls, and swinging as high as they could. When they saw an adult walking around, they all began shouting the same thing: "Look at me." They wanted their achievement to register with someone, to be held and valued, so they would ask it over and over as a single word: "Lookit me. Lookit." (I remember reading of one person barraged with this request who finally replied in frustration, "I'm lookit-ing as fast as I can.")

One step removed from the innocence of this pastime, though still relatively benign, is what might be described as "showing off."

Mark Twain has a wonderful passage about the universality of this behavior. Tom Sawyer's Sunday school is visited by a

> prodigious personage—no less a one than the county judge—altogether the most august creation these children had ever looked upon.... Mr. Walters [the Sunday school superintendent] fell to "showing off," with all sorts of official bustlings and activities.... the librarian "showed off"— running hither and thither, with his arms full of books, and making a deal of the splutter and fuss that insect authority delights in. The young lady teachers "showed off"—bending sweetly over pupils that were lately being boxed, lifting pretty warning fingers at bad little boys, and patting good ones lovingly. The young gentlemen teachers "showed off" with small scoldings and other little displays of authority and fine attention to discipline.... The little girls "showed off" in various ways, and the little boys "showed off" with such diligence that the air was thick with paper wads and the murmur of scufflings. And above it all the great man sat and beamed a majestic judicious smile upon all the house, and warmed himself in the sun of his own grandeur—for he was "showing off," too.

Vast amounts of human behavior, though painstakingly disguised, are simply attempts at showing off. We want to impress other people without letting on that we're trying to impress them. Approval addiction is the full-blown disease of which showing off may be just one minor symptom. Approval addiction involves not just trying to attract attention for what we do well, but also avoiding saying what we truly think if we believe speaking up could draw disapproval.

> **Vast amounts of human behavior, though painstakingly disguised, are simply attempts at showing off.**

The central character in Jerzy Kosinski's novel *Being There* is a variation on this theme. His very name—"Chance, the gardener"

—reflects the random nature of his existence. He has no opinions, no convictions. He is a man without a self. But he becomes a beloved public figure, advisor to presidents and interviewed on television, celebrated for his wisdom and charm, because he simply allows others to project on him whatever opinions or qualities they want to see. Even though they can't even get his name right, calling him "Chauncy Gardiner," he usually does not bother to correct the mistake. Indeed, he seems largely unaware that they do not even know his real name. His whole life—though wildly successful by external standards—is a failure in personhood, in "being there."

Receiving praise gracefully, without becoming an addict, requires a well-ordered heart.

Receiving praise gracefully, without becoming an addict, requires a well-ordered heart. It means loving the right thing in the right way to the right degree with the right kind of love. It is not always possible to know when we have crossed the line to addiction, but there are some indicators.

Comparison

Approval addicts find themselves measuring their accomplishments against those of other people. A businessman told me that when he reads success stories of corporate leaders or entrepreneurs, the accounts always include their age. "When I was younger," my friend said, "I could always tell myself that if someone had been more successful than I it was because they were older, and when I reached that age I'd exceed them. But now the ages in those stories are starting to be younger than mine, and I find it's getting harder to read them."

Ironically, this friend is probably more successful in financial terms than the vast majority of businesspeople. But that's the nature of comparison. It is a form of spiritual bulimia—always craving more, but never satisfied.

Deception

If we are approval addicts, our concern for what others think about us inevitably leads us to shade the truth.

One day I was late for an appointment with an officeholder in our town. I began to search for credible reasons that might excuse my tardiness, when the truth was I had simply not allowed enough time to make the trip to his office. Because I happened to be writing about approval addiction at the time, I realized what I was doing, swallowed hard, and decided I would simply apologize for being late without offering some lame excuse.

Believe it or not, the official was even later than I. And he spent the first five minutes running through precisely the same set of excuses I had been manufacturing in my mind and, under different circumstances, would have offered myself.

This sort of thing happens so often that psychologists say many of us suffer from a syndrome sometimes called the "imposter phenomenon." We know that the truth about ourselves and the image we project are incongruent, and many people go through life with a lurking fear that one day the truth will come out.

Resentment

Oddly enough, when we crave approval too strongly, we inevitably come to resent the very person whose approval we seek. We don't want our sense of well-being to rest in their hands. So even as we long to receive approval, we also resent our need for it.

The Practice of Secrecy

There is an enormously helpful practice for gaining freedom from this addiction. It doesn't generally get much attention as a spiritual discipline, but it is one and is, in fact, recommended by Jesus himself. It is what might be called the practice of secrecy. Jesus spoke of doing good deeds and making sure no one finds out about them. His examples involved fasting, praying, and giving money. "When you give money, don't hire the University of Southern California Marching Band to make sure everybody notices." Of course, not many people actually hire trumpet players to accompany their offering. This command is absurdly easy to observe in the literal sense.

But Jesus' point is that we are prone to try to impress others by our very nature. We don't hire marching bands, because we wouldn't think such a move effective. But we blow our own horns all the time. Sometimes a strategically raised eyebrow can do the trick.

> **True spiritual maturity means that we don't feel the need to congratulate ourselves because we've gotten something right.**

Jesus said, "When you give alms, do not let your left hand know what your right hand is doing." The command is not quite so easy to dismiss as hiring a marching band. Jesus' point is that true spiritual maturity means that we don't feel the need to congratulate ourselves because we've gotten something right. We come to see that it *really is* better to give than receive. Giving no longer looks *extraordinary* to us now; it just looks sane. It seems like the natural thing to do.

When Jesus said to do these things in secret, he was not making a law binding for all times and places. He often gave himself to prayer in front of his friends. Also, King David gave explicit details about how much he gave for the building of the temple, and one result was that his subjects were motivated to give generously as well. Rather, Jesus was giving advice to people who had a problem that could hinder their pursuit of spiritual life.

Jesus prefaced his instructions by announcing who would benefit most from them: "Beware of practicing your piety before others in order to be seen by them." The practice of secrecy exists to liberate those who are trapped by the desire "to be seen," to impress others. "Lookit me!" these pious people say to all who pass by their religious playgrounds. The practice of secrecy is Jesus' gift to approval addicts.

Here is this practice in a nutshell: Every once in a while do something good and try to make sure no one finds out about it. Join the club for recovering approval addicts that might be called "Righteous Anonymous."

We can give up trying to control what other people think of us. We can give up the whole business of trying to convince them that our motives are pure, that our accomplishments are impressive, or that our life is in better shape than it seems.

Resign from Impression Management

The technical term for this habit is "impression management." If we take notice, we will see that a vast amount of what we say generally includes a great deal of impression management. For instance, if we tell someone about a television program, we may preface our report with a disclaimer: "I don't watch much TV, but the other night ..."

Why do we do this? How much television we watch has nothing to do with what we are about to say, so why do we throw in that information? This is merely an exercise in impression management. We do it because if we don't, the listener might think we just sit around eating bonbons and watching sitcoms. And of course, it's unbearable that someone might think that about us. So we reel off the disclaimer to make sure the other person is thinking rightly about us—or, to put it more accurately, to make sure the other person is thinking about us the way we want to be thought about. Practicing secrecy means that we simply describe what we saw on TV without commenting on our viewing habits.

College students play the same game. The most common comment before a test—or after it has been graded and returned—is "I hardly even studied for it." Why do students say that? They want to make sure others know that a potential bad grade on the test is no reflection of their intelligence. That is, if they had studied as expected, they would have done better.

If we begin listening for these kinds of comments, we will discover that attempting to control the way others think of us is one of the primary uses we put words to in contemporary society. Human conversation is largely an endless attempt to convince others that we are more assertive or clever or gentle or successful than they might think if we did not carefully educate them.

The Secret Practice of Good Deeds

The opportunities for practicing secrecy are all around. Pick someone in your life and immerse that person in prayer—and don't tell anyone. Make a lavish donation to an organization, or send a sacrificial gift to a person in need—and keep it anonymous. Live so deeply with a portion of Scripture that it becomes etched on your mind and heart—and don't tell anyone you have memorized it. Mow your neighbor's lawn. Follow the bumper sticker that says, "Commit random acts of kindness and senseless beauty."

The Great Rewards of Secrecy

One way, mentioned earlier, that I have tried to practice secrecy is to take a day off and make it a "secret service" day around the house. The purpose is to have no agenda of my own, but simply to be home and available to my children and my wife to do what needs to be done, to play what they would like to play, but not to tell them that it's part of a "project."

I am always humbled by how quickly I begin to construct my own little agenda even when I am trying to devote the day to others. One time I did voluntary lawn service, and it was all I could do to resist the temptation to tell somebody—anybody—what a marvelous act of servanthood I had performed.

Jesus said there is a reward that we forfeit when we neglect the practice of secrecy: "Beware of practicing your piety before others in order to be seen by them; for then you have no reward from your Father in heaven."

Of course, exactly what Jesus had in mind with that reward we can only guess. Surely part of it consists of our one day hearing that heavenly "Well done, good and faithful servant" that the best praise on earth only dimly foreshadows.

But I believe there also is a present aspect of God's reward, which is lost when we do good deeds to impress others. Acts of servanthood done to impress others lose *their intrinsic power to help us enter the life of the kingdom*. Think back to the distinction between training and trying. Activities such as prayer, fasting, and giving can be training exercises. If we give away some money, for example, we become less enslaved by it and can experience freedom and joy. If we do it secretly, we learn it is possible to survive without saying, "Lookit me!" If we do it enough, we may gradually be freed from the *inner need* to let people know. We may one day find that we can do good simply because it really is the most liberating, joyful way to live.

But if we choose to impress people by making sure they know of our generosity, the nature of our action changes. We settle for the narcotic of approval. Instead of becoming a little more free, we become a little more enslaved. *Acts done to impress cease to have value as training for life in the kingdom.*

Sometimes when we pray, we may have an intimate experience of being held by God, or a particularly vivid sense of his speaking to us. It may be a very good thing to keep this to ourselves—between God and us. To talk about such things too much changes the nature of the experience. Instead of being a gift from God, it becomes one more weapon in our arsenal for impressing people.

> **Acts of servanthood done to impress others lose their intrinsic power to help us enter the life of the kingdom.**

The Desert Fathers had a saying for the connection between secrecy and a heart that is warm toward God. If you want to keep the fire hot, they said, you must not open the door of the furnace too often.

There may be certain occasions when it is especially important for us to practice secrecy, or certain persons with whom we want to exercise it. I was talking about this with a friend, and we both noticed that when we were at a certain gathering, with people we considered important (our "generalized others"), we were most apt to talk about important things we had accomplished, in the hopes of impressing them. My friend and I agreed that we would attempt to practice secrecy at this meeting. That is, we would decide ahead of time that throughout the meeting we would say nothing about accomplishments or good things we had done.

One of the wonderful gifts of this practice is to begin to see how silly the whole enterprise of impression management is. Winston Churchill once described his political rival, Clement Atlee, as "a modest little man, with much to be modest about." I already have the second half of that description down. The practice of secrecy offers the hope that one day the first half might be attainable as well.

<CHAPTER 11>

AN UNDIVIDED LIFE
The Practice of Reflection on Scripture

Woe to those weak and timid souls who are divided
between God and their world! They want and they do not
want. They are torn by desire and remorse at the same
time. . . . They have a horror of evil and a shame of good.
They have the pains of virtue without tasting its sweet
consolations. O how wretched they are.
FRANÇOIS FÉNELON

Purity of heart is to will one thing.
SØREN KIERKEGAARD

Purity is a wonderful thing. When something is pure, it exists in its
essential nature—undefiled, unblemished, uncontaminated.

We are serious about some forms of purity in American society.
A whole department of the federal government, the Food and Drug
Administration, is charged with monitoring and protecting the
purity of what we eat. But our standards of purity are not always
what we might hope. Here are the federal guidelines of purity for a
few familiar products:

Apple butter: If the mold count is 12 percent or more, if it averages 4 rodent hairs per 100 grams or more, if it averages 5 or more
whole insects (not counting mites, aphids, or scale insects) per 100

grams, the FDA will pull it from the shelves. Otherwise, it will go right onto your English muffins.

Coffee beans: (Caffeine addicts beware!) Coffee beans will get withdrawn from the market if an average of 10 percent or more are insect-infested or if there is one live insect in each of 2 or more immediate containers. (The FDA says people just don't like getting too many live insects with their coffee beans—one container is okay, but with more than that we draw the line.)

Mushrooms: Mushrooms can't be sold if there is an average of 20 or more maggots of any size per 15 grams of dried mushrooms.

Fig paste: If there are more than 13 insect heads per 100 grams of fig paste in each of 2 or more subsamples, the FDA ruthlessly tosses the whole batch. (Apparently other insect body parts are tolerable, but we don't want to be staring at too many insect heads.)

Hot dogs: You don't want to know about it.

If anything is really good, we long for it to exist in its pure form: oxygen without exhaust fumes; snow unmixed with slush.

This holds true of the people we know. Purity is a word greatly prized in the New Testament. Unfortunately, in our day it has been largely lost. It sounds quaint, Victorian, prudish, bloodless. It sounds as if a person isn't fully human, when actually God's call for us to be *pure* is precisely his call for us to be *purely human*—humanity as he intended it to be, uncontaminated by sin. The opposite of this uncontaminated condition is what the apostle James called "double-mindedness."

Double-Mindedness

Another way to think of double-mindedness is to regard a life of divided loyalties. James used the image of a person being "like a wave of the sea, driven and tossed by the wind."

Every once in a while we observe someone whose life is about one thing. That person has a singleness of purpose and focus that gives consistency to his or her choices and commitments.

Some public figures are so closely associated with a single-minded purpose—in image if not reality—that their names bring to mind one overriding word: Donald Trump (money), Napoleon (power), Hugh Hefner (lust), Imelda Marcos (shoes).

> **"The secret of life is pursuing one thing."**

In the movie *City Slickers*, Billy Crystal plays a confused, dissatisfied thirty-something character with a vague sense that life is passing him by. Jack Palance—ancient, leathery, wise to the ways of the world ("a saddlebag with eyes")—asks Crystal if he would like to know the secret of life.

"It's this," Palance says, holding up a single finger.

"The secret of life is your finger?" asks Crystal.

"It's one thing," Palance replies. "The secret of life is pursuing one thing."

Somehow this resonates deeply with Billy Crystal's character. His life is scattered. He is torn between his obligation to his family and his desire for career advancement; between his need for security and his appetite for excitement. He is divided somehow. His life is about many things, and so, he senses, it is about nothing.

So what is that one thing? Jack Palance can't tell Billy Crystal. "You have to find it for yourself."

Søren Kierkegaard saw double-mindedness as the essential disease of the human spirit. His book *Purity of Heart Is to Will One Thing* is a reflection on a statement by James: "Purify your hearts, you double-minded." The disease diagnosed by Kierkegaard is the failure to achieve simplicity—to have a life that is integrated, that is focused on one thing. It is the failure to make an ultimate commitment to what Kierkegaard calls "the Good"—what Jesus spoke of as "seeking first the kingdom."

Multiplicity and Duplicity

The enemies of simplicity are multiplicity and duplicity. (The concepts, although not the terms, come from Clifford Williams's book *Singleness of Heart*.) Multiplicity is a life marked by ambivalence—pulled and pushed. It is expressed in Augustine's famous request, when he both longed for sexual purity and innocence and yet was not ready to change his lifestyle and feared losing pleasure: "Lord, give me chastity, but not yet."

When we live a life of multiplicity, we both desire intimacy with God and flee from it. We long to be generous, but we also hoard and covet. We sometimes attempt to be servants and sometimes are driven by arrogance and self-serving. Even the apostle Paul faced this struggle: "I do not do what I want, but I do the very thing I hate."

Duplicity adds a note of falseness. In duplicity there is a discrepancy between the reasons we give for doing something and the *real* reasons why we are doing it. We gossip to tear someone down so we can feel superior, but we do it in the name of "praying more intelligently." We say something that sounds humble, but secretly know that we are trying to impress people with our apparent humility. "Mendacity," Big Daddy growls in the Tennessee Williams play *Cat on a Hot Tin Roof*. Everybody is filled with mendacity. Nobody is really what he or she seems to be.

A few years ago, a middle-aged man stood up as the Sunday morning worship service was coming to a close in a small church in the Pacific Northwest. This man, whom I have known all my life, was devoted to the church. He raised his family in it, taught Sunday school, served as a deacon, fixed coffee for the fellowship hour, and cleaned up afterward. As he stood there that Sunday, he began to weep. Between sobs he told the congregation, which had known him since he was a teenager, that he had sexually abused his children. It began when they were very young, and now they were almost all grown. When his wife found out, he moved out of the house and got into counseling. He was not sure what was going to happen. This man—a nice person to all who knew him—had to confess to his friends that he was a child molester.

Human beings have a remarkable capacity for self-deception.

All those years the man kept going to church, and all those years he kept violating his own children. He was a wave driven on the sea. Why? What did he think when he heard sermons, sang hymns, and taught Sunday school? What did he think when he looked into the eyes of his children?

The capacity of the human for duplicity is staggering. It usually takes different, much less dramatic forms than it did for this man, but the duplicity is there nonetheless.

Duplicity can be aimed at other people, but it can even be aimed at ourselves. Human beings have a remarkable capacity for self-deception.

Simplicity of Heart

The alternative to duplicity and to multiplicity is a life characterized by simplicity. Clifford Williams writes,

> We possess singleness when we are not pulled in opposite directions and when we act without wanting something further for ourselves. Our inner drives do not conflict; they are aimed in one direction. The motives we appear to have are the ones we really have. Our inner focus is unified and our public posture corresponds with it. We are not, in short, divided.

Jesus could have used the words of Jack Palance. What he said was, "Strive first for the kingdom of God and his righteousness."

There is an echo of this thought in Jesus' words to a friend named Martha. This follower "was distracted by her many tasks" and resented her sister, Mary, who had chosen simply to sit in the presence of Jesus. "Martha, Martha, you are worried and distracted by many things; there is need of only one thing." The secret of life is—one thing.

There is unbelievable relief in being delivered from double-mindedness, in finally deciding on the focus of life. Going to a restaurant with a double-minded person can be torture: soup or salad, potatoes or rice, coffee or tea, cash or credit. Some of you reading these words wrestle with double-mindedness. And some of you can't make up your mind whether you have it or not!

Most of us know what it is to be a wave on the sea, to be pulled toward this life of Christ and yet held back by a secret sin we haven't been willing to renounce or get help for. We long to be servants but are unwilling to leave the comfort of the lounge chair. We'd like to be humble—but what if no one notices? So we go back and forth.

It is a miserable way to live, Jesus said. "The secret of life is pursuing one thing."

The Bible and Transformation

If we want to be saved from double-mindedness, we must "be transformed by the renewing of your minds." An indispensable practice is to have our minds re-formed by immersing them in Scripture. The psalmist writes of hiding God's Word in our hearts so that we might not sin. So how do we read the Bible in a way that will purify our hearts and help us live as Jesus would in our place? Let us start by looking at a metaphor from the Bible itself.

When Paul wrote to the church at Ephesus, telling the husbands to love their wives, he used this analogy: ". . . just as Christ loved the church and gave himself up for her, in order to make her holy by cleansing her with the washing of water by the word, so as to present the church to himself in splendor, without a spot or wrinkle or anything of the kind—yes, so that she may be holy and without blemish."

We—the new community, the bride—are to be washed by "the Word." What does this mean?

Consider what happens when something doesn't get washed as it should. Two staff members at our church had been roommates in college, and back then they had a contest to see who could go the longer without washing his sheets. One year later they decided to call it a draw. You can imagine the consequences.

By contrast, think of what happens when something *does* get washed. Soap and water move through the fibers of the dirty fabric at the deepest level, lifting out the impurities and removing them. Only after the washing can we see the fabric in the state for which it was originally designed. When we come to God, our minds and hearts are like that, cluttered with "false beliefs and attitudes, deadly feelings, misguided plans and hopes and fears."

I readily recall a few "deadly feelings" that I expressed in the course of a single day. Once when I was walking downtown, a street person was sitting where I wanted to walk and was holding a little sign asking for money. The thought ran through my mind, *He's dirty. I resent that he's here. Not only will I not give him money, but I won't make eye contact with him—I don't want to have to feel guilty. I want to keep my money.*

A little later, I made a purchase in a convenience store. I was in a hurry, and the line was not moving quickly enough to suit me. The man behind the counter spoke English with difficulty and was communicating slowly to the person at the head of the line. I thought, *Why can't they hire people who speak English? Just give me my change and let me get out of here.* Given these thoughts, I felt no love for this man. He was different from me—he was "other"—and I wished he weren't there.

Another moment with another person that same day produced another thought: *Here's an important person. Let me think what I might say that could get some good out of this person. How can I make a strategic connection?*

Heading back to my office, I walked through the church, but I had no keys with me and the door to the auditorium was locked, so I had to walk downstairs and back up. *That's so frustrating,* I whined to myself. *Look at all this time I have to waste now.* I could have had other thoughts: I could have been grateful that I have legs and am able to walk. I could have been speaking with God about my day. Instead, I was angry about a locked door and a flight of stairs.

There's more. As I was reading Scripture early in the morning, I gained an insight about the passage. My very next thought drifted to a staff meeting scheduled for later in the day: *I can tell them about this insight I've had. They will be impressed that I thought of it, particularly when they know it came out of this time that I have devoted to being with God. It may cause them to think of me as a spiritually advanced person.* Of course, the thought wasn't articulated quite that clearly or brazenly even in my own mind. But that was the gist of my quick fantasy about how to use this moment as an exercise in impression management. Ironically, the "insight" involved the nature of humility.

Those experiences from one day are typical of the thoughts that inhabit my mind time after time. My mind is like—to use a wonderful image from Henri Nouwen—a banana tree filled with monkeys constantly jumping up and down. It is rarely still or quiet. All these thoughts, like so many chimps, clamor for attention: "How can I get ahead? Is someone trying to hurt me? How will I handle this problem?"

> **One moment I want to hear from God; the next I want to use what I have heard to impress people with how spiritual I am.**

These thoughts are just a little soiled. I have some much darker thoughts that resemble big clods of dirt. The Desert Fathers had a word for them: *logismoi*. This Greek word refers to the false thoughts and desires that lead us to sin and despair. They are subtle and relentless. In an image less charming than Nouwen's monkeys, one ancient writer, John Climacus, compared the *logismoi* to maggot eggs that incubate in the soil of our fallenness.

What I lack is precisely "purity of heart." I do not will one thing. One moment I want to hear from God; the next I want to use what I have heard to impress people with how spiritual I am.

These *logismoi* are the infernal counterparts to Scripture. They equip us for bad works. They make corrupt words and actions inevitable. They also make it difficult for us to meditate or reflect on Scripture. Dietrich Bonhoeffer confessed,

> Often we are so burdened and overwhelmed with other thoughts, images, and concerns that it may take a long time before God's Word has swept all else aside and come through. . . . This is the very reason why we begin our meditation with the prayer that God may send His Holy Spirit to us through His Word and reveal His Word to us and enlighten us.

A Cleansed Mind

It is a frightening thing to begin to see the truth about your own mind and its need for cleansing. This is why Martin Luther used to spend so much time in the confessional. He often spent several hours there for several days in a row. His fellow monks used to ask him what he was doing. (After all, he lived in a monastery. What did he have to confess: short-sheeting the other monks? chanting off-key?)

But Luther was frightened by his own cleverness at self-justification. He knew that the first commandment is to love God with heart, soul, body, and strength—and he couldn't even keep this injunction for five minutes.

Imagine having a mind cleansed of all the debris that blocks our best intentions. Imagine if each time you saw another person your first thought was to pray for him or bless her. Imagine what it would be like if, any time you were challenged or anxious, your reflexive response would be to turn to God for strength. Imagine, if you're a married man, that whenever you looked at any woman other than your wife you would see her as if she were your sister or your daughter. Imagine genuinely wishing your "enemies" well.

That's what it would be to have the mind "washed by the Word." This is what it means to "let the word of Christ dwell in you richly." This is how we are to be transformed by Scripture. This is our great need.

So the Bible is to help us learn how to live in the kingdom of God here and now.

> The purpose of knowing Scripture is not to help us get a 100 score on the heavenly entrance exam. It is to help us become equipped for good works.

It teaches us how to morph. It is indispensable for this task. I have never known someone leading a spiritually transformed life who had not been deeply saturated in Scripture.

Paul writes about this role of Scripture in this famous statement: "All scripture is inspired by God and is useful for teaching, for reproof, for correction, and for training in righteousness, *so that everyone who belongs to God might be proficient, equipped for every good work."*

Paul does not say that the purpose of knowing Scripture is to enable us, when we go to heaven, to get a 100 score on the entrance exam. He says the purpose is for us to become equipped for good works. Or, to put it another way, it is for us to become transformed into the kind of people from whom goodness flows like an unceasing stream of water.

Prepared for Good Works

How many good works will we be prepared for? Every one. We won't miss a trick. The idea is not that we will be trying to accumulate a vast assortment of "good deeds" each day, like some Boy Scout always on the lookout for a senior citizen to help across the street. It is that every moment of our lives will be an occasion for reflecting in external, visible ways the richness of the inner life shared between us and our Father.

If the Bible were to completely fulfill its mission, our minds would be so transformed—so filled with thoughts and feelings of truth, love, joy, and humility—that our lives would become one uninterrupted series of acts of grace and moral beauty. Every moment would be a miniature reflection of life in the kingdom of God.

So we need to develop the practice of meditating on the Scriptures. This is not quite the same thing as Bible study, although that is critically important, too. The purpose of meditation is to have our minds "washed by the Word." Here are some suggestions for the practice of meditating on Scripture.

1. Ask God to Meet You in Scripture

Before you begin reading, take a moment to ask God to speak to you. Then as you read, anticipate that he will do so.

Through the centuries Christians have told many stories of how they met God through the Bible. Augustine, in the best-known passage of his *Confessions*, tells of sitting under a fig tree and hearing a voice repeat, "Take it and read, take it and read." It seemed clear to him that this was the voice of God calling him to pick up the Bible. And when he had read a brief section from Paul's letter to the Romans, Augustine wrote, "I had no wish to read further; there was no need to.... it was as though my heart was filled with a light of confidence and all the shadows of my doubt were swept away."

God still meets people in such ways. A friend of our family named Eileen was upset when her daughter told her that someone had been talking to her about God. Although she was disappointed with her life—trapped on her own suburban island—Eileen wanted nothing to do with God. That night Eileen couldn't sleep. At midnight she went downstairs and picked up a Bible. She couldn't remember the last time she had been to a church; nor had she ever opened a Bible on her own. When she opened it now, she noticed it was divided into an "old" part and a "new" part. She decided to start with the "new" part, figuring the book may have been updated.

So in the still of the night she sat on her living room floor and began to read the gospel of Matthew. By 3 a.m. she was in the middle of John's gospel and found, as she puts it, that she had fallen in love with the character of Jesus. "I don't know what I'm doing," she prayed to God, "but I know you are what I want."

It is uniquely in the Bible that we encounter Jesus. The message of the Bible is not just that help is coming—it has arrived: "The kingdom of heaven is at hand," Jesus said. So before you begin to read, acknowledge that Jesus is present with you. Ask him to begin to wash your mind, your thoughts—even if the cleanser stings a bit.

As you read, certain ideas may strike you. You may be moved in reading about God's love, or feel convicted about some sin, or be prompted to take some course of action. Be open to the possibility that God really is speaking to you through his Word.

2. Read the Bible in a Repentant Spirit

Read the Bible with a readiness to surrender everything. Read it with a vulnerable heart. Read it wisely, but understand that reading for transformation is different from reading to find information or to prove a point. Resolve that you will be obedient to the Scriptures.

People who read the Bible in the wrong way, for the wrong reasons, can actually be damaged by their reading. Philipp Spener wrote wonderful advice about how *not* to read the Bible:

> How may readers . . . do harm to themselves?
>
> If . . . they read the Scriptures without sincere prayer and the purpose to obey God, but only to get knowledge, to make a show, and to exercise their curiosity upon them. . . . If they do not observe what is useful for *their edification*, but only what they can use for *their glory and against others*. . . . If they *despise* what the Scriptures simply stated and what is *easy to comprehend*. If, on the contrary, they take up only *difficult passages*, about which there is much dispute, in order to discover in them something unusual and to make a show before others. If they use what they have learned with *pride* and for *their own* glory. If they *think they alone are wise*, obstinately refuse better instruction, love to quarrel, and receive nothing from others with modesty.

To be filled with knowledge about the Bible but to be unwashed by it is worse than not knowing it at all. One Sunday after church I was accosted by a man who was greatly admired for his knowledge of the Bible. He more or less appointed himself the watchdog of the church's doctrinal purity. It was a matter of deep importance to him that people know how well he knew the Scriptures. He loved to get into theological debates because they offered an opportunity to display his knowledge.

Read the Bible wisely, but understand that reading for transformation is different from reading to find information or to prove a point.

This man began to recite to me a long litany of complaints. He said he had been praying about them to the Lord, who agreed with him on so very many things: The young people in the church were not as devoted as they should be; the leaders of adult classes were not sufficiently in line with his favorite radio Bible teacher; he had seen little children (including mine) running irreverently in the sanctuary. And he wasn't too sure about my preaching either.

"Now remember," he said, as a final note, "I don't like a lot of what you do, but I love you in the Lord."

This man knew so very much about what the Bible said about love. The only thing he forgot was to practice it.

I began to reflect on this little biblical phrase—to love someone "in the Lord"—and it occurred to me how often we misuse it. "I don't like someone and I don't hope the best for them, but I'm a Christian, and of course, Christians love everyone, so this must be 'loving them in the Lord.'" The phrase becomes a way to spiritualize our lack of love. By contrast, loving someone "in the Lord" means to love them as the Lord himself would love them if he were in our place. Loving me "in the Lord" is precisely what this man didn't do.

It didn't take much reflection to realize the sad truth that I didn't love him, either. I didn't wish the best for him. I wanted to hear bad things about him. And the even more humbling truth is that the main reason I didn't love him is simply that he didn't like me. If he had had the same disposition but had been a fan of mine, I would have found myself prepared to overlook almost anything. I realized anew how much I need to be washed.

When a mind is washed—when someone begins to be filled with the very thoughts of God—it is a gift to the world. Some years ago when I was in Ethiopia, I learned about one such mind. It belonged to a ninety-nine-year-old woman who lived about two hours outside Addis Ababa, the capital city. This woman had become a follower of Christ in middle age, and she was both blind and illiterate. She lived in a little hut, where she kept two Bibles on her table—one in Amharic (the official language of Ethiopia), one in English. Whenever someone came to visit her, she would ask the person to read. Over time, her favorite passages became so familiar that she could recite them from memory, and if her visitors couldn't read, she would recite as a kind of gift to them.

People would come from far away just to visit her. Why would they make the journey for an elderly, illiterate, blind widow? Because somehow in her presence, through her voice, the words "The LORD is my shepherd" ceased to be just words. Those thoughts had washed over her mind so deeply, so often, that there was simply no way that anxiety-producing thoughts could survive. In purity of heart she willed one thing. People flocked to her because it was impossible to hear her say those words without being filled with the hope that perhaps one day they would be as real to them as they were to her.

> **When it comes to reading Scripture, the key question is not "how much," but "how."**

Why did reading the Bible have such a different effect on this Ethiopian woman than it did on the man in my church? It is because, when it comes to reading Scripture, the key question is not "how much," but "how."

It is possible to read Scripture without being "washed by the Word." Scripture itself speaks of just such a condition. Jesus addressed religious leaders who prided themselves on how well they knew the sacred writings. "You search the Scriptures," Jesus said, "because you think that in them you have eternal life; and it is they that testify on my behalf. Yet you refuse to come to me to have life." The religious leaders thought their great knowledge of Scripture was proof of their spiritual greatness. But they never allowed the Bible's teachings on humility to cleanse their mind of pride, never allowed its teachings on love to purge their judgmentalism, so they did not recognize the truth of Jesus' teaching.

3. Meditate on a Fairly Brief Passage or Narrative

It is important to be familiar with all of the Bible. In times of study we will need to read broadly and cover a great deal of material. But in reading for transformation we have to go slowly.

Madame Guyon wrote,

> If you read quickly, it will benefit you little. You will be like a bee that merely skims the surface of a flower. Instead, in

this new way of reading with prayer, you must become as the bee who penetrates into the depths of the flower. You plunge deeply within to remove its deepest nectar.

So immerse yourself in a short passage of Scripture—perhaps a few verses. Read it slowly. Read it the way you would read a love letter at the height of romance. Certain words may stand out to you; allow them to sink into your heart. Ask if perhaps God wants to speak to you through these words. The question that always lies behind such reading is, "God, what do you want to say to me in this moment?"

The goal is not for us to get through the Scriptures. The goal is to get the Scriptures through us.

If you are reading a story in Scripture, you may want to use your imagination to try to recapture the setting and what was happening in the text. What do the arms of the aging father feel like as they wrap around his prodigal son? How do the fish and bread taste that Jesus multiplied to feed the five thousand?

If you are like me, this kind of reading means that you will have to adjust your attitude. Success is not measured by the number of pages read. Sometime ago I set a goal of praying through the psalms, one psalm a day. This is an ancient practice because the psalms have traditionally been the great prayer book of the people of God. They cover the whole range of the human heart's expression toward God: awestruck praise, bitter complaint, soul-rattling confusion, exuberant gratitude.

But a strange thing happened. I found that my goal became to get through the psalms. Each day that I did one, I could chalk it off my list, for I was one step closer to the goal. This meant, of course, that I never wanted to get stuck on one psalm two days in a row—that would keep me from my goal.

It was as if in my mind God had a great big Behavior Modification chart on the refrigerator of heaven, and each time I made it through a psalm I got a gold star. Naturally, this utterly sabotaged

God's real purpose in giving the psalms in the first place. God wants to speak to us, to renew us. And if he is using one psalm, or even one word, to do this, our job is to stick with it as long as it takes to learn what we need to learn.

The goal is not for us to get through the Scriptures. The goal is to get the Scriptures through us.

Some churches give people the idea that the only way to transformation is knowledge. There is an assumption that as people's knowledge of the Bible rises, their level of spiritual maturity rises with it.

A friend who had just started attending church asked a wonderful question about the role of knowledge in spiritual transformation. "Now, as I understand it, one reason people devote so much time to listening to preaching and teaching is to be able to understand the Bible better, right?" he asked.

"That's right." "And the reason for people to be able to understand the Bible better is . . . ?"

We don't have to reflect on his question very long to see the implications. Take any person you know whose knowledge of the Bible is, say, ten times greater than that of the average unchurched person. Then ask yourself if this person is ten times more loving, ten times more patient, and ten times more joyful than the average unchurched person.

Both human experience and the Bible teach that increased knowledge—even knowledge of the Scriptures—does not automatically produce transformed people.

Knowledge about the Bible is an indispensable good. But knowledge does not *by itself* lead to spiritual transformation. When Paul urged the Christians at Rome to "be transformed by the renewing of your minds," he was thinking of far more than just the acquisition of information. "Mind" refers to a whole range of perceiving, understanding, valuing, and feeling that in turn determines the way we live. (Calvin commented on this verse: "It means that we will think, speak, meditate, and do all things with a view to

God's glory.") This renewal will only take place when we, to echo Paul's words, "present our bodies as living sacrifices"—as we arrange our lives around those practices, relationships, and experiences through which God produces transformation.

Moreover, while knowledge is vital and should be prized, it also poses some dangers. It often demolishes humility. The sobriquet "know-it-all" is never used as a compliment. The Bible itself contains some warnings: "Knowledge puffs up, but love builds up."

Both human experience and the Bible teach that increased knowledge—even knowledge of the Scriptures—does not automatically produce transformed people.

1. Take One Thought or Verse with You Through the Day

The psalmist says that fruitful living comes to the person who meditates on the law "day and night." That appears to cover every part of the day.

We can't meditate fast. The idea of meditation comes from an era less frenzied than ours. There were no "Evelyn Wood courses in speed-meditation" in the psalmist's day: "I can meditate at 700 words a minute with a 90 percent comprehension rate."

Meditation is as slow as the process by which the roots draw moisture from the flowing river to bring nurture and fruitfulness to a great tree. Meditation is important enough to be mentioned more than fifty times in the Old Testament. It means not only to think about God's Word, but also to read it aloud. Reading the Scriptures out loud gives the reader focused attention and the advantage of learning by both eye and ear. Meditation is likened in Scripture to a young lion growling over its prey, or the low murmur of a dove, or a cow chewing its cud.

Meditation is not meant to be esoteric or spooky or reserved for gurus reciting mantras in the lotus position. It merely implies sustained attention. It is built around this simple principle: *"What the mind repeats, it retains."*

To begin, choose a single piece of Scripture—one "thought" of God's—that you will live with for one day. Select this verse or phrase before you go to sleep at night or as soon as you wake up in the morning.

Take, for example, this thought from Psalm 46:10: "Be still, and know that I am God!" For one day, live with these words. Let your mind continually return to them in secret:

"Today, as best I can, I am going to be still. I am not going to chatter thoughtlessly. I will remember that I don't have to defend myself or make sure people think of me the way I want them to. Today I don't have to get my way. Today, before I make decisions, I will try to listen for God's voice. Today I am not going to be tossed around by anxiety or anger—I will take those feelings as prompts from the Spirit to listen first. In each of these situations I will ask God, 'How would you like me to respond?' I will live in stillness."

Do you know what it is like to be still? Do you know how others in your life might love it if you were still, just for a day?

As you do this, a wonderful thing will happen. You will discover that you really do *want* to be still. You will really *want* to know that the Lord is God.

5. Allow This Thought to Become Part of Your Memory

Memorizing Scripture is one of the most powerful means of transforming our minds. "I have hidden your word in my heart," the psalmist wrote, "that I might not sin against you."

Memorize statements from Scripture that will help you in matters in which you need it most. For instance, if you wrestle with fear, you may want to memorize Psalm 27:1: "The LORD is my light and my salvation; whom shall I fear?" If pride is a problem, try Philippians 2:3: "Do nothing from selfish ambition or conceit, but in humility regard others as better than yourselves."

And if you are concerned that you have a memory like a steel sieve, don't be. What matters is not how many words we memorize, but what happens to our minds as we immerse them in Scripture. As with any other "spiritual discipline," memorization is only a means to an end.

One of my earliest memories of church involves a contest to see who could memorize the most Bible verses. We each had a poster on the wall with our name on it. The poster had a picture of a mansion, and every verse memorized meant a sticker—a little room to add on to our mansion. Whoever got the most rooms in his or her mansion won a prize: A white Bible—with our name printed on the cover—in gold.

> **What matters is not how many words we memorize, but what happens to our minds as we immerse them in Scripture.**

Eventually the contest narrowed down to me and another kid—a freckle-faced, dark-haired little girl with great big glasses, who was named Louise. For weeks it was nip and tuck, until the last month when she began to pull away. In the last week it was clear she would win.

I began to wonder: What could I do about Louise?

So I killed her.

At least, in my mind I did. I did not like her. I would have done almost anything to hear my name called as the winner and get that Bible. Church was becoming a place where I could shine and prove how good and smart I was. So I did not rejoice when Louise's name was called.

That wasn't the only time I have turned church into a contest. Sometimes I still act as if I'm trying to earn a big white Bible.

To memorize Scripture—to "hide it in our hearts"—can be a great help, but only if it serves the divine purpose: "that I might not sin against you."

Be a "Person of One Book"

If you were marooned on a desert island and could have only a single book with you, what would you choose?

Somebody once asked this question of G. K. Chesterton. Given his reputation as one of the most erudite and creative Christian writers in the first half of the twentieth century, one would naturally expect his response to be the Bible. It was not. Chesterton chose *Thomas' Guide to Practical Ship-building*.

That makes sense, of course. When we're trapped on an island, we want a book that will help us get home. We don't want to be entertained or even informed. We want a book that will show us how to be saved.

The truth is that we *are* trapped—trapped in patterns of thought and behavior that lead to death. Chesterton himself once said that the doctrine of the Fall is the one Christian belief that is empirically verifiable. We are all trapped, as Eugene Peterson put it, on an "I-land," where we know neither ourselves nor God and are looking for a message that help is on the way.

So the followers of Christ have historically sought to be a people devoted to the Word. John Wesley said that a pivotal moment of his life came when he prayed to become a "*homo unius libri*, 'a man of one book.'"

Let us not forget that "the secret of life is pursuing one thing." And as Kierkegaard said, "Purity of heart is to will one thing." The words that bombard us all day long from billboards and tabloids and talk shows pull us in a thousand directions. But the word God speaks to us from his Word can renew our minds. As he said to Augustine, so God says still: "Take it and read. Take it and read."

CHAPTER 12

LIFE WITH A WELL-ORDERED HEART

Developing Your Own "Rule of Life"

Above all else, guard your heart,
for it is the wellspring of life.
PROVERBS 4:23 NIV

In Arthurian legend, certain people devoted their lives to the great quest for the Holy Grail. They sacrificed their bodies, purified their hearts, and gladly renounced all they had—for what? To gain a glimpse of the ultimate symbol of communion with Christ. Of course, this quest was about more than the momentary sight of a relic. It was about the pursuit of union with God. It was the pursuit of life in the kingdom of God, the kingdom of which Camelot itself was only a faint echo.

This pursuit was not a casual undertaking. It demanded—indeed, largely consisted of—preparation of the spirit. This quest could only be fulfilled by someone who was humble and true and pure in heart. As one version expresses it, "On the sole condition of leading a life of purity in thought, word, and deed."

However, no matter how difficult the task, no true knight questioned whether it was worth the cost. This was the Quest, beside which all others—conquering great enemies or gathering great wealth or building great kingdoms—paled in comparison. This was, to use one of Jesus' metaphors, the "pearl of great price," for which any rational person would joyfully give up everything.

In our time, the great quest is for a "balanced lifestyle." Ask most people in American society today what they are after, and they will say something about the need for balance. The Merlins of our day are time management consultants; books of incantations have been replaced by Day-Timers.

Even so, balance is not the Holy Grail. A balanced lifestyle is not an adequate goal to which to devote our lives. The problem with that goal is not that it is too difficult, but that it is too slight. Balance is not the most helpful paradigm for an ideal life.

Beyond Balance

The quest for balance can contribute to a tendency to compartmentalize our faith. Often a balanced life is pictured as a pie chart with life divided into seven or eight slices, one labeled "financial," another "vocational," and so on, with one of the slices reserved for "spiritual." This paradigm encourages us to think of matters such as finances or work as "nonspiritual activities." It blinds us to the fact that God is intensely interested in our every moment and activity.

A Balanced Life

Another problem with the goal of balance is that it doesn't allow much room for people in desperate situations—those in crisis or the poor or the oppressed. What does it mean to tell someone with a terminal disease or a street person or a single mother with a physically challenged child that she needs "more balance"?

"Balance" tends to carry with it the notion that we are trying to make our lives more manageable, more convenient, more pleasant. After all, we ultimately decide for ourselves what balance looks like. On a vacation we discovered the world's greatest peach cobbler at a restaurant called Bob Evans, and we spent the rest of our trip looking for Bob Evans three or four times a day. We decided that for that week a balanced life looked like this:

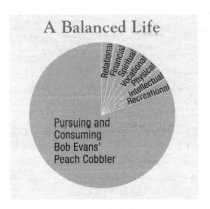

A Balanced Life

Relational
Financial
Spiritual
Vocational
Physical
Intellectual
Recreational

Pursuing and Consuming Bob Evans' Peach Cobbler

At a deeper level, the paradigm of balance simply doesn't capture the sense of compelling urgency worthy of human devotion. It is largely a middle-class pursuit. It lacks the notion that my life is to be given to something bigger than myself.

As George Bernard Shaw said,

> This is the true joy in life, the being used for a purpose recognized by yourself as a mighty one; the being thoroughly worn out before you are thrown on the scrap heap; the being

a force of nature instead of a feverish selfish little clod of ailments and grievances complaining that the world will not devote itself to making you happy.

The quest for balance lacks the notion that life is to be given to something bigger than ourselves. It lacks the call to sacrifice and self-denial—the wild, risky, costly, adventurous abandon of following Jesus. Ask hungry children in Somalia if they want to help you achieve balance, and you will discover that they were hoping for something more from you. And I believe that, deep down, *you* are probably hoping for something more from yourself.

> **The quest for balance lacks the notion that life is to be given to something bigger than ourselves.**

So is God. Jesus never said, "If any want to become my followers, let them deny themselves, take up their cross and lead a balanced life." He said to follow him. He wants us to do what he would do if he were in our place.

I sometimes try to imagine a conversation between the apostle Paul and a twentieth-century time management consultant (TMC). It starts something like this:

TMC: Paul, if you look at this pie chart, I think you'll agree with me that your spiritual life is going pretty well. But vocationally, your tent-making has seriously fallen off. This has led to some downsizing in your financial portfolio. Let's take a look at the time log I asked you to keep since our last meeting.

PAUL: "Five times I have received . . . the forty lashes minus one. Three times I was beaten with rods. Once I received a stoning. Three times I was shipwrecked; for a night and a day I was adrift at sea; on frequent journeys, in danger from rivers, danger from bandits, danger from my own people, danger from Gentiles, danger in the city, danger in the wilderness, danger at sea, danger from false brothers and sisters; in toil and hardship, through many a sleepless night, hungry and thirsty, often without food, cold and naked."

I have a hard time coming up with the TMC's next line. Paul's ultimate aim in life was something beyond balance.

Unbalanced Living Is Not the Answer!

The point to all this is not that we ought to live an unbalanced life. Being unbalanced is not the answer. When our son John was three years old, he became deeply attached to an old Disney movie called *The Love Bug*. The character he identified with was not the hero, played by Dean Jones, nor the comic sidekick, played by Buddy Hackett. It was the race car, Herbie. (There were actually four Herbie movies—the original and three sequels. We saw them all, often enough to memorize the scripts.)

This attachment became an obsession. Johnny wore a shirt with Herbie's name and number (53) on it. Every time we got in the car, Johnny would sit next to me; our car was Herbie, and we were in a race against every other car, each one driven by Herbie's nemesis, Thorndike. To let another car pass us was unthinkable. We lived for speed. Every moment was a race.

> There used to be a saying among hyperactive preachers: "I'd rather flame out than rust out." The problem with this is that either way, they're out.

One time, visiting a church, we picked up John from the child-care area after the service and discovered that he had gotten a scratch. The attendants filled out an "ouchie report" for him, and under "name" it read: "Herbie Ortberg." He *was* Herbie.

Life is hard when we live like Herbie. The race can provide a rush—a "high"—for a while, but eventually it becomes exhausting.

Years ago, the founder of what became a large parachurch ministry used to travel the globe and in doing so neglected his wife, his children, and his own soul. He lived like Herbie. He said his continuing prayer was "Okay, God, I'll take care of your lambs; you take care of mine." In other words, "I will neglect the people to whom I have made the most basic commitment of my life, but because I'm doing it in the name of ministry, you take care of them." His wife and children paid a high price.

There used to be a saying among hyperactive preachers: "I'd rather flame out than rust out." The problem with this is that either way, they're out. Once we're out, it doesn't matter much how we got there.

The Quest for a Well-ordered Heart

But there *is* a pursuit that is worthy of our devotion. There is a goal that is achievable even in the most desperate of situations. It will produce good far beyond our own little sphere of influence. It is something that our souls long for: the life we've always wanted.

It is the quest for what might be called a well-ordered heart. The balance paradigm assumes that our problem is external—a disorder in our schedule or our job or our season of life. But the truly significant disorder is internal.

What does it mean to have a well-ordered heart? Augustine suggested that to have a well ordered-heart is to love

— the right thing
— to the right degree
— in the right way
— with the right kind of love.

The effect of the Fall is that we have disordered affections. For

When the heart is well-ordered, we are not only increasingly free from sin, but also increasingly free from the *desire* to sin.

instance, beauty is God's handiwork and therefore it is good, but when we love it so much that we worship supermodels and ignore those whom American society regards as "plain," we do not love beauty rightly. Augustine wrote, "When the miser prefers gold to justice, it's through no fault of the gold. For although it's good, it can be loved with an evil as well as a good love." Money itself is a good thing, but that does not absolve of blame those who love it *so much* that they will oppress or hoard or cheat to obtain it.

Augustine wrote further, "It seems to me that a brief but true definition of virtue is this: 'It is well-ordered love.'"

Another writer expressed the idea nearly a thousand years before that: "Keep your heart with all vigilance, for from it flow the springs of life."

When the heart is well-ordered, we are not only increasingly free from sin, but also increasingly free from the *desire* to sin. If the heart were truly well-ordered, we would love people so much we would not *want* to deceive or manipulate or envy them. We would be transformed from the inside out.

Imagine what the world would be like if it were filled with people who had well-ordered hearts. Television programs such as *Miami Vice* would be replaced by *Miami Virtue*. Tabloids sold at grocery stores would be filled with stories about acts of lavish generosity and spontaneous sacrifice committed by noncelebrities we have never heard of. Television talk shows would feature men who secretly enjoy dressing as men.

We would sleep at night the untroubled sleep of innocence—no staring at the ceiling at two o'clock in the morning because of regrets. We would have no need for "do-overs" or mulligans.

A Game Plan for Morphing

How do we go about transforming ordinary, fallen hearts into hearts that love the right thing in the right way to the right degree with the right kind of love? It requires a plan of action; otherwise it will never happen. William Paulsell advises us,

> It is unlikely that we will deepen our relationship with God in a *casual* or *haphazard manner*. There will be a need for some intentional commitment and some reorganization in our own lives. But there is nothing that will enrich our lives more than a deeper and clearer perception of *God's presence in the routine of daily living*.

The CEO of a Fortune 500 company would never try to grow an organization without some strategic planning. A coach serious about winning would never enter a season in a "casual or haphazard manner." We understand the need for wise, flexible planning in other important matters such as finances. The need is just as great in pursuing spiritual life.

> **Spiritual transformation cannot be orchestrated or controlled, but neither is it a random venture.... We need a plan.**

Spiritual transformation cannot be orchestrated or controlled, but neither is it a random venture. We need some kind of support or structure, much as a young vine needs a trellis. We need sails to help us catch the winds of the Spirit. All of us know the frustration of random, haphazard efforts that lead nowhere in spiritual life. We need a plan for transformation—for morphing.

For Jesus' disciples, as we have seen, the "plan" consisted simply of following the Master around and learning from him how to live. In groups such as Alcoholics Anonymous, the plan for transformation involves working through the twelve steps as often as necessary.

I believe it is at just this point that many contemporary Christ-followers become frustrated. *"How do I know that I am living as a disciple? What is it, precisely, that disciples do?"*

There is a name for this process. Historically, when Christians sought to order the events of ordinary life around growing in Christ-likeness, they would develop what is called a "rule of life." Various monastic orders each had a rule. This was not simply a set of laws. The Latin word for rule is *regula*—that is, something done regularly.

A rule involves a rhythm for living in which we can grow more intimately connected to God. In particular, finding a strategy for transformation will involve questions such as

— How and when will I pray?
— How will I handle money in a way that draws me closer to God?
— How can I approach work in a way that will help Christ to be formed in me?
— How am I involved in Christian community (such as corporate worship, fellowship, and confession)?
— How can I fill my daily tasks with a sense of the presence of God?

Living "in the Name of Jesus"

Consider how you might arrange your day around the pursuit of a well-ordered heart. Paul writes to the church at Colossae, as the climax of instruction on transformed living: "Whatever you do, in word or deed, do everything in the name of the Lord Jesus, giving thanks to God the Father through him."

What does it mean to do something "in the name of Jesus"? Generally speaking, in the Bible a person's name has to do with his or her character. So doing something in Jesus' name means to do it in his character. It means doing it as Jesus himself would do it if he were in your place. This flows right out of our understanding of discipleship.

But what is really striking here is the comprehensive nature of what Paul says: "Whatever you do. . . ." Lest there be any

> Doing something in Jesus' name means to do it in his character. It means doing it as Jesus himself would do it if he were in your place.

confusion, Paul explains what he means: "Whatever you do *in word or deed....*" That covers it all. But again, in case we are tempted to allow for loopholes, Paul says it once more: "Whatever you do, in word or deed, do *everything....*"

We tend to read rather quickly over statements like this, but Paul's repetition should cause us to linger a while on this thought.

Next, we need to design some concrete activities to achieve our goal. In that case we must, first, understand clearly what doing them in Jesus' name involves, and second, find out how to rearrange our lives accordingly.

What would it mean for us to "wake up in Jesus' name"? Some of us, by the nature of our genetic wiring, wake up differently from other people. We could divide the human race into two categories: the people who *love* to get up in the morning, and people who *hate* the people who love to get up in the morning. (Someone asked my wife once, "Do you wake up grumpy in the morning?" "No," she said, "I let him sleep.")

If Jesus held unhindered sway when the alarm clock goes off, what kind of thoughts would pass through the mind? Would our heads be filled with anxieties about today and regrets about yesterday? Or would our first thoughts be the assurance as to who holds the day and who holds us?

I have made it a point recently to take a few moments before I get out of bed to greet God. I tell him that my day belongs to him. I invite him to go through it with me. I believe that is one way to wake up "in Jesus' name."

How we greet the people closest to us is crucial. The first fifteen seconds that we spend with them really sets the tone for an entire day. How would Jesus greet our spouse, or our children or our roommate? What words would he use, in what tone of voice, with what expression on his face?

My son came bounding into our bedroom well before dawn one day because overnight we had the first snowfall of the season. "I'm so excited," he bubbled. "I can't decide whether I want to play outside in the snow or watch the Weather Channel." I won't write my response, but I don't think it is what Jesus would have said. This doesn't mean that the right thing is to let the kids come barging in any time they want. But in general, I think Jesus would treat these first moments of the day with great value. I think he would greet household members with words that would express joy. If we want to greet people in Jesus' name, it means doing radical things such as *looking right at them* and actually noticing them.

What would it mean for us to drive in Jesus' name? If Jesus were behind the wheel of our car, would the vehicle behave any differently than usual? On matters like this, people tend to laugh at the suggestion of acting in Jesus' name, but it is in just such ordinary, seemingly "nonspiritual" activities as these that "doing everything in Jesus' name" *must* make a difference if it is to mean anything at all. Would Jesus listen to worship tapes as he drove? Would he sometimes listen to country western music? I think he might sometimes listen to the news—and pray for the state of the world as he listens. I suspect that sometimes he would drive in silence.

This brings us to an important point. Doing things in Jesus' name doesn't mean always doing them the same way. We should exercise some discernment.

How do we watch television in Jesus' name? Nearly everyone I know watches TV, and a good many of us wonder whether we watch too much at times. Would Jesus watch only PBS? Might he sometimes watch a show that is funny and simply receive the joy of it as kind of a gift? As my children and I watched part of a tennis tournament on TV, we marveled at the excellence of the players and were inspired to go out and practice. Yet there is a harder question: How much and what kinds of TV programming can I watch before it begins to create in me a disordered heart?

What does it mean to do household chores in Jesus' name? How do I do laundry or rake the leaves or wash dishes as he would in my place?

One night soon after we moved into our home, Nancy and I were lying in bed when we heard a tremendous whirring sound, as if there were a jet engine up on the roof. "What's that noise?" Nancy asked. I knew that if I acknowledged the noise it would be my job to check it out.

"What noise?" I said, although I had to say it very loudly so she could hear me over the roar of the jet engine.

"That tremendous whirring noise," she yelled.

"Oh, that!" I shouted back. "Probably it's just a low-flying plane resting on its way to O'Hare."

Eventually I got around to trying to track down the problem. It turned out to be an aberrant exhaust fan up in the attic that I couldn't get to turn off. I wanted to shoot it. Generally, in such moments I am easily frustrated and tend to snap at people, even if they want to help. But to respond in Jesus' name would mean reflecting on how fortunate I am to have a nice place to live. It would mean recognizing that this task can help me to remember that I am not the Messiah, and the earth won't stop spinning if I have to take some time out to fix something.

In a sense, each of us chooses a "spiritual strategy" whether or not we are intentional about it. We can choose it by default.

How do I work in Jesus' name? Our jobs might bring us into contact with many people in the course of a day, whether as customers or colleagues. To work in Jesus' name would involve viewing them not *just* as customers or accounts or production-units, but as *people*. We might say a quick prayer for each person we encounter. We might take a geniune interest in their lives. Do they have a family? What are their interests?

If we work with our hands, we might reflect on the fact that Adam was a gardener. When we spend physical energy to create something, we do a good thing. We can say a quick prayer at the end of each task and offer it as a gift to God. We might reflect that Jesus spent most of his adult life as a carpenter. When he did this, we can be sure that he was expressing his character—glorifying his Father—every bit as much as when he was traveling as a teacher.

How do we spend money in the name of Jesus? When we enter a mall, how do we shop in the name of Jesus? Part of the answer involves noticing and treating with kindness the people who work there. It may also involve enjoying colors and fabric out of a sense of beauty and artistry. We could get confused here and think that to dress "in Jesus' name" means to wear ugly clothes. This is a distorted understanding of spirituality. Beauty is a good thing; to appreciate and enjoy it is good. Jesus pointed out that God himself has such an eye for beauty that common flowers are better dressed than Solomon—the best-dressed man in the history of Israel. The work of Givenchy and Yves St. Laurent pale by comparison with God's designs.

However, shopping in Jesus' name will surely mean saying no to certain purchases. It will mean realizing that we are not called to be the ultimate fashion statement. To live with a well-ordered heart in this regard means to realize that beauty is good, but it is not the *deepest* good.

Now we begin to get a sense of the radical nature of what Paul means when he says, "*Whatever* you do, in *word or deed*, do *everything* in the name of Jesus." We sometimes miss the point because we tend to divide up life like a pie. But I believe Paul is quite serious about what he says. He is not simply using spiritual-sounding language. He really means it. We are invited to do *life* in Jesus' name.

Choosing a "Plan for Transformation"

In a sense, each of us chooses a "spiritual strategy" whether or not we are intentional about it. We can choose it by default. How much and when we pray, how we handle money, how and when we worship—these are all elements in the process of transformation.

Jesus' followers are those who intentionally arrange their lives around the goal of spiritual transformation—the development of a well-ordered heart. We can learn to be intentional. We might want to write down, on a single sheet of paper or in a journal, our own "rule of life." It doesn't have to be elaborate. In fact, such a rule works best if we keep it quite simple and practical.

Living in Jesus' Name

"Whatever you do, in word or deed, do everything in the name of the Lord Jesus."

In the Bible, names often reflect a person's character. So to do something in Jesus' name means to do it in a way consistent with his character — to do it the way Jesus himself would.

Every moment is an opportunity to live in Jesus' name. All the everyday stuff of life can be filled with his presence — if you are.

Start by thinking about what it would mean to do each of these activities in Jesus' name:

Waking up
Greeting those you see first thing in the morning
Eating
Driving
Working outside the home, or caring for children
Shopping
Watching television
Doing household tasks
Reading
Going to sleep

Keep it simple. Focus on Jesus' presence with you as you go through these seemingly inconsequential moments of the day. Keep directing your thoughts back to him. Ask for his help or his guidance, or simply share your heart with him.

Memorize Colossians 3:17 as a way of helping you do this exercise. Ask God to bring these words back to your mind continually.

Keep track of how this experiment goes. Talk about it with a spiritual mentor or friend.

For example, Pope John XXIII, a Christian leader who had a profound impact on the church in the twentieth century, began to follow this daily practice when he was quite young:

Spending fifteen minutes in silent prayer the first thing in the morning

Spending fifteen minutes in reading spiritual literature

Before bed, spending a few moments examining his conscience and making a confession to God; then identifying the issues he wanted to pray about in the morning

Setting aside specific times for prayer, study, recreation, and sleep

Making a habit of turning his mind to God in prayer through the day

Each Day an Adventure with God

You and I are invited to make each moment of every day an opportunity to learn from Jesus how to live in the kingdom of God. Every minute counts, as Frank Laubach explains so well:

For do you not see that God is trying experiments with human lives? That is why there are so many of them. He has one billion seven hundred million experiments going around the world at this moment. And his question is "how far will this man and that woman allow me to carry this hour? . . . For I who pushed life up through the protozoan and the tiny grass, and the fish and the bird and the dog and the gorilla and the man. . . . I have not become satisfied yet. I am not only willing to make this hour marvelous. I am in travail to set you akindle with the Christ-thing which has no name. How fully can you surrender and not be afraid?

CHAPTER 13

A LIFE OF ENDURANCE
The Experience of Suffering

It is said of God that no one can behold his face and live.
I always thought this meant that no one could see his
splendor and live. A friend said perhaps it means that no
one could see his sorrow and live. Or perhaps his sorrow
is his splendor.

NICHOLAS WOLTERSTORFF

A friend of mine ran in the Los Angeles marathon, so I followed the event quite closely. There were 18,000 runners—18,000 brave, motivated, skinny, overachieving, masochistic people.

With the event being held in California, we can expect that some of the runners were a little out of the ordinary. One guy ran in full circus makeup and called himself "T-bone the Clown." Another contestant ran as "Flower Man." Thirteen people draped themselves in a specially designed costume and competed as a human centipede.

The starting line was a sight to behold. T-bone was shaking hands with the crowd and laughing and waving. The centipede looked friskier than any centipede has a right to be.

Then the race began. The first phase of such a race might be called the pleasure stage. At this point running is fun. Your body is loose, your heart is pumping, you are "one with the cosmos": The blood is flowing, the head is clear, the lungs are breathing deeply, the birds are singing, the sun is shining, the fish are jumping, the cotton is high, Daddy's rich, and Momma's good-looking. You are functioning like a well-oiled machine.

How long this stage lasts depends on the runner's conditioning. For me, it lasts twelve or thirteen feet.

After the initial rush of pleasure, running becomes drudgery. After drudgery it becomes effortful and laborious. And if you keep going long enough, you reach the point when the temptation to stop is overwhelming. Your feet are protesting vigorously, knives of pain are stabbing through your calves, your lungs have burning coals at the bottom of them. Runners speak of this experience as "hitting the wall."

To run at this stage—to hit the wall and keep going—is the ultimate test of a runner. Races are won or lost, completed or abandoned, at "the wall."

At this stage, the LA marathon really became interesting. T-bone wasn't laughing with the crowd anymore. The human centipede was hanging over the fence, and it didn't look good—all thirteen centipedal stomachs united in collective revolt.

At the finish line, people came dribbling in one at a time. Some didn't make it at all.

The start of a race is enjoyable. It is easy. Finishing is hard work. To finish well—that's glory. Finishing well is what counts.

How will we run the race of life? Will we finish well?

The capacity to finish well is what the New Testament writers called endurance, or perseverance. It is the virtue by which we become increasingly able to honor commitments that ought to last a lifetime. It is especially the ability to honor commitments when honoring them becomes difficult.

A wife says to her husband of fifty years as they lie in bed one night, "When we were young, you used to hold my hand each night." Slowly, a little irritably, his hand reaches out until it finds hers.

"And when we were young," she goes on, "you used to snuggle up against me in bed." A little more slowly, her husband's body creaks and turns until it is nestling against hers.

"And when we were young, you used to nibble on my ear." Abruptly the covers are thrown back, and the man lurches out of bed.

"Where are you going?" she asks, a little hurt.

"To get my teeth," he grumbles.

> **Any truly meaningful human accomplishment will require perseverance.... Spiritual transformation won't happen without it.**

To nibble on an ear when you are young and full of romance and bubbling hormones and the room is scented with eau de something or other is one thing. To still be nibbling when the ear holds a hearing device and the room is scented with Ben-Gay and you have to get up to get your teeth—that's something else.

Perseverance is not a panacea. We have limits that the desire to endure alone will not transcend. We will be both enabled and limited by a host of factors that perseverance alone will not overcome.

But any truly meaningful human accomplishment will require perseverance. Gifts, talents, IQ—these are to some extent beyond our control. Endurance is the gift that *we* can offer. Spiritual transformation won't happen without it.

"Let us run with perseverance the race that is set before us," the writer of Hebrews said. In other words, just don't quit.

Perseverance Through Suffering

How do we develop perseverance? There is more than one way, but one course is repeatedly affirmed by the New Testament writers and others who are wise in the way of spiritual life. This involves endurance in the midst of hardship. "My brothers and sisters," James said, "whenever you face trials of any kind, consider it nothing but joy, because you know that the testing of your faith produces endurance; and let endurance have its full effect, so that you may be mature and complete, lacking in nothing."

I was recently involved in a survey in which hundreds of people were asked to identify the factors that were most formative in their spiritual growth. The number one response overwhelmingly involved times of suffering and pain. Ironically, the role of suffering is one of the most neglected issues in spiritual growth, because we do not arrange for

> **Suffering always changes us, but it does not necessarily change us for the better.**

it to happen as we might Bible study or prayer. Instead, life inevitably arranges it for us. So if we are going to be transformed, we must look at how suffering benefits us, or at least how to respond to it.

Suffering always changes us, but it does not necessarily change us for the better. In his book *A Grace Disguised*, Gerald L. Sittser, who lost his wife, his mother, and a daughter in a head-on collision, poignantly writes of the struggle to make sense of tragedy:

> Loss creates a barren present, as if one were sailing on a vast sea of nothingness. Those who suffer loss live suspended between a past for which they long and a future for which they hope. They want to return to the harbor of the familiar past and recover what was lost. . . . Or they want to sail on and discover a meaningful future that promises to bring them life again. . . . Instead, they find themselves living in a barren present that is empty of meaning.

This uncertain result is the reason that the writer of Hebrews urges us to take our lead from the "cloud of witnesses"—that great number who have endured before us. The primary champion—the one who gets the most space in the cloud—is Abraham. Let us consider how this Old Testament saint endured the most difficult stage of his race.

The Road to Moriah

God said to Abraham, "Take your son, your only son Isaac, whom you love, and go to the land of Moriah, and offer him there as a burnt offering on one of the mountains that I shall show you."

It is a dark road to Moriah. It is dark because it means giving up what Abraham loves most in the world. But the darkness is more than that. Isaac is not just Abraham's child, but also the fulfillment of the promise from God: "I have made you the ancestor of a multitude of nations." Isaac is Abraham's hope for the future.

The time has come for Abraham to walk a while in darkness.

What do we do when we walk in the darkness and God seems distant and remote and silent? Gerhard von Rad suggests that Abraham is going out onto the road of "God-forsakenness," where God seems to contradict himself, appears to want to remove the salvation that he himself began in human history.

You may know what it is to walk in darkness. Sometimes faith is walking in darkness and simply refusing to quit. Sometimes faith is just hanging on. The character of the faith that allows us to be transformed by suffering and darkness is not doubt-free certainty; rather, it is tenacious obedience.

The Role of Testing

"After these things God *tested* Abraham." That is the way the story begins. The first thing the writer does is to assure us that Isaac is never in any real danger. We have a perspective that Abraham does not have. We know something he does not know.

Have you ever had a really hard test?

A college sophomore sweats all semester in anticipation of the notoriously difficult final exam in his ornithology class. Having made what he regards as the ultimate effort, he is stunned when he walks into the classroom to take the exam. There is no blue book, no multiple-choice questions, no text booklet at all—just twenty-five pictures on the wall. And they are not photos of birds in resplendent color, but pictures of birds' *feet*. The test is to identify the birds.

"This is insane," the student protests. "It can't be done."

"It must be done," says the professor. "This is the final."

"I won't do it," the frustrated student says. "I'm walking out."

"If you walk out, you fail the final."

"Go ahead and fail me," the boy says, heading for the door.

"Okay, you have failed. Tell me your name," the professor demands.

The boy rolls his pants up and takes his shoes off to reveal *his* feet: "You tell me!"

A test is a difficult experience through which a person's true values, commitments, and beliefs are revealed. *Test* became a very important word in the Old Testament, and the way it is used there reveals something about how endurance develops.

1. It is used only in reference to the people of God, never to heathen nations.

2. It is applied only to people of faith, never to the ungodly.

Testing is reserved for those in a covenant relationship with God. Even though it is painful, testing is an act of love. Suffering serves to test our faith. James wrote, "You know that the testing of your faith produces endurance; and let endurance have its full effect, so that you may be mature and complete, lacking in nothing."

A Voice cries out, "Abraham!"

And Abraham responds, "Here I am." Abraham is not telling where he is. He has heard this Voice before. The Voice made wonderful promises about his destiny. It asked him to do the most difficult things he has ever done.

The Voice told him to leave his homeland, all the familiar surroundings—and he did.

The Voice told him that he and God were in a covenant, bound by indissoluble ties, and that they would have a sign of their relationship. Abraham was to be circumcised. And he was. (Perhaps he wondered why the sign couldn't be a secret handshake or decoder ring, but he obeyed.)

The Voice told him he and his wife would have a son even though their combined ages equaled 190. He laughed. But apparently he was obedient once again—because Sarah did bear a son.

And now the Voice comes once more. As far as we know, this is the last time Abraham is to hear it on earth. It asked him once before to give up everything in his life for the sake of a promise. Now it asks one more thing. The Voice is asking him to give up the promise.

Abraham's response is an offering of himself: "Here I am." It is a succinct way of saying, "I will not run or evade or hide. I am wholly available. I am at your service."

"Abraham, . . . Take your son, your only son Isaac, whom you love. . . ."

Take this child—as Frederick Buechner so wonderfully puts it—born in the geriatric ward for which Medicare picked up the tab, this child named Isaac—which means "laughter." Abraham and Sarah laughed at first because they didn't believe; they laughed at the sheer impossibility of it. They laughed because they were told they would have a son when they had reached an age when they didn't even dare to buy green bananas. And after the child was born, they laughed because they *did* believe. They laughed that when Sarah went to Wal-Mart, she was the only shopper to buy both Pampers and Depends. They laughed that both parents and baby had to eat the same strained vegetables because nobody in the whole family had a single tooth.

Enduring in Confusion

But now the Voice had spoken one last time, and Abraham isn't laughing anymore. The laughter is going out of his life.

For he is losing a dream along with his son. God had promised that Isaac would be the beginning of a new community for humankind. This was to be God's great Experiment—one final chance for human beings to live as family.

Imagine planting a church in response to what we take to be a clear call from God. We didn't want to, but out of sheer obedience we do. We spend twenty-four years on our own—as Abraham spent twenty-four more years childless after receiving God's promise. No one joins our newly planted church. We keep going to conferences, where we are asked repeatedly, "How many people attend your church?"

"Just me." That kind of response doesn't get us invited to speak in many places.

Then we get one. One member. All our dreams for the future, God's whole promise, ride on that solitary person. Then the Voice says, "Take him out to the parking lot, and put him down."

Our only member?

Imagine if we were to lose our dream.

Can we let go of what we love the most?

Abraham lives in this torment for three days. We want to cry out to him, "It's all right. It will turn out all right. He's not that kind of a God. He will provide."

But life doesn't work that way. We can only proceed one chapter at a time. Every

> **Going in faith does not necessarily mean going with serenity or without doubts. Faith can be difficult.**

journey has a beginning, a middle, and an end. And when we're in the middle, no one is allowed to see what the end will be.

The road to Moriah is very dark; much too dark to see more than a few feet ahead. Those who endure can go only by faith. But going in faith does not necessarily mean going with serenity or without doubts. Faith can be difficult.

Enduring in Doubt

Doubt can be a good thing. I am skeptical of reports that Elvis is alive and well and working as a short-order cook at Taco Bell. I don't believe that aliens periodically land on earth and give rides to humans—how come they never seem to land at MIT to give a ride to a physics professor? I wouldn't want to buy into every infomercial I see on television.

But doubt is not always good. It can hinder our praying. It can trouble us when we see suffering we don't understand. It can tempt us to try to sound more certain than we really are.

So I am comforted by Abraham, because this great paragon of faith in the Old Testament is not doubt-free. Abraham laughs in disbelief. He lies about his wife, placing her in jeopardy to save his skin. He sleeps with his wife's servant because he wants to father a child at any cost. He gets a lot wrong. But he gets one thing right: He just keeps going.

On the way to Mount Moriah, Abraham takes Isaac and leaves the servants behind, telling them, "We will return." Why does he say "we"? Does he want to mislead them or hide what he's really doing? (We know he has lied before.) Does he think that maybe at the last minute he won't be able to go through with it, that it is too horrible to contemplate? Does he think somehow that in spite of it all, God's promise will yet come true—"It is through Isaac that offspring shall be named for you"? We don't know. We do know that even when he doesn't fully understand, Abraham obeys God.

Having faith does not mean never having doubts or questions. It does mean remaining obedient.

Enduring in Loneliness

As Isaac and his father go on alone, Abraham carries the knife and the fire. There is a deep irony here in that the knife and fire are dangerous objects that the boy could hurt himself with. "But it is a father's job to protect his son," he rationalizes.

He makes Isaac carry the wood that will be used for the sacrifice.

Now it is just the two of them: "So the two of them walked on together."

For the second time, a voice calls Abraham. This time it is Isaac: "Father."

And this time Abraham must have wanted to run or hide from the voice. But for the second time he gives the response, "Here I am." That is, "At your service, my son."

Isaac is old enough to notice that although his father said they are going to offer a burnt sacrifice, they have no animal. His father is strangely silent. So Isaac asks the question, "The fire and the wood are here, but where is the lamb for a burnt offering?"

Again, Abraham gives an ambiguous answer—prompted by doubt or fear or hope or bitterness or maybe a little of all of them: "The Lord will provide."

Again, "the two of them walked together." Abraham is with his son, yet he is alone. They are separated by an unspeakable barrier and go on in silence.

One of the most painful aspects of suffering is the loneliness of it. Others may offer support or empathy, but no one can walk the road to Moriah in our place.

And then father and son come to the place. The narrator keeps mentioning Abraham's obedience: building an altar, taking the wood from Isaac's back, and stretching out his son upon the sticks and the stones.

Now it is time. This is Isaac his son, the promise of the new community, the dream of God, the reason he has left everything, his one hope. This boy is all that, but not just that. And Abraham ties up his son's legs and binds his arms so there will be no struggle at the end. Then he picks up his son—bone of his bone and flesh of his flesh—and holds the same body that he held on the first day it came from Sarah's womb, the little body that he used to feed and bathe and rock and tell stories of a home somewhere far behind him and a greater home somewhere in the future that Abraham would never know but maybe

> Having faith does not mean never having doubts or questions. It does mean remaining obedient.

Isaac would, the little body he would check on at night to make sure it was still breathing and hold sometimes just to laugh with at the sheer impossibility of it all. He holds that body one last time, then lowers it again to the wood. He reaches toward heaven with the knife in his hand, to destroy with a single move the life that he had created, and with it all his hope and joy and future.

Enduring Unanswered Prayer

And now we need to linger a little bit. We want to hurry on and get to the happy ending. We want to be assured that suffering is serving a larger purpose—bringing transformation, producing the quality of endurance.

But if pain is, in C. S. Lewis's famous metaphor, "God's megaphone to rouse a deaf world," that is not the whole truth. Like Abraham, we haven't reached the end of our story, and we need to be honest about what it is like in the land of Moriah.

A couple come in for counseling. They desperately want to have a baby. They have waited and prayed for twelve anxious, doubting years. They see other people with baby carriages and bassinets and they wonder why they are denied. They trudge on year after year as barren as Abraham and Sarah.

Then one day, after they have given up on technology, it happens: the liquid in the test tube changes color, and their prayers are answered, and then they have a perfect, healthy baby—a little boy. And they believe.

When he is three years old, this answered prayer is playing with an orange soccer ball. It lands on a crack in the sidewalk and bounces crazily to the left. It didn't have to happen that way—a little more breeze, a little nudge from God, and the ball would miss the crack. It could have bounced to the right, but it doesn't. God doesn't nudge it, and it goes to the left. And that means into the street, and the boy goes in after it, and never sees the car.

And now they are alone again, his mother and father. Their world has landed on a crack and has bounced away with an orange soccer ball. And now their answered prayer hurts more than their unanswered one. The laughter has died.

This is a story for people who doubt sometimes, for people who have heard the laughter die, for people who occasionally wonder why God seems disinterested and remote.

What does it mean to be faithful in the dark land of Moriah?

Enduring When All Seems Lost

Abraham raises his hand in the air to destroy everything. And yet even now, even at this moment, he somehow believes. Not perfectly—he has never in his life believed perfectly. He lied and feared and impregnated Hagar and laughed all along the way. Such is the great irony of Abraham, that the journey of faith has been riddled with doubt every step of the way.

But the reason that Abraham did not run or hide and kept taking step after horrible step was his hope against hope that somehow this strange and distant God who seemed so remote and terrifying would yet turn out to be the God who spoke to him so many years ago. There was the hope that somewhere in this story of bloodshed and death would emerge the God who makes impossible promises and keeps them and names them laughter. The man keeps hoping even when from human perspective the situation seems most hopeless.

This faith beyond reason is why Søren Kierkegaard gives Abraham the title of "Knight of the Absurd." Abraham is not stoic about it; he has never resigned himself to calm acceptance. When Socrates took the hemlock that ended his life, he did it calmly, nobly. He was a model of resignation. Abraham is no Socrates. Abraham, obedient to the end, gives up everything, yet still hopes—even when hope seems absurd—that God will yet deliver him.

Abraham does not have perfect faith. He just hangs on. He places himself in God's hands. He just keeps running.

God's Call in the Midst of Suffering

Then Abraham is called a third time. The narrator says that it is an angel of the Lord calling from heaven. The angel calls the name twice, as if he wants to make sure it is not too late: "Abraham, Abraham!"

And for the third time Abraham responds, "Here I am." He might well add, "I will not run, for I have nowhere else to hide. I have nothing else to give. You have nothing left with which to hurt me. Here I am."

And finally the Voice speaks: "Do not lay your hand on the boy or do anything to him." And in an instant Abraham is given back his laughter, his dream, his son.

> Abraham does not have perfect faith. He just hangs on. He places himself in God's hands. He just keeps running.

He is not given everything. He doesn't see the fulfillment of his dream—not nearly. He is counted by the writer of Hebrews among those who "did not receive what was promised."

He just hangs on. Suffering alone does not produce perseverance, only suffering that is endured somehow in faith.

Start with Small Trials

To be formed and transformed through trials, the place to start is with
little ordeals. The place is when "*all kinds* of trials and temptations"
crowd into our lives, as the Phillips version expresses James 1:2.

Often I am humbled by my failure to endure even the smallest
trials. I am writing these words as I ride on a crowded flight. When
I received my seat assignment, I was slightly chagrined to find I had
the middle seat in a row of three. My chagrin grew to irritation
when I found out who my companions would be: a single mother
holding a cranky three-month-old baby on
one side of me, and her young daughter on
the other side, with her two little boys in the
seats right in front of us. "I hope you don't
mind the baby," the mother said.

> Suffering alone
> does not produce
> perseverance, only
> suffering that is
> endured somehow
> in faith.

As a matter of fact, I *did* mind the baby.
I wished the baby were far away, in another
row, on another flight. I did not think about
the trial of a mother traveling alone with
three small children and an infant. All I thought about was how this
would keep me from accomplishing my agenda for the flight—
writing this book to tell people all about how to live as Jesus would
in their place.

I sent out all the body-language signals that I could that I was
not open to communication. I was devoted to my laptop computer.
But it was all to no avail. The little girl sitting on my right asked
me, "What are you doing?"

"Writing," I said, summarizing admirably.

"What are you writing?"

"A book."

"What's the book about?"

Ouch!

Here was a tiny trial. In fact, for someone further along than me, it wouldn't have been a trial at all but an opportunity to serve someone with far greater needs. But I'm not that far along yet. So I suddenly had an opportunity to practice patience as graciously as I could in a situation I didn't want to be in.

Life is filled with minitrials. When someone interrupts me, I can learn to graciously hold my tongue. When my co-worker borrows something and doesn't return it immediately, I can learn patience. When I have a headache, I can discover that it is possible to suffer and not tell everybody about it. As simple as it sounds, the place to start being formed by trials is with the mini variety.

> We do not keep the faith from sheer strength of will. The reason we can trust God is that he understands what it is to walk in darkness.

But we need to add persistence for the large trials. Perhaps you need to identify the greatest challenge of your life right now, or a dilemma you are about ready to give up on. Make a commitment that you are going to relentlessly persevere in prayer.

Perhaps the challenge is relational. Is someone you love far from God and you have about given up hope? Is it a pattern of sin in your life that you haven't been able to break and you feel as if you will be in its grip forever? Is it a new habit you would do well to cultivate? Is it a family rupture that has been going on for years?

Are we on the road to Moriah? Surely we will experience suffering of one sort or another. Yet the question remains: How will we run the race? Will we finish well? Will we keep the faith?

We do not accomplish this from sheer strength of will. The reason we can trust God is that he understands what it is to walk in darkness. One message of the Cross is that God chooses not to stand apart from our suffering. He is not unmoved by the pain of the creatures he loves. He embraces that pain and suffers with us. Karl Barth wrote that God would rather be unblessed with his creatures than to be the blessed God of unblessed creatures.

Jesus, too, walked to the place of sacrifice carrying on his own back the wood on which he was to be put to death. Jesus, like Abraham, had to walk the road of "God-forsakenness." He cried out, "My God, my God, why have you forsaken me?"

When Jesus was bound, no voice cried out to stay the ropes. When the blade went to pierce his body, no power held it back. This time, no other sacrifice was provided. This time, the Son died. This time, the Father grieved.

But then the third day came. As it will come someday for you and me. In the meanwhile, just don't quit.

It's morphing time.

SOURCES

All italics in quotations have been added by the author and are not in the original unless otherwise noted.

Chapter One: *"We Shall Morph Indeed"*

11: *Kierkegaard:* Søren Kierkegaard, *The Prayers of Kierkegaard*, ed. Perry LeFevre. Chicago: University of Chicago Press, Chicago, 1956, 147.

11: *Conroy:* Pat Conroy, *Beach Music*. New York: Doubleday, 1995.

12: *Keillor:* Garrison Keillor, *Lake Wobegon Days*. New York: Penguin Books, 1986, 333.

14: *Smedes:* Lewis B. Smedes, *Shame and Grace*. San Francisco: Harper Collins, 1993, 145.

14: *Kierkegaard:* Kierkegaard, *The Prayers of Kierkegaard*, 147.

14: *"The pain of childbirth":* Galatians 4:19.

15: *"God's workmanship":* Ephesians 2:10 NIV

15: *"Fill the earth":* Genesis 1:28.

16: *Buechner:* Frederick Buechner, *Telling the Truth: The Gospel as Tragedy, Comedy, and Fairy Tale*. San Francisco: Harper & Row, 1977.

16: *Tolkien: J. R. R. Tolkien*, quoted in Buechner, *Telling the Truth*, 82.

16: *MacDonald:* George MacDonald, *The Princess and Curdie*. Baltimore: Puffin Books, 1976.

16: *Buechner:* Buechner, *Telling the Truth*.

17: *"The kingdom of God":* Mark 1:15.

17: *Lewis:* C. S. Lewis, *The Weight of Glory*. New York: Macmillan, 1980, 11.

18: *"I must turn aside":* Exodus 3 *passim*.

18: *"I am slow of speech":* See Exodus 4:10.

20: *Beck:* Aaron Beck, *Love Is Not Enough*. New York: Harper & Row, 1988. See discussion on 155ff.

20: *"Until Christ is formed":* Galatians 4:19.

20: *"Conformed to the image":* Romans 8:29.

20: *"Transformed by the renewing":* Romans 12:2.

21: *Browning:* Elizabeth Barrett Browning, *Aurora Leigh*, Book vii, Line 820.

22: *Schmidt:* Tom Schmidt, *Trying to be Good*. Grand Rapids: Zondervan, 1990, 180–83. Used by permission.

24: *"Jesus is all the world":* Words and music by Will Lamartine Thompson (1847–1909).

25: *"The LORD is my shepherd":* Psalm 23:1.

Chapter Two: *Surprised by Change*

27: *Laubach:* Frank Laubach, "Game with Minutes," in *Man of Prayer*. Syracuse: Laubach Literacy International, 1990, 205.

27: *Willard:* Dallas Willard, *The Spirit of the Disciplines*. San Francisco: Harper & Row, 1988, 81.

29: *Gallup poll:* George Gallup and Jim Castelli, *The People's Religion: American Faith in the 90's*. New York: Macmillan, 1989.

30: *Iverson:* William Iverson, in *Christianity Today*, 6 June 1980, 33.

30: *Lewis:* C. S. Lewis, *The Weight of Glory*. New York: Macmillan, 1980, 4.

31: *Dunn:* James Dunn, *Romans 1–8*, Word Biblical Commentary, vol. 38. Dallas: Word Books, 1988. See especially his discussion of Paul and Pharisaic Judaism on lxiv–lxxii of the introduction.

31: *"Hear, O Israel":* Deuteronomy 6:4–5.

32: *"Love God, love people":* See Matthew 22:37–39.

32: *"If I speak":* 1 Corinthians 13:1–2.

32: *"Everyone who loves":* 1 John 4:7–8.

33: *"Not to bring peace":* Matthew 10:34.

34: *"Tax collectors":* Matthew 21:31.

34: *Twain:* Mark Twain. Source unknown.

34: *Churchill:* William Manchester, *The Last Lion: Winston Spencer Churchill*. New York: Bantam Books, 1983, 34.

35: *Vanauken:* Sheldon Vanauken, *A Severe Mercy*. San Francisco: Harper & Row, 1977, 85.

35: *Willard:* Willard, *The Spirit of the Disciplines*, 80, 91.

35: *"Woe to you":* Matthew 23:25.

36: *"They love to have":* Matthew 23:6.

36: *St. John of the Cross:* St. John of the Cross, *The Dark Night of the Soul*. London: Harper Collins, 1995, 11.

37: *Simpson:* From the weekly television program *The Simpsons*.

37: *Caussade:* Jean Caussade, *The Sacrament of the Present Moment.* San Francisco: Harper & Row, 1987, 42.

37: *"They love . . . to have":* Matthew 23:6–7.

38: *"They tie up":* Matthew 23:4.

38: *Mosley:* Steven Mosley, *A Tale of Three Virtues.* Sisters, Ore.: Questar, 1989, 17.

38: *Mosley:* Ibid., 19.

38: *"You blind guides!":* Matthew 23:24.

39: *"But God, who is rich":* Ephesians 2:4.

40: *"Sleeper, awake!":* Ephesians 5:14.

Chapter Three: *Training Vs. Trying*

41: *Bonhoeffer:* Dietrich Bonhoeffer, *The Cost of Discipleship.* New York: Macmillan, 1976, 64.

43: *Willard:* Dallas Willard, *The Spirit of the Disciplines.* San Francisco: Harper & Row, 1988.

43: *"Train yourself":* 1 Timothy 4:7.

43: *"Everyone who competes":* 1 Corinthians 9:25 NIV.

43: *Fee:* Gordon Fee, *1 Corinthians,* New International Commentary of the New Testament. Grand Rapids: Wm. B. Eerdmans, 1987, 433ff. See also Acts 18:1-3.

44: *"So that after proclaiming":* 1 Corinthians 9:27.

44: *Foster:* Richard Foster, *Celebration of Discipline.* San Francisco: Harper & Row, 1978.

45: *Luther:* Martin Luther, *The Freedom of the Christian,* as quoted in *Selected Writings of Martin Luther,* ed. Theodore Tappert. Philadelphia: Fortress Press, 1967.

47: *Bonhoeffer:* Bonhoeffer, *The Cost of Discipleship,* 60.

47: *Frog and Toad Together:* Arnold Lobel, *Frog and Toad Together.* New York: Harper & Row, 1979.

49: *Time:* 24 April 1989, 58ff.

49: *Ballie:* John Ballie, *A Diary of Private Prayer.*

49: *"I will both lie down":* Psalm 4:8.

49: *"I lie down":* Psalm 3:5.

49: *Elijah:* 1 Kings 19:1–9, especially 5–6.

49: *Disciples in Gethsemane:* Matthew 26:36–46, especially 40, 43–45.

49: *"It is in vain":* Psalm 127:2.

51: *"The wind blows":* John 3:8.

51: *"Rest for your souls"*: Matthew 11:29.

51: *Laubach:* Frank Laubach, *Letters from a Modern Mystic.* Syracuse, N.Y.: Laubach Literacy International, 1990, 22ff. Laubach says that what is most needed is "a gentle pressure of the will" (46).

53: *Lincoln:* Source unknown.

53: *Lewis:* C. S. Lewis, *The Screwtape Letters.* New York: Macmillan, 1969, 37–38.

54: *Lewis:* Ibid.

56: *Mr. Missouri:* Source unknown.

57: *"Pearl of great value"*: Matthew 13:45.

57: *Willard:* Willard, *The Spirit of the Disciplines,* 172.

Chapter Four: *A "Dee Dah Day"*

59: *Lewis:* C. S. Lewis, *Letters to Malcolm, Chiefly on Prayer.* New York: Harcourt, Brace & World, 1964, 93.

60: *Percy:* Walker Percy, *Lost in the Cosmos: The Last Self-Help Book.* New York: Farrar, Straus and Giroux, 1983, 71.

61: *Chesterton:* G. K. Chesterton, *Orthodoxy.* New York: Dodd, Mead, 1943.

62: *"God said, . . . And"*: Genesis 1:29, 30–31.

62: *"God said, 'Let there'"*: Genesis 1:3–4.

63: *"God is the happiest"*: Dallas Willard, "Wide Awake," *Leadership,* Fall 1994.

63: *"A man of sorrows"*: Isaiah 53:3 KJV.

63: *"Which comes out"*: Psalm 19:5.

63: *"I have said these things"*: John 15:11.

63: *Smedes:* Lewis B. Smedes, *How Can It Be All Right When Everything Is All Wrong?* San Francisco: Harper Collins, 1992, 17.

63: *Lewis:* Lewis, *Letters to Malcolm,* 93.

63: *"Rejoice in the Lord"*: Philippians 4:4.

64: *Joyce:* James Joyce, *A Portrait of the Artist as a Young Man.* 1916. Reprint, New York: Viking, 1956, 160, 161.

64: *Francis:* Francis de Sales, *Introduction to a Devout and Holy Life.* New York: Doubleday, 1989, 254.

64: *Chuck:* Chuck has always had a penchant for the absurd. In our high school reunion book—where most people list their impressive accomplishments—Chuck glossed over the fact that he was a medical doctor and noted eloquently his proudest achievement: "I've learned to play the harmonica through my nose."

66: *"This day is holy"*: Nehemiah 8:9–10.

66: *Willard*: Dallas Willard, *The Spirit of the Disciplines*. San Francisco: Harper & Row, 1988, 81.

67: *"Choice food"*: Nehemiah 8:10 NIV.

67: *"This is the day"*: Psalm 118:24.

68: *Bonhoeffer*: Dietrich Bonhoeffer, *Life Together*. New York: Harper & Row, 1956, 58.

68: *Barth*: Karl Barth, *The Epistle to the Philippians*, trans. J. W. Leitch. Richmond: John Knox Press, 1962, 120.

69: *"Smiling faces"*: Proverbs 15:30 Good News Bible.

70: *Bonhoeffer*: Dietrich Bonhoeffer, *Life Together*, 68.

70: *"Every good and perfect"*: James 1:17 NIV.

71: *Lewis*: C. S. Lewis, *The Screwtape Letters*. New York: Macmillan, 1969, 40.

71: *Nielson et al.*: Charles Swindoll, *The Seasons of Spiritual Life*. Waco, Tex.: Word Books, 1987, 326.

72: *Curren*: Dolores Curren, *Traits of a Healthy Family*. New York: Ballantine, 1983.

72: *Egeland*: Cited in Siang-Yang Tan and John Ortberg, *Understanding Depression*. Grand Rapids: Baker, 1995, 33.

73: *Hughes*: Robert Hughes, *The Culture of Complaint*. Oxford: Oxford University Press, 1993.

73: *Fulghum*: Robert Fulghum, *It Was on Fire When I Lay Down on It*. New York: Villard Books, 1989, 10–15.

75: *"Let us rejoice"*: Revelation 19:7.

75: *"You shall go out"*: Isaiah 55:12.

75: *"He will dwell with them"*: Revelation 21:3–4.

Chapter Five: *An Unhurried Life*

76: *Kelly*: Thomas Kelly, *A Testament of Devotion*. New York: Harper Bros., 1941, 54.

77: *Jung*: Carl Jung, quoted in Richard Foster, *Celebration of Discipline*. San Francisco: Harper & Row, 1978, 13.

77: *Time*: Date unknown.

78: *USA Today*: Date unknown.

78: *Carroll:* Lewis Carroll, *Alice in Wonderland*. Reprint, Philadelphia: John H. Winston, 1957.

78: *Banks:* Robert Banks, *All the Business of Life*. Claremont, Calif.: Albatross Books, 1987, 9.

78: *Friedman:* Meyer Friedman and Diane Ulmer, *Treating Type A Behavior—And Your Heart*. New York: Fawcett Crest, 1984, 33.

78: *"The cares and riches":* Luke 8:14.

79: *"Come away" and "many were coming":* Mark 6:31.

80: *Pearsall:* Paul Pearsall, *Super Joy*. New York: Doubleday, 1988, 134.

81: *Foster:* Richard Foster, *Celebration of Discipline*. San Francisco: Harper & Row, 1978, 1.

81: *Donald:* David Donald, *Lincoln*. New York: Simon & Schuster, 1995, 29.

81: *Herndon:* William H. Herndon and Jesse E. Weik, *Herndon's Lincoln*. Chicago: Belford-Clarke Co., 1890, 477.

82: *Grant:* Lewis Grant, quoted in Dolores Curren, *Traits of a Healthy Family*. New York: Ballantine, 1983.

84: *Researchers:* Friedman and Ulmer, *Treating Type A Behavior—And Your Heart*, 179ff.

84: *Jesus in solitude:* See, for example, Matthew 4:1ff.; 14:13; 14:23; 26:36ff.

84: *Frog in boiling water:* The troubling aspect of this analogy, of course, is to wonder whether anyone has even tried it. What kind of sick-minded frog-hater would devise two methods for boiling frogs? How many other animals did he try it with first? Actually, a friend once sent me an article that featured interviews with Harvard biologists and an experiment involving an MIT research associate; it turns out that under test conditions the frog really *did* jump out of the gradually heated pot. So there you are.

85: *Merton:* Thomas Merton, *The Wisdom of the Desert*. New York: New Directions, 1960, 3.

85: *"Don't let the world":* Romans 12:2 *Philipps*.

85: *Mice on amphetamines:* Cited in Dallas Willard, *The Spirit of the Disciplines*. San Francisco: Harper & Row, 1988, 160.

86: *Kierkegaard:* Søren Kierkegaard, *Purity of Heart Is to Will One Thing*. New York: Harper & Row, 1956, 107.

86: *Nouwen:* Henri Nouwen, *The Way of the Heart*. New York: Ballantine, 1981, 15.

88: *Francis:* Francis de Sales, *Introduction to a Devout and Holy Life*. New York: Doubleday, 1989, 271.

89: *Carney:* Glandion Carney and Coleman Moore, *The Spiritual Formation Toolkit*. Grand Rapids: CentrePointe, n.d.

90: *Brother Lawrence:* Brother Lawrence, *The Practice of the Presence of God*. Springdale, Pa.: Whitaker House, 1982. See the fifth letter.

Chapter 6: *Interrupting Heaven*

91: *Julian of Norwich:* Julian of Norwich, *Showings*, trans. Edmund Colledge and James Walch. New York: Paulist Press, 1978, 253.

92: *Willard:* Dallas Willard, *Divine Conspiracy*. San Francisco: HarperSanFrancisco, 1998, 244.

93: *"There was silence":* Revelation 8:1.

93: *"The smoke of the incense":* Revelation 8:4.

93: *Wink:* Walter Wink, *Engaging the Powers*. Minneapolis: Fortress Press, 1992, 301.

94: *"It is Christ Jesus":* Romans 8:34.

94: *"Will you indeed sweep away":* Genesis 18:23–25 NRSV with paraphrasing.

95: *Wink: Ibid.*

95: *Merton:* Thomas Merton, *The Seven-Storied Mountain*. New York: Harcourt, Brace, 1948, 325, 332.

95: *"As he was praying":* Luke 9:29 NIV.

96: *"Lord, teach us":* Luke 11.1.

96: *Merton:* Thomas Merton, *Contemplative Prayer*. New York: Doubleday, 1969, 37.

96: *Martin:* Linette Martin, *Practical Praying*. Grand Rapids: Eerdmans, 1997, 21–22.

97: *"Very early in the morning":* Mark 1:35.

97: *"Come with me by yourselves":* Mark 6:31–32.

99: *"God made many":* Martin, *Practical Praying*, 27.

99: *Nouwen:* Taped address (title and date unknown).

100: *Foster:* Richard Foster, *Prayer: Finding the Heart's True Home*. San Francisco: HarperSanFrancisco, 1992, 9.

100: *Willard:* Willard, *Divine Conspiracy*, 242.

101: *"Did I conceive?":* Numbers 11:11–12.

101: *Lewis:* C. S. Lewis, *Letters to Malcolm, Chiefly on Prayer*. New York: Harcourt, Brace, & World, 1964, 22.

104: *Bonhoeffer:* Dietrich Bonhoeffer, *Life Together,* trans. Donald Bloesch. Minneapolis: Fortress Press, 1996, 90.

104: *Campolo:* Tony Campolo, *You Can Make a Difference.* Waco, Tex.: Word, 1984, 24–25.

106: *Willard:* Willard, *Divine Conspiracy,* 323.

106: *Foster:* Foster, *Prayer,* 3–4.

Chapter Seven: *"Appropriate Smallness"*

107: *Churchill:* Violet Bonham Carter, *Winston Churchill: An Intimate Portrait.* New York: Harcourt, Brace & World, 1965, 4.

107: *Rokeach:* Milton Rokeach, *The Three Christs of Ypsilanti.* New York: Alfred A. Knopf, 1964.

109: *"For God knows":* Genesis 3:5.

109: *"One who is often reproved":* Proverbs 29:1.

110: *Jesus said:* See, for example, Mark 12:30.

110: *Two men at prayer:* Luke 18:9–14.

110: *"Who were confident":* Luke 18:9 NIV.

111: *Lasch:* Christopher Lasch, *The Culture of Narcissism.* New York: W. W. Norton, 1978.

111: *"All who humble themselves":* Matthew 23:12.

112: *Luther:* Martin Luther, cited in Philip Watson, *Let God Be God: An Interpretation of the Theology of Martin Luther.* Philadelphia: Fortress Books, 1970.

113: *"Their end is destruction":* Philippians 3:19.

113: *The prodigal son:* See Luke 15:11–32.

113: *Foster:* Richard Foster, *Celebration of Discipline.* San Francisco: Harper & Row, 1978, 113–14.

113: *"Not to be served":* Matthew 20:28.

114: *Hawthorne:* Gerald Hawthorne, *Philippians,* Word Biblical Commentary, vol. 43. Waco, Tex.: Word Books, 1983, 85.

116: *"Argued with one another":* Mark 9:34.

116: *Bonhoeffer:* Dietrich Bonhoeffer, *Life Together.* New York: Harper & Row, 1956, 90.

116: *"Jesus took a little child":* Mark 9:36–37.

117: *Kurtz:* Ernest Kurtz, *Not-God: A History of Alcoholics Anonymous.* San Francisco: Harper Collins, 1991, 27ff. Kurtz offers a fascinating look at the role of Christian spiritual disciplines in the AA movement.

118: *Jesus took a little child:* See Matthew 18:1–5; Mark 9:36–37; Luke 9:46–48.

119: *Boyer:* Ernest Boyer, *A Way in the World: Family Life as a Spiritual Discipline*. San Francisco: Harper & Row, 1984.

120: *Jesus said the last:* See Matthew 20:25–28; Mark 10:42–45.

120: *Edwards:* Tilden Edwards, *Soul Friend*. New York: Paulist Press, 1980, 56.

121: *Lincoln:* Source unknown.

121: *Bonhoeffer:* Bonhoeffer, *Life Together*, 91.

123: *Bonhoeffer:* Ibid., 91–92.

123: *Francis:* Francis de Sales, *Introduction to a Devout and Holy Life*. New York: Doubleday, 1989, 135–36.

124: *Smedes:* Lewis B. Smedes, *How Can It Be All Right When Everything Is All Wrong?* San Francisco: Harper Collins, 1992, 27.

124: *"Bearing":* See Galatians 6:2.

126: *"In the flesh":* See 1 John 4:2–3.

Chapter Eight: *Life Beyond Regret*

127: *Bonhoeffer:* Dietrich Bonhoeffer, *Life Together*. New York: Harper & Row, 1956, 110.

128: *Plantinga:* Cornelius Plantinga, *Not the Way It's Supposed to Be: A Breviary of Sin*. Grand Rapids: Wm. B. Eerdmans, 1995, ix–x.

130: *Fadiman:* Clifton Fadiman, *The Little, Brown Book of Anecdotes*. Boston: Little, Brown, 1985, 573.

131: *"But who can detect":* Psalm 19:12.

131: *Francis:* Francis de Sales, *Introduction to a Devout and Holy Life*. New York: Doubleday, 1989, 95.

132: *Hammond:* James Hammond, as quoted in James McPherson, *Drawn with the Sword*. New York: Oxford University Press, 1996, 46–47.

133: *"Why do you see the speck":* Matthew 7:3–5.

134: *Prostitutes and cheats:* See Matthew 9:10–13; Mark 2:15–17; Luke 5:30–32.

135: *"Cleanse your hands":* James 4:8–9.

135: *Two kinds of sorrow:* See 2 Corinthians 7:10.

138: *Zacchaeus:* See Luke 19:1–10, especially v. 8.

138: *Smedes:* Lewis B. Smedes, *Forgive and Forget*. San Francisco: Harper & Row, 1984, 68.

138: *De Niro: The Mission* (Goldcrest Productions, 1986; directed by Roland Joffé).

Chapter Nine: *The Guided Life*

140: *Kelly:* Thomas Kelly, *A Testament of Devotion.* New York: Harper Bros., 1941, 12.

141: *"He who keeps you":* Psalm 121:3–4.

142: *Fox:* Rufus Jones, ed., *The Journal of George Fox.* Richmond, Ind.: Friends United Press, 1983.

142: *Calvin:* John Calvin, *Institutes of the Christian Religion.* Philadelphia: Westmisnter Press, 1960. See especially the discussion of the Spirit in Book 3.

142: *Ignatius:* Ignatius of Loyola, *The Spiritual Exercises of St. Ignatius.* Chicago: Loyola University Press, 1992. See especially the comments on discernment, 313–27.

142: *The still, small voice:* See 1 Kings 19:11–12 King James Version. NRSV: "a sound of sheer silence." NIV: "a gentle whisper."

142: *Newsweek:* "Talking to God: An Intimate Look at the Way We Pray," *Newsweek,* 6 January 1992.

143: *Tomlin: The Search for Signs of Intelligent Life in the Universe,* a one-woman play written by Jane Wagner 1986 for Lily Tomlin, who received a Tony Award for her performance on Broadway.

143: *Foster:* Richard Foster, *Celebration of Discipline.* San Francisco: Harper & Row, 1978, 150.

144: *Shaw:* George Bernard Shaw, *St. Joan.*

145: *"Surely the LORD":* Genesis 28:16 NIV. See vv. 10–22.

147: *Lewis:* C. S. Lewis, *The Problem of Pain.* New York: Macmillan, 1962, 30.

147: *Samuel:* See 1 Samuel 3.

149: *Balaam and his donkey:* See Numbers 22–24, especially 22:22–40.

150: *Kelly:* Kelly, *A Testament of Devotion,* 12.

152: *Laubach:* Frank Laubach, *Letters from a Modern Mystic.* Syracuse, N.Y.: Laubach Literacy International, 1990, 14.

153: *"I will be with your mouth":* Exodus 4:12. See also v. 15.

153: *"The Holy Spirit will teach":* Luke 12:12.

153: *Paul also said:* See, for example, Ephesians 1:17.

156: *"The Word made flesh":* See John 1:14.

Chapter Ten: *A Life of Freedom*

157: *St. John of the Cross:* St. John of the Cross, *The Dark Night of the Soul.* London: Harper Collins, 1995, 123.

158: *Nouwen:* Henri Nouwen, *The Return of the Prodigal Son.* New York: Doubleday, 1992, 42.

158: *Smedes:* Lewis B. Smedes, *How Can It Be All Right When Everything Is All Wrong?* San Francisco: Harper Collins, 1992, 49.

159: *"But with me it is":* 1 Corinthians 4:3–4.

159: *Cain and Abel:* See Genesis 4:1–16.

160: *"Am I now seeking":* Galatians 1:10.

160: *"They loved praise":* John 12:43 NIV.

160: *Field:* Sally Field, Academy Award for Best Actress, *Places of the Heart,* 1984.

161: *Mead:* George Herbert Mead, *Mind, Self and Society.* Chicago: University of Chicago Press, 1934.

161: *Siskel and Ebert:* Gene Siskel and Roger Ebert, partners as movie critics.

161: *Nouwen:* Henri Nouwen, *The Way of the Heart.* New York: Ballantine, 1981, 10–11.

162: *Ahabs and Jezebels:* See 1 Kings 16:29–19:18.

162: *Burns:* David Burns, *Feeling Good: The New Mood Therapy.* New York: NAL/Dutton, 1981.

163: *Adams:* Quoted in Paul Nagel, *Descent from Glory.* New York: Oxford University Press, 1983, 193.

164: *"We take every thought":* 2 Corinthians 10:5. See vv. 1–6.

164: *Lewis:* C. S. Lewis, *Mere Christianity.* New York: Macmillan, 1960, 112.

165: *Twain:* Mark Twain, *Tom Sawyer.* Philadelphia: John C. Winston, 1957, 34.

165: *Kosinski:* Jerzy Kosinski, *Being There.* New York: Harcourt, Brace, 1971.

167: *Jesus on doing good deeds:* See Matthew 6:1–6, 16–18.

168: *"When you give alms":* Matthew 6:3.

168: *King David:* See 1 Chronicles 29:1–9.

168: *"Beware of practicing":* Matthew 6:1.

170: *"Well done, good and faithful":* Matthew 25:21, 23; see vv. 14–29.

171: *The Desert Fathers:* Quoted in Henri Nouwen, *The Way of the Heart,* 11.

172: *Churchill:* William Manchester, *The Last Lion: Winston Spencer Churchill.* New York: Bantam Books, 1983, 34. Churchill also called Atlee "a sheep in sheep's clothing."

Chapter Eleven: *An Undivided Life*

173: *Fénelon:* François Fénelon, *Christian Perfection,* quoted in Richard Foster and J. B. Smith, eds., *Devotional Classics.* San Francisco: Harper Collins, 1993, 48.

173: *Kierkegaard:* Søren Kierkegaard, *Purity of Heart Is to Will One Thing.* New York: Harper Bros., 1938.

174: *"Double-minded":* See James 1:8.

174: *"Like a wave":* James 1:6.

175: *"Purify your hearts":* James 4:8.

175: *"Seeking first the kingdom":* See Matthew 6:33.

175: *Williams:* Clifford Williams, *Singleness of Heart.* Grand Rapids: Wm. B. Eerdmans, 1994.

175: *Augustine: The Confessions of St. Augustine,* trans. Rex Warner. New York: Signet Books, 1960.

176: *"I do not do":* Romans 7:15.

177: *Williams:* Williams, *Singleness of Heart,* 10.

177: *"Strive first":* Matthew 6:33.

177: *Mary and Martha:* See Luke 10:38–42.

178: *"By the renewing of our minds":* See Romans 12:2.

178: *Hiding God's Word in our hearts:* See Psalm 119:11.

178: *"Just as Christ loved":* Ephesians 5:25–27.

178: *"Washed by 'the word'":* The author is indebted here to Dallas Willard and his book *In Search of Guidance.* San Francisco: Harper Collins, 1993.

178: *"False beliefs and attitudes":* Ibid., 161.

180: *Nouwen:* Henri Nouwen, from a talk.

180: *John Climacus:* Quoted in James Houston, *The Heart's Desire.* Colorado Springs: NavPress, 1996, 192.

180: *Bonhoeffer:* Dietrich Bonhoeffer, *Life Together.* New York: Harper & Row, 1956, 82–83.

181: *Luther:* Quoted in Roland H. Bainton, *Here I Stand: A Life of Martin Luther.* Nashville: Abingdon Press, 1950, 40ff.

181: *"Let the word of Christ":* Colossians 3:16.

181: *"All scripture is inspired":* 2 Timothy 3:16–17.

182: *Augustine: The Confessions of St. Augustine*, 183.

183: *"The kingdom of heaven"*: Matthew 3:2; 4:17 KJV.

184: *Spener:* Philipp Spener, *The Spiritual Priesthood*, in *Pietists— Selected Writings*. New York: Paulist Press, 1983, 58.

186: *"The LORD is my shepherd"*: Psalm 23:1.

186: *"You search the scriptures"*: John 5:39–40.

186: *Madame Guyon:* Madame Guyon, *Experiencing the Depth of Jesus Christ*. Goleta, Calif.: Christian Books, 1975, 16.

187: *Prodigal son:* See Luke 15:11–32, especially v. 20.

187: *Feeding the five thousand:* See, for example, Mark 6:30–44.

188: *"Be transformed"*: Romans 12:2.

188: *Calvin:* John Calvin, *Golden Booklet of the True Christian Life*. Grand Rapids: Baker, 1952.

189: *"Present our bodies"*: See Romans 12:1.

189: *"Knowledge puffs up"*: See 1 Corinthians 8:1.

189: *Meditates "day and night"*: Psalm 1:2.

190: *"I have hidden your word"*: Psalm 119:11 NIV

191: *Chesterton:* G. K. Chesterton, quoted in Clifton Fadiman, *The Little, Brown Book of Anecdotes*. Boston: Little, Brown, 1985, 117.

192: *Peterson:* Eugene Peterson, *Working the Angles*. Grand Rapids: Wm. B. Eerdmans, 1987, 98.

192: *Wesley:* This was one of Wesley's favorite phrases. See Colin Williams, *John Wesley's Theology Today*. Nashville: Abingdon Press, 1982, 24.

Chapter Twelve: *Life with a Well-ordered Heart*

193: *"On the sole condition"*: Source unknown.

194: *"Pearl of great price"*: See Matthew 13:45–46 KJV.

195: *Shaw:* George Bernard Shaw, introduction to his play *Man and Superman*.

196: *"If any want to become"*: See Matthew 16:24.

196: *"Five times I have received"*: 2 Corinthians 11:24–27.

198: *Augustine:* Augustine, *The City of God*, Great Books, vol. 18. Chicago: Encyclopedia Britannica, 1952, 416.

199: *"Keep your heart"*: Proverbs 4:23.

200: *Paulsell:* William Paulsell, "Ways of Prayer: Designing a Personal Rule," *Weavings* 2, no. 5 (Novermber–December 1987): 40.

201: *"Whatever you do"*: Colossians 3:17.

204: *Jesus as a carpenter:* See Matthew 13:55; Mark 6:3.

205: *Better dressed than Solomon:* See Matthew 6:28–29.

207: *Pope John:* See Marjorie Thompson, *Soul Feast: An Invitation to the Christian Spiritual Life.* Louisville, Ky.: Westminster/John Knox, 1995.

207: *Laubach:* Frank Laubach, *Letters from a Modern Mystic.* Syracuse, N.Y.: Laubach Literacy International, 1990, 15–16.

Chapter Thirteen: *A Life of Endurance*

208: *Wolterstorff:* Nicholas Wolterstorff, *Lament for a Son.* Grand Rapids: Wm. B. Eerdmans, 1987, 81.

210: *"Let us run":* Hebrews 12:1.

210: *"My brothers and sisters":* James 1:2–4.

211: *Sittser:* Gerald L. Sittser, *A Grace Disguised: How the Soul Grows Through Loss.* Grand Rapids: Zondervan, 1996, 56.

211: *"Cloud of witnesses":* Hebrews 12:1; see 11:1–39.

211: *"Take your son":* Genesis 22:2. See vv. 1–19 for the account of the road to Moriah.

212: *"I have made you the ancestor":* Genesis 17:5.

212: *"God-forsakenness":* Gerhard von Rad, *Genesis: A Commentary.* Philadelphia: Westminster Press, 1972, 236ff.

213: *"You know that the testing":* James 1:3–4.

214: *Buechner:* Frederick Buechner, *Telling the Truth: The Gospel as Tragedy, Comedy and Fairy Tale.* San Francisco: Harper & Row, 1977.

216: *"It is through Isaac":* Genesis 21:12.

218: *Lewis:* C. S. Lewis, *The Problem of Pain.* New York: Macmillan, 1943.

219: *Kierkegaard:* Søren Kierkegaard, *Fear and Trembling,* trans. Walter Lourie. Princeton, N.J.: Princeton University Press, 1974. Kierkegaard writes, "Abraham believed, therefore he was young; for he who always hopes for the best becomes old, and he who is always prepared for the worst grows old early, but he who believes preserves an eternal youth" (33).

219: *"Did not receive":* Hebrews 11:39.

220: *"All kinds of trials":* James 1:2 *Phillips.*

221: *Barth:* Karl Barth, cited in a lecture by Nicholas Wolterstorff.

222: *"My God, my God":* Mark 15:34.

STUDY GUIDE

Written by Kevin G. Harney

Chapter 1: "We Shall Morph Indeed"

Small Group Discussion Questions

1. John talks about the reality that we all live with disappointment. He writes of having "a nagging sense that all is not as it should be." What is one disappointment you live with as you look back over your life?

2. Søren Kierkegaard prayed, "And now Lord, with your help I shall become myself." In the moments you get a glimpse and vision of what God wants you to be, what do you see?

Read: Exodus 3:1–15.

3. How did Moses turn aside from his daily routine in this passage and how did this willingness to turn aside impact the rest of his life?

   How might Moses' life, and the history of Israel, have been different if he had not bothered to turn aside when God spoke to him?

4. Describe a time when you slowed down and turned aside to see what God was doing.

   How did your slowing down and turning toward God impact your life?

Read: Exodus 3:11–15 and 4:1–17.

5. Moses and God have an enlightening conversation in these passages. What arguments does Moses present to God to explain why he should not lead the people of Israel out of Egypt?

   How does God respond to each of Moses' efforts to avoid this calling for his life?

6. Describe a time you felt a deep desire to see God transform your life so that you would "morph" and become more of who God wants you to be.

   How is this desire becoming a reality?

7. Tom Schmidt tells a story of Mable, an elderly woman who was bedridden for almost twenty-five years. Though blind and nearly deaf, she was a staggering example of the power of Jesus to transform a life. Tell about a person in your life who exemplifies the power of Jesus to bring beautiful and lasting change.

Group Prayer Direction

Take time as a small group to pray in two directions:

First, lift up prayers of thanks and praise for the many ways God has brought transformation in your life as you have followed Jesus.

Second, pray for continued morphing experiences where God will move, transform, and shape your life!

Living the Life

The burning bush was a powerfully transforming moment in Moses' life. His willingness to turn aside and meet with God made all the difference. Like Moses, we need to learn to turn aside and meet with God. We need to arrange our lives in such a way that there is space for God to speak. We should be intentional about taking time to slow down and notice how God wants to move in our hearts and lives.

Look back over the past week. If you keep a daily calendar, take this out and review it closely. Do you see times where you turned aside to meet with God? Does your schedule allow the freedom to turn aside as God prompts you?

Look at the coming week and find places you can set aside space to meet with God, to listen, and to invite his morphing power and purposes in your life this week.

Personal Reflection

What is one area of your life you know God wants to transform but you honestly don't want to change (or have given up hope of ever changing)? Take time to pray for the Holy Spirit to give you a renewed desire to be changed in this area of your life and to give you hope in his power to bring transformation.

Additional Small-Group Questions

1. What can make people feel like Popeye and simply resigned to saying, "I yam what I yam and that's all that I yam"?

2. On page 17 there is a quote by C. S. Lewis. Have a group member read this out loud.

3. If you truly believed "you have never talked to a mere mortal," how might your behavior change toward one of the following people:

   - A close friend

   - A bitter enemy

   - Your spouse

   - A parent

   - A co-worker or schoolmate

Chapter 2: Surprised by Change

Small-Group Discussion Questions

1. We have all had the experience of relating to cranky, complaining, Hank-like people in our lives. Without using a name, how have you been impacted by a Hank in your life?

2. What are some of the possible consequences if we expect people in the church to follow a list of rules and regulations but fail to call them to a life that is becoming progressively more and more like Jesus?

3. C. S. Lewis said that each of us is "like an ignorant child who wants to go on making mud pies in the slum because he cannot imagine what is meant by the offer of a holiday at the sea. We are far too easily pleased." In what ways is this true of your life?

Read: Matthew 23:1–28.

4. Jesus tells us a great deal about the teachers of the law and the Pharisees. These leaders all had doctorates in the study and application of boundary-marker spirituality. What were some of their boundary markers?

   How did Jesus feel about their approach to faith?

   What are some examples of how these boundary markers exist today?

5. Sometimes our spiritual tanks are full to overflowing. At other times we feel spiritually depleted as if we are running on fumes. Which tank below reflects how full your tank is today and what has brought you to this point?

6. What fills your tank and gives you fuel for authentic spiritual growth?

   What causes your tank to empty?

   What can you do in the coming week to make sure your tank is being filled for authentic Christian living, and who will keep you accountable in this growth area?

7. Imagine if someone were to ask you, "How is your spiritual life?" What would you use to measure and determine the condition of your spiritual life?

What are healthy and Christ-honoring measures of our spiritual health?

Group Prayer Direction

Take time to pray for your group members who feel spiritually depleted and whose tanks are running low. Pray for a fresh filling of the presence of God and for renewed and authentic faith.

Living the Life

Take time in the coming week to help fuel up one of your small-group members through praying daily for them, through an affirming note, or by some creative means of encouragement.

Personal Reflection

John writes of boundary-marker spirituality. What are some of the boundary markers that reflect the spiritual culture of your church or community?

- Vocabulary
- Dress
- Major dos
- Major don'ts
- Worship style

How are you avoiding the pitfalls of boundary-marker spirituality and seeking to grow in authentic faith?

Personal Disciplines

John calls Jesus the most approachable person who ever lived. Rich people and poor people, women and men, educated and simple people were all drawn to him. Mark on the scale below how you see yourself in terms of being approachable.

1	2	3	4	5	6	7	8	9	10

People tend
to avoid you

People are
comfortable
with you

People seek
you out

What can you do to grow in your approachability and be more like Jesus?

Additional Small-Group Questions

1. What are some of the tell-tale signs that we are settling for pseudo-transformation rather than a true and life-changing work of God within us?

Read: Deuteronomy 6:1–9 and Matthew 22:37–40.

2. How do these passages fly in the face of boundary-marker spirituality and call us to authentic faith?

3. Put an X where you see yourself in this picture. What is it going to take for you to move more intentionally toward God's will for your spiritual life?

Legalistic,
boundary
marker faith

Genuine love
for God
and others

4. John writes about the tendency to become judgmental and exclusive. What are some of the consequences if we let the poison of judgmental pride fill our hearts:

- For us

- For the church

- For those outside of the church

Chapter 3: Training vs. Trying

Small-Group Discussion Questions

1. Describe a time when you failed to train and discovered that no matter how hard you tried, you could not accomplish your goal.

   What did you learn from this experience?

2. John talks about the need to train for things like competing in an athletic event, learning an instrument or a new language, or running a business. What might happen if a person takes training seriously in one of these areas?

   Tell about a time you trained and prepared and how you felt when you were able to accomplish your goal.

3. John points out that there are certain disciplines needed to train for a triathlon and a very different set of disciplines needed to prepare for a pie-eating contest. Every area of life demands different disciples for growth. What are some of the core elements of a disciplined training regiment that will help you prepare for spiritual vitality and maturity?

4. Read the story of Frog and Toad (pp. 47–48). Describe a time you have felt like these two discipline-challenged friends?

5. One definition of spiritual discipline is "any activity that can help you gain power to live life as Jesus taught and modeled it." Take time as a group to walk through the process below:

   • To get a taste of how broad this is, work as a group to form a list of at least twenty examples of things you can do that will help you gain power to live the life Jesus intended.

   • To help you think creatively and deeply, once you are out of ideas, try to come up with three more!

   • Use your group's brainstorming list above to identify one new spiritual discipline you want to develop in your life.

- Tell your small-group members what new discipline you will be practicing and how you hope it will impact your spiritual life.

- Invite them to encourage you and pray for you in the coming weeks as you grow in this area.

Read: Psalm 127:1–2.

6. John talks about how being a parent can become God's training-school for spiritual maturity in a person's life. What are some of the unique spiritual lessons that can be learned in this season of life?

   What title would you give for the unique season of life you are in now and how can this season become a time of growth and formation in becoming all God wants you to be?

7. We all know what it feels like to be rested and what it feels like to be very tired. How do you change for the worse when you are tired and how do you change for the better when you are rested?

   How might adjusting your present sleep patterns help you grow in your ability to love God and others?

Group Prayer Direction

Many of your group members communicated that they are making a commitment to specific disciplines that will help them overcome barriers and grow in spiritual maturity. Pray for each of your group members to stay committed to these new disciplines. Pray for them to experience joy and encouragement as they begin this journey.

Living the Life

John writes about the reality that people don't just drift into a life of training. They must be committed. What is one specific step you need to take to begin your training toward developing a new area of spiritual discipline? Who will you invite to encourage you, challenge you, and keep you accountable in this area of commitment?

Personal Reflection

John says that if keeping the spiritual disciplines makes us less loving, rather than more loving, we would be better off not practicing them. Are there disciplines you need to stop because they are driving love out of your life?

Additional Small-Group Questions

1. What are some of the possible implications for a person who decides to only try hard but never train?

2. If we make personal spiritual advancement a legalistic program, how can this lead to guilt and sadness rather than joy?

3. How have you found joy and peace during the times you have developed disciplines that train you for godliness?

4. What are some of the signs that the wind of the Spirit is blowing and that you should raise your sails?

Chapter 4: A "Dee Dah Day"

Small-Group Discussion Questions

1. If you were having a Dee Dah Day, how would people know it? What would be the outward signs that give you away?

   Tell about your last Dee Dah Day moment. What brought you joy and caused you to really celebrate life?

2. What are some of the ways we tend to squelch the spirit and enthusiasm of those around us who seem to have more than their fair share of Dee Dah Day moments?

3. Who is one person in your life who models the Dee Dah Day spirit? What have you learned about joy by watching this person? (Remember, this person can be any age.)

Read: Nehemiah 8:9–12.

4. What is one place in God's creation that gives you a profound sense that God is a joyful God and the happiest of all beings in

the universe? When you are in this place, how is his joy passed on to you?

How does living in the joy of the Lord bring strength to you?

5. Describe a time when life circumstances brought you unexpected joy. What are some practical things we can do to seek joy on a more regular basis?

6. Read the quote from Dallas Willard on page 66. Willard is making two points. First, when we are joy-filled, we are less likely to be drawn into temptation. Second, when we are joy-deprived, we are more likely to fall into temptation. How have you experienced these two principles in your life?

7. Some people have a contagious joy that makes them "joy-carriers." What characteristics mark the lives of these people?

What are some practical steps you can take to develop these characteristics in your life?

8. Read the story from Robert Fulghum about the bride and the lesson, "In the end, the bride got the groom!" (pp. 73–74). What are some of the unchangeable and eternal joy-gifts God has given you that no one can ever take away?

How can these be a regular source of joy . . . even when times are tough?

Group Prayer Direction

Lift up specific prayers of thanks for the joy-giving gifts God has poured into your life.

Living the Life

Consider one of the following exercises in the coming weeks:

- Write a letter or note to a person who has been a joy-mentor in your life. Thank them and ask if they will continue in this capacity.

- Consider turning off the TV for a week, two weeks, or even a month.

- Set aside a whole day as your personal Dee Dah Day. What would you do? (Dare to dream a little.) What would keep you from doing this? If there is something your small-group members could do to help you plan a day like this (child care, cover a responsibility, or provide a material resource), think about inviting them to help you plan your Dee Dah Day.

Personal Reflection

John writes, "Here is a key for spiritual vitality: We must arrange life so that sin no longer looks good to us." What might you rearrange in the coming week to make one specific area of temptation look less enticing?

Additional Small-Group Questions

1. John writes about people who have a unique ability to destroy joy. Without using any names, how have people like this impacted your life? What can we do to keep these people from robbing us of joy?

2. Impatience kills both joy and time. How have you seen impatience kill time in your life?

3. Read the quote from G. K. Chesterton on page 61. How does Chesterton's vision of a youthful and joy-filled God affirm or clash with your vision of God?

A joyless, angry and harsh God	A stoic and unconcerned God	A joy-filled and embracing God

What kind of a picture of God were you given as a child growing up in your home or church? (Put an X on the line above to indicate what best represents your childhood vision of God.)

A joyless, angry   A stoic and   A joy-filled and
and harsh God   unconcerned God   embracing God

What kind of a picture of God do you have today? (Put an X on the line above to indicate what best represents your vision of God at this time in your life.)

4. If you asked the members of your small group to describe your joy-quotient, what do you think they would say about you in terms of joy or non-joy?

5. John says, "Joylessness may be the sin most readily tolerated by the church." Why do you think the church is so quick to accept and even encourage joylessness?

6. What are some of the natural and joy-filled moments that occur in your week that you need to begin noticing and celebrating?

7. John says, "Often it is the people closest to suffering who have the most powerful joy." Tell about a person who has modeled this truth and what you have learned from his or her life.

Chapter 5: An Unhurried Life

Small-Group Discussion Questions

1. If you were to take this exhortation with all seriousness, "to be spiritually healthy, you must ruthlessly eliminate hurry from your life," what is one thing you would need to change in your life so you could slow down?

2. John writes, "Hurry is the great enemy of spiritual life in our day. Hurry can destroy our souls. Hurry can keep us from living well." How have you experienced the destructive power of hurry in your life?

3. How can busyness cause us to settle for mediocrity in our faith rather than a deep experience of God's presence and power?

How have you experienced this reality in your life during times of intense busyness?

Read: Mark 1:32–39 and Luke 5:15–16.

4. From these two passages and other stories in the Gospels, what are some examples of how Jesus modeled an unhurried life?

5. Take a few moments and have your small-group members take this brief survey. Circle yes or no for each question.

- Do you live with a daily sense that there is *not* enough time to get done with everything you need to accomplish? YES   NO

- Do you find yourself talking faster because there is so much to say? YES   NO

- Do you nod a lot when a person is talking slowly in an effort to keep them moving along? YES   NO

- When people are talking too slowly, do you ever find yourself wanting to (or actually) finishing their sentences? YES   NO

- Do you ever drive faster than is safe (even sometimes when you are not in a hurry)? YES   NO

- When you stop at a red light with two or more lanes with cars in them, do you ever try to anticipate which car looks faster so you can get behind that car and save a few seconds when the light turns green? YES   NO

- Do you ever try to gauge which line at the grocery store will be the quickest and get in that line? And, if it turns out you picked the slower line, does it bother you? YES   NO

- Do you multiple-task and try to get more than one thing done at a time on a regular basis? YES   NO

- Do you have a big pile of magazines, newspapers, and books that you hope to read "some day"? YES   NO

- Do you live your life driven by schedules, organizers, and to-do lists? YES   NO

- Do you find it difficult to say no when others ask you to do things that will add one more item to your schedule? YES   NO

Share how many times you circled yes to the questions above, and tell your group what you think this reveals about the place of hurry in your life.

6. John says, "Love and hurry are fundamentally incompatible." How is hurry the enemy of love in one of these relationships?

   - Your relationship with God

   - Your relationship with your family members

   - Your relationship with other followers of Christ

   - Your relationship with those who don't yet know Jesus

7. What are some of the values and attitudes in our society that drive us to a hurried lifestyle?

   What are some biblical truths we can hold on to that will counteract these values and attitudes?

Group Prayer Direction

Pray that God's Spirit of peace will fill your hearts, homes, workplaces, and thought patterns. Ask God to teach you the life-giving discipline of slowing down.

Living the Life

Take time in the coming days to implement one of these challenges:

- Drive in the slow lane for a week and say a prayer for each person who passes you.

- Eat your meals slowly (not in a car or on the fly) and be sure to chew each bite fifteen times in order to actually taste the food.

- Don't wear a watch for a day.
- Commit to a day of extended solitude. (Use the guideline given on page 89.)

Personal Reflection

If I have identified a high level of busyness in my life, what is it that is driving me to push so hard all the time? What am I trying to accomplish? Who am I trying to impress? Does God really ask me to do all I am doing?

Additional Small-Group Questions

1. Identify a time in your life when you really slowed down and enjoyed each experience that came your way.

   What helped lead you to this time of slowing?

2. How do you feel during the times you are not working or producing something?

Chapter 6: Interrupting Heaven

Small-Group Discussion Questions

1. If we turn to prayer as a final desperate measure, only after all our own efforts have been exhausted, what does this reveal about our view of the following:

   - Prayer
   - Ourselves
   - God

2. Have a group member read the quote by Dallas Willard on page 92. If you truly believed that your prayers make no difference and that "everything would happen exactly as is does" without you praying, how would this impact your prayer life?

3. Describe a time you prayed and saw clear and definite results. How did this answered prayer spur you on to pray more passionately?

4. Walter Wink writes, "History belongs to the intercessors . . . those who believe and pray the future into being." If Wink is right, what implications would this have on one of the following:

- Your personal commitment to pray

- The power of a praying church

- What you teach your children about prayer, if you are a parent

Read: Luke 11:1–4 and Matthew 6:9–13.

5. What core issues does Jesus address as he teaches his followers to pray?

Which of these areas do you tend to focus on the most when you pray?

Which do you need to focus on more?

6. What situations and life-experiences most naturally move you to pray? How can you use these God-given moments to propel you into more frequent and passionate prayer?

What situations and life-experiences tend to keep you from praying? What can you do to make these moments an opportunity to seek God in prayer?

7. What are some of the values of setting a specific time and place for prayer?

If you have a time and place you have set aside for prayer, tell your group members how this has helped you in your prayer life.

If you have not established a specific place and time for prayer, but want to, tell your group members where and when you plan to pray. Invite them to encourage you in this new discipline.

Group Prayer Direction

Take time to thank God for inviting you into relationship with him. Sometimes we forget what an amazing honor and privilege it is to talk to God in prayer. Thank Jesus for making a way for us to speak with the Father in prayer.

Living the Life

Take time this week to sit down with a paper and pencil or at a computer terminal uninterrupted for at least twenty minutes. Identify one specific area of life or one need that you have been praying about consistently. Write out two prayers focused on this area of need or concern.

First, write out a safe, polite, cautious prayer. Play it close to the vest and don't get too passionate. Don't be too expectant and don't expect God to be very responsive or extravagant.

Second, write a prayer that reflects the attitude Walter Wink suggests in this chapter. Be bold, fearless, and expectant. Ask in a way that takes you beyond your own comfort zone and ask in anticipation.

After you are done writing both prayers, read each one out loud and ask yourself which of these prayers most reflects what God wants to hear from his children.

Personal Reflection

The first disciples were face-to-face with Jesus, the master prayer. As you think through the life of Jesus as recorded in the Gospels, identify what you can learn about prayer and how these lessons should impact your prayers. If nothing comes to mind, consider reading through the Gospels in the coming month and focusing on the prayer life of Jesus.

Additional Small-Group Questions

1. How have you seen prayer used as a last resort and a desperate "Hail Mary" pass at the end of the game?

2. Tell about a time you were forced to your knees in prayer because you realized you had nowhere else to go. What happened once you hit your knees and began praying?

Chapter 7: Appropriate Smallness

Small-Group Discussion Questions

Read: Genesis 3:1–7.

1. How did Satan use the human tendency for vanity as leverage in his temptation of Adam and Eve?

   How does the enemy still use this same tactic for temptation in the world today?

2. John says, "Pride is essentially comparative in nature." How does comparing ourselves to others do one of the following:

   - Breed pride
   - Destroy community
   - Function as a kind of anti-love

3. How does our society affirm and even encourage a prideful spirit?

   What consequences does this pride-affirming ethos have on the fabric of our culture?

4. Invite a group member to read the quote by Richard Foster on page 113. How can service—and specifically *hidden* service—act as a remedy for pride?

   What keeps us from offering more acts of secret service?

Read: Mark 10:45 and Philippians 2:6–11.

5. What are some of the acts of service Jesus offered when he walked on this earth?

   What was his heart and attitude when it came to serving?

6. John talks about how we can be swept into busyness and get our motors running too fast. Using the odometer below, where do you see yourself running your RPMs right now? Respond to one of the following questions that apply to you:

- If your RPMs are too slow, what needs to happen to help you pick up the pace?
- If you feel your RPMs are at a good place, what can you do to be sure you maintain health and balance and not get revved up too fast?
- If your RPMs are hitting the red line and danger zone, what can you do to slow down and find restored health and balance in your life?

7. If you could form a personal schedule team made up of people who care about you, know you, and would speak honestly to you, what kind of evaluation do you think they would make if they reviewed your schedule from the past month?

   What might they tell you to stop?

   What might they encourage you to begin?

Group Prayer Direction

Read: Mark 10:45.

Pray for God to give each of your small-group members a growing desire to serve in humble secrecy. Pray for the heart of Jesus when it comes to your acts of service.

Living the Life

What is an example of the ministry of the mundane that you can offer in one of the following areas this week?

- In a friendship
- In the work place

- In your home

- In your neighborhood

- In your church

Take a moment and identify one or two simple chores, tasks, or jobs that you know (and others may know) you really *don't* enjoy. What might you learn if you commit to one of these tasks on a regular basis for the coming months, seeking the Spirit's leading in your life as you enter into these simple tasks?

Personal Reflection

What can you do to keep the latch off your door and make yourself more available to others in how you do the following:

- Schedule your day

- Project approachability and availability

- Set up your home, office, and other places people connect with you

Additional Small-Group Questions

1. Not only can vanity strike in the secular parts of life, it can hit at the core of our spiritual life. What are some signs or indicators that spiritual pride is creeping in?

Read: Luke 18:9–14.

2. What is Jesus teaching us about the condition of our heart in relation to our actions?

3. Have a member of your small group read the possible responses to a sincere compliment (p. 111). What does genuine and authentic humility look like?

    What does false humility look like and how can you tell the difference?

4. Read the Bonhoeffer quote on page 123. Tell about a time you should have held your tongue, but failed to. What were some of

the repercussions? Tell about a time you did hold your tongue and had the wisdom and self-control to be silent. What did God accomplish through your silence?

Chapter 8: Life Beyond Regret

Small-Group Discussion Questions

1. We all have our own mauve sofa story of when we had a chance to confess, but chickened out. Tell about a time you stood on the edge of confession, but just couldn't do it.

   What is it that makes confession so hard and painful for us?

2. Read the Plantinga quote on page 129. What are some of the euphemisms for sin that we use in an effort to keep from calling sin exactly what it is?

   Why is it so important that we learn to identify sin in ourselves and call it sin?

3. When writing about confession, John says, "When we practice confession well, two things happen. The first is that we are liberated from guilt. The second is that we will be at least a little less likely to sin in the same way in the future than if we had not confessed. Sin will look and feel less attractive." How have you experienced the liberating power of confession?

   How have you seen confession reduce your desire to continue in a sinful practice in your life?

4. John says, "At the heart of it, confession involves taking appropriate responsibility for what we have done." What are the consequences of confessing but refusing to take responsibility for the impact of our sinful choices?

   How can taking responsibility help us turn away from sin and walk in deeper places of holiness?

5. When we see sin through our own eyes, it is easy to excuse ourselves and justify our sin. When we see sin through the eyes of those we have sinned against and hurt, our perspective begins

to change. When we see through the lens of God's vision and heart, we get a whole new perspective. Why is it essential for us to learn to see our sin through the eyes of those we have sinned against and through the eyes of God?

6. How can God use tears, mourning, and brokenness over our sins as a tool for his will to be done in our lives?

John talks about the "gift of tears." Have you ever experienced this and how did this gift make you more the person God wants you to be?

7. Describe a time when you hurt someone through a sinful choice, humbly confessed, and saw God bring healing and restoration. How did this experience act as a catalyst for future obedience and willingness to confess when you recognized your sins?

Group Prayer Direction

Read: James 5:16.

Spend time offering prayers of confession. It is important that group members understand that all that is communicated in a small group (including in prayer) is confidential.

Living the Life

Identify where you might need to confess sin in each of the following areas using the seven deadly sins as a guideline or tool to help you.

Area of sin:	Confession:
Pride	
Anger	
Lust	
Envy	
Greed	
Sloth	
Gluttony	

Personal Reflection

In the story on pages 130–131 you read about Charles Steinmetz charging $9,999.00 for knowing where to put the X. Take a moment and ask the Holy Spirit to examine your life. Where does the Holy Spirit want to put an X on your life today to show where there needs to be confession and repentant action?

Additional Small-Group Questions

1. Why is it so critical for us to seek the filling and leading of the Holy Spirit as we grow in our understanding of confession?

2. What possible extremes might we face if we confess on our own without the leading of the Holy Spirit?

Read: Psalm 51.

3. What do you learn about the heart of true confession from David's prayer?

4. Restitution is the process of making things right with the person you have sinned against. If someone has stolen, they give back what they took. If someone has lied, they tell the truth ... even if it hurts. Why is restitution essential for the confession and healing process to be complete?

Chapter 9: The Guided Life

Small-Group Discussion Questions

1. Have a group member read the quote by Thomas Kelly on page 140. Describe a time, even if it was only a brief moment, when you experienced this ability to live on two levels at once.

2. What are some of the things that can get in the way of this kind of ongoing awareness of God's presence and closeness?

   What have you discovered that has helped you grow in your awareness of your life in God, even in the midst of your daily responsibilities?

Read: Psalm 121.

3. Take a few minutes and write down what you think God *sees* and *thinks* when he looks at you while you are sleeping.

   Invite your small-group members to read what they wrote.

   What can you learn about your perspective on the heart of God for his children?

Read: John 10:1–4.

4. In light of this passage, respond to one of the questions below about the Shepherd and his sheep.

   - What does this passage teach you about God as our shepherd?

   - What does it teach about us as his sheep?

   - Tell about how you hear the Good Shepherd's voice and how you receive his leading in your life.

5. What are some modern day "pillars" we can set up to help remind us to be attentive to God and ready to hear his Spirit speak?

Read: 1 Samuel 3:1–10.

6. Tell about a time when God was speaking to you and trying to get your attention, but it took a long time for you to tune in and realize God was seeking to move you.

   What finally got your attention and helped you recognize that God was speaking to you?

7. John tells the story of how God spoke to him on a number of occasions through a dear woman named Lorraine. Tell about a time you heard God speak to you through the words of another person. How did you respond to this leading or prompting?

Group Prayer Direction

Take time to thank God for the many ways he speaks through his Word, through others, through his creation, through life circumstances, and through the still small voice of his Spirit. Also, pray and ask for the ability to recognize the voice of the Good Shepherd with greater and greater clarity.

Personal Reflection

What are some of the things that get in the way of you being attentive to God? What can you do to remove some of these roadblocks in the coming week?

Additional Small-Group Questions

1. Why are so many followers of Christ cautious about speaking of God actually leading them or giving them promotions in life?

2. What practices, habits, or disciplines have you learned that have helped you grow in attentiveness to God?

Chapter 10: A Life of Freedom

Small-Group Discussion Questions

1. Invite one of your small-group members to read the quote by Henri Nouwen on page 158. What are some of the signs that one of the following people might be struggling with "approval addiction"?

   - A child
   - A teen
   - An adult

Read: 1 Corinthians 4:3–5 and Galatians 1:10.

2. How might your life change if you had the same attitude as the apostle Paul when it comes to being judged and criticized by other people?

   Why is it so hard to maintain this kind of attitude day in and day out?

3. John writes about our human tendency to "confuse our performance in some aspect of life with our worth as a person." What

are some of the most common areas of life that people tend to use as a measure of their personal worth?

What areas of performance are you most tempted to use as a measure of your worth and what are you doing to fight this tendency?

4. Read the quote by John Quincy Adams on pages 163–64 (and the list of his personal accomplishments that follows the quote). Tell about a time you have dealt with similar feelings about your own value and accomplishments in life.

What does God have to say to us about these kinds of feelings?

Read: Matthew 6:1–6, 16–18.

5. What is Jesus trying to teach us about secrecy in our faith?

What are some other areas of our spiritual lives (besides praying, giving, and fasting) that this same lesson should impact?

6. What do we lose as soon as we begin to announce or flaunt our acts of service and our spiritual accomplishments?

What are some of the rewards and blessings when we are able to maintain secrecy in our acts of service?

7. John gives some wonderful ideas for secret service such as immersing a person in prayer but telling no one, making a lavish donation in complete secret, and cleaning a neighbor's yard when they are away and leaving no trace it was you. What are some other secret service project ideas?

Group Prayer Direction

Pray for single-mindedness in who you want to please with your life and acts of service. Ask God to help each member of your group live with a profound awareness that God is the only audience that really matters.

Living the Life

Plan a secret service day. Don't tell anyone that you have this planned or when you have accomplished the mission! Just do it for God's glory and let that be the whole reward!

Personal Reflection

When you close your eyes and imagine a jury box filled with the people who you want to please and impress, who is in this jury box and why do you want to please them? What will your life look like if you live for these people rather than for Jesus?

Additional Small-Group Questions

Have a member of your small group volunteer to read the short section by Mark Twain on page 165. What are some of the ways we are prone to show off and try to impress others?

How can this showing off become a hazard to our spiritual health?

Chapter 11: An Undivided Life

Small-Group Discussion Questions

1. Have someone in your group read the FDA regulations for food purity at the beginning of this chapter. How do you feel when you realize that these are the real standards for the food you buy at the local grocery store?

   If there was an organization like the FDA that established national standards for moral and spiritual purity, what might these standards look like?

2. John writes about the movie *City Slickers* and the message that life should be centered on "One Thing." When you look around you, what are some examples of the "One Thing" people seem to be seeking?

   Why is it deeply important that we pick the right "One Thing"?

Read: Romans 7:14–20.

3. Describe the condition of the apostle Paul's heart in this passage.

   Describe a time you felt the way Paul feels in this passage.

4. When defining multiplicity, John gives three examples: "We desire both intimacy with God and we flee from it. We long to be generous, but we also hoard and covet. We sometimes attempt to be servants and sometimes are driven by arrogance and self-serving." What are some other areas of multiplicity followers of Christ can face?

5. Tell about a time when you experienced a spiritual washing as you studied God's Word. How did God bring cleansing and refreshment to your life through his Word?

Read: 2 Timothy 3:16–17.

6. What are some of the specific kinds of work God can do in our lives through study of his Word, and how have you experienced one of these in the past month?

7. Why are a repentant spirit and a soft heart essential when we read the Scriptures?

   What are some of the dangers when a person reads the Bible simply to accumulate knowledge?

8. What is one passage in the Bible that has sunk deep into your heart and how has this portion of Scripture brought transformation to your life?

Group Prayer Direction

Pray that God will meet each of your small-group members through the presence of his Holy Spirit each time you open his Word. Pray for undivided lives that are shaped by Scripture.

Living the Life

Take time in the coming week and memorize one of the following passages:

- Hebrews 4:12–13
- 2 Timothy 3:16–17
- Psalm 119:105

Personal Reflection

Take time to read John's examples of "deadly feelings" on pages 179 and 180. What are some similar feelings you deal with and what does God's Word have to say about these kinds of attitudes and hidden thoughts? What passages in the Bible might you meditate on to counteract these feelings?

Additional Small-Group Questions

1. In no more than one or two sentences, what is the "One Thing" you want to pursue with all your strength and life?

   What are you doing to pursue this one thing?

2. Tell about a time God encountered you and confronted you as you studied his Word. How did this experience impact your life?

Chapter 12: Life with a Well-ordered Heart

Small-Group Discussion Questions

1. Look at the graph on page 194. When we organize our lives in this "balanced" way, what are some of the possible consequences?

2. Look at the graph on page 195. Describe a time when your life looked like this. What was your "Peach Cobbler" and how did this version of a "balanced life" impact your spiritual life?

Read: 2 Corinthians 11:23–28.

3. Have two members of your small group read the discussion between the apostle Paul and the Time Management Consultant (p. 196). How does Paul's life serve as an example of shattering the boundaries of balance and entering a life beyond balance?

   What are some healthy modern-day examples of a life beyond balance?

4. John gives examples of five questions we can ask ourselves as we begin to establish a "rule of life" (p. 201). Choose one of these questions and tell your small-group members how you are *presently* developing in this area of your spiritual growth.

5. Choose another question from page 201 and explain how you hope to grow in this area of your spiritual life.

6. How do you think Jesus would do one of the following:

   • Wake up in the morning

   • Greet those he would first see in the morning

   • Eat

   • Drive

   • Work

   • Shop

   • Use the Internet

   • Watch television

   • Go to bed at night

7. What will you do in the coming week to be more like Jesus in one of these areas?

   How can your small-group members pray for you and keep you accountable as you grow in this area of your life?

Group Prayer Direction

Pray for your small-group members in the specific area of life where they expressed a desire to be more like Jesus (Question 7). Pray for their attitudes and actions to reflect the heart of Jesus more and more with each passing day.

Living the Life

Use the simple process on page 206 as a guideline to begin establishing a rule of life.

Personal Reflection

Of all the activities listed on page 206, which one do you find the most difficult to do in Jesus' name? Commit to pray for a dramatic change in this area of your life. What practical steps can you take (even if you don't feel like it) to more reflect the heart of Christ in this activity?

Chapter 13: A Life of Endurance

Small-Group Discussion Questions

1. John writes about the stages a person faces when running a marathon:

   - Pleasure
   - Drudgery
   - Effortful labor
   - Temptation to quit—"hitting the wall"
   - Either endurance or quitting

   If you look at your spiritual life as a race, describe what phase you are in and how it feels right now.

2. Tell about a time when you "hit the wall" in some area of your life and kept pressing on.

   What did you learn from this experience?

Read: James 1:2–4.

3. We all face times of struggle and pain. What counsel does James give us that will help us make it through these times?

   Tell about a time when you were able to experience joy even though you were going through a time of trial.

Read: Genesis 22:1–14.

4. Imagine you were Abraham and had to walk through this life experience. What are some of the feelings you would face?

5. Years later, as Abraham looked back on this whole experience, how might it have impacted his life and faith?

   Now think about this experience from Isaac's perspective (remember, he was the one that was placed on the altar as a young boy). How might this whole experience have impacted Isaac's life and faith?

6. John points out that the word "testing" (a difficult experience through which a person's true values, commitments, and beliefs are revealed) is only used in reference to the people of God. Why would God reserve testing for his children?

   How can testing be a form of true love?

7. What is one prayer you have been lifting up for a long time but have not seen the answer your heart longs for? What have you learned through this process of consistent prayer over time?

Group Prayer Direction

Take time to pray for your small-group members who have hit the wall in some area of their life. Pray for them to experience a new strength and power to press on and endure, even when it is painful. Pray for this process to draw them closer to Jesus more than they have ever been before.

Living the Life

Consider training for some kind of physical challenge. A marathon might be asking too much (or maybe not). But set a goal to train to be able to run or walk five miles in a certain time, ride a bike for twenty miles, or swim twenty laps in a specific time. Be sure to pick something that will stretch you! As you train to accomplish this physical goal, ask God to help you discover parallels and lessons for your spiritual life. There are many to be learned in this kind of an exercise.

Personal Reflection

When do I tend to quit or give up instead of endure? What needs to change in my actions or attitudes so I can be sure I will endure in a way that honors God the next time I hit this wall? Who can encourage me and help me in my training in this area of my life?

Additional Small-Group Questions

Describe a time when you faced deep loneliness (remember, you can be lonely even when people are around you). How did God use this experience to draw near to you and to draw you closer to him?

JOHN ORTBERG

Author of If You Want to Walk on Water, You've Got to Get Out of the Boat

WHEN THE GAME IS OVER

IT ALL GOES

BACK IN THE

LEARN RULE 1

This is our predicament. Over and over again,
we lose sight of what is important and what isn't.
EPICTETUS[1]

My grandmother had just gotten out of jail.

She was a roll away from the yellow properties. And the yellow properties meant trouble. They were mine. And they had hotels. And Gram had no money. She had wanted to stay in jail longer to avoid landing on my property and having to cough up dough she did not have, but she rolled doubles, and that meant her bacon was going to get fried.

I was a ten-year-old sitting at the Monopoly table. I had it all— money and property, houses and hotels, Boardwalk and Park Place. I had been a loser at this game my whole life, but today was different, as I knew it would be. Today I was Donald Trump, Bill Gates, Ivan the Terrible. Today my grandmother was one roll of the dice away from ruin. And I was one roll of the dice away from the biggest lesson life has to teach: the absolute necessity of arranging our life around what matters in light of our mortality and eternity. It is a lesson that some of the smartest people in the world forget but that my grandmother was laser clear on.

For my grandmother taught me how to play the game. . . .

Golda Hall, my mother's mother, lived with us in the corner bedroom when I was growing up. She was a greathearted person. She was built soft and round, the way grandmothers were before they took up aerobics. She remains, at least in the memories of my boyhood, the most purely fun person I have known. She let us stay up later than we were supposed to on Friday nights when our parents were gone. She peeled apples for us, told us ghost stories and scary old poems ("Little Orphan Annie came to our house to stay . . .") that kept us awake for hours. She baked banana bread that was like having dessert for breakfast and made us red velvet cake— which consists mostly of butter—on our birthdays.

And she taught me how to play the game.

My grandmother was a game player, and she did not like to lose. She didn't get mean or mad, but she still (to use an expression from her childhood world) had some snap in her girdle. It was part of her charm. Every Friday night as long as my grandfather was alive, the whole family, including spouses, would gather to play a card game called Rook; and if you were Gram's partner, it was not wise to miss a trick or lose the bid. Everyone's favorite old home movie featured Gram playing in a softball game at a family picnic in her younger days. She made contact with the ball and ran the bases with such singleness of purpose—a large woman coming at you like Bronco Nagurski—that no one got in her way. Home run. When she played Chinese checkers with small grandchildren, she was not one of those pushover grandmothers who would lose on purpose to make the grandchildren feel better about themselves. Gram believed before Max De Pree ever said it that a leader's first task is to define reality. She was the leader, and the reality was that she played to win. Pouting and self-pity, two of my spiritual gifts, did not elicit sympathy from her, for even when she was playing, she kept an eye on what kind of person you were becoming. And my grandmother taught me how to play the game.

The Master of the Board

Grandmother was at her feistiest when it came to Monopoly. Periodically leaders like General Patton or Attila the Hun develop a reputation for toughness. They were lapdogs next to her. Imagine that Vince Lombardi had produced an offspring with Lady MacBeth, and you get some idea of the competitive streak that ran in my grandmother. She was a gentle and kind soul, but at the Monopoly table she would still take you to the cleaners.

When I got the initial $1,500 from the banker to start the game, I always wanted to hang on to my money as long as possible. You never know what Chance card might turn up next. The board is a risky place. I am half Swedish (on my father's side), and Swedes are not high rollers.

But my grandmother knew how to play the game. She understood that you don't win without risk, and she didn't play for second place. So she would spend every dollar she got. She would buy every piece of property she landed on. She would mortgage every piece of property she owned to the hilt in order to buy everything else.

She understood what I did not—that accumulating is the name of the game, that money is how you keep score, that the race goes to the swift. She played with skill, passion, and reckless abandon. Eventually, inevitably, she would become Master of the Board. When you're the Master of the Board, you own so much property that no one else can hurt you. When you're Master of the Board, you're in control. Other players regard you with fear and envy, shock and awe. From that point on, it's only a matter of time. She would watch me land on Boardwalk one time too many, hand over to her what was left of my money, and put my little race car marker away, all the time wondering why I had lost yet again. "Don't worry about it," she'd say. "One day you'll learn to play the game."

I hated it when she said that.

Then one year when I was ten, I spent a summer playing Monopoly every day with a kid named Steve who lived kitty-corner from me. Gradually it dawned on me that the only way to win this game was to make a total commitment to acquisition. No mercy. No fear. What my grandmother had been showing me for so long finally sank in.

By the fall, when we sat down to play, I was more ruthless than she was. My palms were sweaty. I would play without softness or caution. I was ready to bend the rules if I had to. Slowly, cunningly, I exposed the soft underbelly of my grandmother's vulnerability. Relentlessly, inexorably, I drove her off the board. (The game does strange things to you.)

I can still remember—it happened at Marvin Gardens.

I looked at my grandmother—this was the woman who had taught me how to play. She was an old lady by now. A widow. She had raised my mother. She loved my mother, as she loved me. And I took everything she had. I destroyed her financially and psychologically. I watched her give up her last dollar and quit in utter defeat.

It was the greatest moment of my life.

I had won. I was cleverer, and stronger, and more ruthless than anyone at the table. I was Master of the Board.

But then my grandmother had one more thing to teach me. The greatest lesson comes at the end of the game. And here it is. In the words of James Dobson, who described this lesson from Monopoly in playing with his family many years ago: *"Now it all goes back in the box."*

All those houses and hotels. All that property—Boardwalk and Park Place, the railroads and the utility companies. All those thousands of dollars. *When the game is over, it all goes back in the box.*

I didn't want it to go back in the box. I wanted to leave it out as a perpetual memorial to my skill at playing the game—to bronze it, perhaps, so others could admire my tenacity and success. I wanted the sense of power that goes with being Master of the Board to last forever. I wanted the thrill of winning to be my perpetual companion. I was so heady with victory after all these years that for a few moments I lost touch with reality. None of that stuff was mine—not really. Now, for a few moments, it was my turn to play the game. I could get all steamed up about it for a while and act as if the game were going to last forever. But it would not. Not for me. Not for you either. Plato said that the entire task of philosophy can be summed up as *melete thanatou*—"mindfulness of death."[2]

I am a Christian, and I seek to write this book from the perspective of faith. I believe that you are a ceaseless being with an eternal destiny in the universe of an unimaginably good God. But you don't even have to believe in the Bible to understand the lesson of the box. Comedian Jerry Seinfeld put it like this:

> To me, if life boils down to one significant thing, it's movement. To live is to keep moving. Unfortunately, this means that for the rest of our lives we're going to be looking for boxes.
>
> When you're moving, your whole world is boxes. That's all you think about. "Boxes, where are the boxes?" You just wander down the street going in and out of stores, "Are there boxes here? Have you seen any boxes?" It's all you think about.
>
> You could be at a funeral, everyone around you is mourning, crying, and you're looking at the casket. "That's a nice box. Does anybody know where that guy got that box? When he's done with it, you think I could get it? It's got some nice handles on it. My stereo would fit right in there."
>
> I mean that's what death is, really—the last big move of your life. The hearse is like the van, the pall bearers are your close friends, the only ones you could really ask to help you with a big move like that. And the casket is that great, perfect box you've been looking for your whole life.[3]

What Really Matters?

It's not bad to play the game. It's not bad to be really good at it. It's not bad to be Master of the Board. My grandmother taught me to play to win. But there are always more rungs to climb, more money to be made, more deals to pull off. And the danger is that we forget to ask what really matters. We race around the board with shallow relationships, frenzied schedules, preoccupied souls. Being smart or strong does not protect you from this fate. In some ways, it makes the game more dangerous, for the temporary rewards you get from playing can lull you into pretending that the game will never end.

As a student in school, I may think that the game is won by getting better grades or making first string or getting elected class president. Then comes graduation and the pressure to win at my job, to get promoted, to have enough money to feel safe, and to be able to think of myself as successful. I pass somebody up and feel pleasure. Someone passes me, and I feel a stab of pain. Always I hear this inner voice: *Is it enough? Did I do good?* And sometimes if I'm quiet: *Does it mean anything?*

Then the chase is for financial security, a well-planned retirement in an active senior community where Botox and Grecian Formula 44 and ginko biloba and Lipitor and Viagra bring chemically induced temporary immortality.

Then one day it stops. Other people keep going. Somewhere on the board, somebody is just getting started. But for you, the game is over. Did you play wisely? We all want God, Anne Lamott writes, but left to our own devices, we seek all the worldly things—possessions, money, looks, and power—because we think they will bring us fulfillment. "But this turns out to be a joke, because they are just props, and when we check out of this life, we have to give them all back to the great prop master in the sky. They're just on loan. They're not ours."[4] They all go back in the box.

Live Differently—Starting Now

Human beings are the only creatures whose frontal lobes are so developed that they know that the game will end. This is our glory, our curse, our warning, and our opportunity. In Jerusalem, hundreds of synagogues have been built by Jews from around the world. One was built by a group from Budapest, and according to an ancient custom, they had a coffin built into the wall. There is no body in it, they explain to visitors; it is present as a silent witness to remind us that it all goes back in the box.

The Talmud teaches that every person should fully repent one day before his death. When a visitor asked, "But how will I know when that day is?" he was told: "Treat every day as if it were the day before your last."[5] Arrange your life around what matters most. Starting today. The box will wait.

This is how my grandmother taught me to play the game of my life, and I talk about that in the pages that follow. My grandmother led, in many ways, a pretty simple life. She never went to high school, never led a company, never wrote a book, never traveled the world. She met her lifelong sweetheart in the eighth grade, her last year of formal education. She gave birth to three sons named—I'm not making this up—Hack, Jack, and Mac (the names Huey, Dewey, and Louie already having been taken by Donald Duck's nephews), and then three girls, including my mother. She never moved outside the state where she was born. The only paid job she ever had that I know of was working behind the counter in a little Swedish bakery.

She was content with her life because she believed she knew what mattered. She had a clear understanding about what she thought was temporal and what was eternal. Everybody has to decide what he or she believes counts as winning and losing in life. One of the smartest men who ever lived told one of his most unforgettable stories about exactly that decision. That's for the next chapter. But I've had a long time to think about it.

My grandmother taught me how to play the game.

Chapter One: Learn Rule #1

1. Epictetus, *The Art of Living: The Classic Manual on Virtue, Happiness, and Effectiveness.* A new interpretation by Sharon Lebell. New York: HarperCollins, 1994, 105.
2. Daniel Goleman, *Vital Lies, Simple Truths.* New York: Simon & Schuster, 1985, 237.
3. *Seinfeld* (television program): www.seinfeldscripts.com/ TheBoyfriend2.htm.
4. Anne Lamott, *Bird by Bird: Some Instructions on Writing and Life.* New York: Doubleday, 1994, 195.
5. Benjamin Blech, *The Complete Idiot's Guide to Understanding Judaism.* New York: Alpha Books, 1999, 157.

WILLOW
Willow Creek Association

Willow Creek Association
Vision, Training, Resources for Prevailing Churches

This resource was created to serve you and to help you build a local church that prevails. It is just one of many ministry tools that are part of the Willow Creek Resources® line, published by the Willow Creek Association together with Zondervan.

The Willow Creek Association (WCA) was created in 1992 to serve a rapidly growing number of churches from across the denominational spectrum that are committed to helping unchurched people become fully devoted followers of Christ. Membership in the WCA now numbers over 10,500 Member Churches worldwide from more than ninety denominations.

The Willow Creek Association links like-minded Christian leaders with each other and with strategic vision, training, and resources in order to help them build prevailing churches designed to reach their redemptive potential. Here are some of the ways the WCA does that.

- **A2: Building Prevailing Acts 2 Churches—Today**—an annual two-and-a-half day event, held at Willow Creek Community Church in South Barrington, Illinois, to explore strategies for building churches that reach out to seekers and build believers, and to discover new innovations and breakthroughs from Acts 2 churches around the country.

- **The Leadership Summit**—a once a year, two-and-a-half-day conference to envision and equip Christians with leadership gifts and responsibilities. Presented live at Willow Creek as well as via satellite broadcast to over one hundred locations across North America, this event is designed to increase the leadership effectiveness of pastors, ministry staff, volunteer church leaders, and Christians in the marketplace.

- **Ministry-Specific Conferences**—throughout each year the WCA hosts a variety of conferences and training events—both at Willow Creek's main campus and offsite, across the U.S., and around the world—targeting church leaders and volunteers in ministry-specific areas such as: evangelism, small groups, preaching and teaching, the arts, children, students, women, volunteers, stewardship, raising up resources, etc.

- **Willow Creek Resources®**—provides churches with trusted and field-tested ministry resources in such areas as leadership, evangelism, spiritual formation, spiritual gifts, small groups, stewardship, student ministry, children's ministry, the use of the arts—drama, media, contemporary music—and more.

- **WCA Member Benefits**—includes substantial discounts to WCA training events, a 20 percent discount on all Willow Creek Resources®, *Defining Moments* monthly audio journal for leaders, quarterly *Willow* magazine, access to a Members-Only section on WillowNet, monthly communications, and more. Member Churches also receive special discounts and premier services through WCA's growing number of ministry partners—Select Service Providers—and save an average of $500 annually depending on the level of engagement.

For specific information about WCA conferences, resources, membership, and other ministry services contact:

Willow Creek Association
P.O. Box 3188
Barrington, IL 60011-3188
Phone: 847-570-9812
Fax: 847-765-5046
www.willowcreek.com

God Is Closer Than You Think

This Can Be the Greatest Moment of Your Life Because This Moment Is the Place Where You Can Meet God

John Ortberg

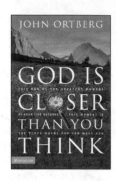

What Are You Waiting For?

Intimacy with God can happen right now if you want it. A closeness you can feel, a goodness you can taste, a reality you can experience for yourself. That's what the Bible promises, so why settle for less? God is closer than you think, and connecting with him isn't for monks and ascetics. It's for business people, high school students, busy moms, single men, single women . . . and most important, it's for YOU.

God Is Closer Than You Think shows how you can enjoy a vibrant, moment-by-moment relationship with your heavenly Father. Bestselling author John Ortberg reveals the face of God waiting to be discovered in the complex mosaic of your life. He shows you God's hand stretching toward you. And, with his gift for storytelling, Ortberg illustrates the ways you can reach toward God and complete the connection—to your joy and his.

Hardcover: 978-0-310-25349-5
Audio CD, Unabridged: 978-0-310-26379-4
Curriculum Kit: 978-0-310-26635-8
DVD: 978-0-310-26637-8
Participant's Guide: 978-0-310-26639-4
Audio Download,
 Unabridged: 978-0-310-26700-5

ebooks:
Adobe® Acrobat®
 eBook Reader: 978-0-310-26336-0
Microsoft Reader®: 978-0-310-26337-9
Palm™ Reader: 978-0-310-26338-7
Mobipocket Reader™: 978-0-310-26339-5

Pick up a copy today at your favorite bookstore!

Normal? Who's Normal?

Everybody's Normal Till You Get to Know Them

John Ortberg

Not you, that's for sure! No one you've ever met, either. None of us are normal according to God's definition, and the closer we get to each other, the plainer that becomes.

Yet for all our quirks, sins, and jagged edges, we need each other. Community is more than just a word—it is one of our most fundamental requirements. So how do flawed, abnormal people such as ourselves master the forces that can drive us apart and come together in the life-changing relationships God designed us for?

In *Everybody's Normal Till You Get to Know Them*, teacher and bestselling author John Ortberg zooms in on the things that make community tick. You'll get a thought-provoking look at God's heart, at others, and at yourself. Even better, you'll gain wisdom and tools for drawing closer to others in powerful, impactful ways. With humor, insight, and a gift for storytelling, Ortberg shows how community pays tremendous dividends in happiness, health, support, and growth. It's where all of us weird, unwieldy people encounter God's love in tangible ways and discover the transforming power of being loved, accepted, and valued just the way we are.

Hardcover, Jacketed: 978-0-310-22864-6
Unabridged Audio CD: 978-0-310-25083-8
Unabridged Audio Download: 978-0-310-26147-6

Pick up a copy today at your favorite bookstore!

If You Want to Walk on Water, You've Got to Get Out of the Boat

John Ortberg

Deep within you lies the same faith and longing that sent Peter walking across the wind-swept Sea of Galilee toward Jesus.

John Ortberg invites you to consider the incredible potential that awaits you outside your comfort zone. Out on the risky waters of faith, Jesus is waiting to meet you in ways that will change you forever, deepening your character and your trust in God. The experience is terrifying. It's thrilling beyond belief. It's everything you'd expect of someone worthy to be called Lord.

The choice is yours to know him as only a water-walker can, aligning yourself with God's purpose for your life in the process. There's just one requirement: *If You Want to Walk on Water, You've Got to Get Out of the Boat.*

Hardcover, Jacketed: 978-0-310-22863-9
Curriculum Kit: 978-0-310-25053-1
DVD: 978-0-310-26180-3
Leader's Guide: 978-0-310-25055-5

When the Game Is Over, It All Goes Back in the Box

John Ortberg

Remember the thrill of winning at checkers or Parcheesi? You become the Master of the Board—the victor over everyone else. But what happens after that, asks best-selling author John Ortberg. You know the answer: It all goes back in the box. You don't get to keep one token, one chip, one game card. In the end, the spoils of the game add up to nothing.

Using popular games as a metaphor for our temporal lives, *When the Game Is Over, It All Goes Back in the Box* neatly sorts out what's fleeting and what's permanent in God's kingdom. Being Master of the Board is not the point; being rich toward God is. Winning the game of life on Earth is a temporary victory; loving God and other people with all our hearts is an eternal one. Using humor, terrific stories, and a focus on winning "the right trophies," Ortberg paints a vivid picture of the priorities that all Christians will want to embrace.

Hardcover, Jacketed: 978-0-310-25350-1
Audio CD, Unabridged: 9780310277330
Audio Download, Unabridged: 9780310277347

Pick up a copy today at your favorite bookstore!

ZONDERVAN®
.com

Faith and Doubt

John Ortberg

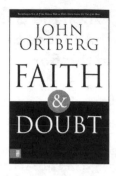

Is it possible to be a thinking person and be completely free of doubt? To believe without question? Author and pastor John Ortberg explores the nature of doubt and finds that it is not only common but inevitable, and in some ways necessary. How do we have unshaken faith in a God who seems to sit idle as an earthquake kills thousands? How can we firmly believe in a God that lets children perish in war or from disease or hunger? Calling on his own faith (and doubt) and the observations of philosophers and theologians, Ortberg grapples with when doubt and uncertainty are obstacles to faith, demonstrating what forms of doubt are damaging, and how we can open ourselves up to the gift of belief. He discusses the faith that hope delivers, a faith so strong and real that "I can let go and trust that Jesus will catch me."

Hardcover, Jacketed: 978-0-310-25351-8

Pick up a copy today at your favorite bookstore!